'Adam shaped my thinking about peace studies and radi‹ else in the whole world! He did so in three ways, (i) as a close personal friend and (iii) as an experienced Quake delighted, therefore, that his life has been captured by T‹ erach in their excellent introduction, and that much of hi and peacemaking has been reproduced in this volume. For those who did not have the good fortune to know Adam, this book demonstrates how he engaged with and contributed to the well being of others through education and peacemaking. It also demonstrates how Adam's own personal and political relationships enriched and enlivened his own deep self aware-ness. Underpinning all the narratives lies Adam's central truth, which is that peacemaking is about understanding that things which seem apart are really part of an interdependent whole. It gives me great delight, therefore, to recommend this book to all those who are interested in learning how to understand and help heal a broken and divided world.'

Professor Kevin P Clements
Chair and Director of The National Centre for Peace and Conflict Studies,
University of Otago, New Zealand.

'This book invites the international community of peace researchers and practitioners to celebrate Adam Curles' 100th birthday in a worthy way. Tom Woodhouse and John Paul Lederach, currently two of the worldwide most eminent voices of our discipline, present a sound compilation of Adam Curle's key publications between 1971 and his death in 2006.

This carefully selected extract of Curle's extensive writings demonstrates impressively the path-breaking and trend-setting importance of his pioneer work for generations of peace workers. And it shows how relevant those writings are still after decades. Curle opened early the field for perceiving peace(s) relationally and valuate the balance between inner and out-er, private and public peace(s). He highlighted the importance of personal and emotional development for would-be peace workers in training and study programs. He pioneered track-two diplomacy and proposed adequate methods of applied peace work based on proved and tested insights of neighboring disciplines such as psychology and anthropology.

A wonderful introduction, written by Tom Woodhouse, about Curle's life as a peace educator and peacemaker demonstrates perfectly the relevancy of the peace worker's per-sonality. Curle is portrayed as an extra-ordinary well-trained and ever searching academic nomad, who found his main inspiration in Quakerism and Tantric Buddhism. While telling us the most important facts about Curle's life, Woodhouse gives the story a very personal touch and makes Curle's "fragile voice of love" vibrate throughout.

In the same way the closing chapter, written by John Paul Lederach, is much more than just a praise of Adam Curle's visionary practical scholarship. Lederach "remembers forward", that is, he draws a beautiful line from Curle's legacy to contemporary approach-es to peace work. Lederach does not write about "elicitive conflict transformation" here, but the book teaches us precisely that, how this key term of contemporary peace work has been prepared in the seminal work of Adam Curle, Lederach's own principal inspiration.

By reading this book one wonders how some branches of the discipline could get lost. Who could assume to do peace research or applied peace work in the 21st century without building on Adam Curle's radical, that is literally, deeply rooted insights into human peace-ability and the many ways to celebrate it?'

Wolfgang Dietrich
UNESCO Chairholder and director of the MA program for Peace Studies at University of
Innsbruck Austria, and founder of the Innsbruck School of Peace Studies.

'This extraordinary man was not only an intrepid transformer of conflicts, a revolutionary thinker and a brilliant professor of peace studies, but he knew the essential value of using the heart as well as the head. This insistence flows through his entire life's work. He recognised early the vital contribution of locally led peace initiatives, and organised support for their inner resources of wisdom, courage and compassionate non violence. This was the inspiration for the formation of Peace Direct and many other peace initiatives. He was also the first to recognise and champion the role of women to "put the brakes on the juggernaut of war". In his later years Adam meditated throughout the Oxford Research Group gatherings of nuclear weapons policy-makers in the UK and in China, inspiring dialogue for potential agreements on disarmament. He influenced many, many thousands throughout the world in developing their inner power alongside their outer work for a better world. This book is an essential manual for building peace in our troubled times, and deserves to be bed-time reading for leaders in the UN, the armed forces and in governments of every nation.'

Dr. Scilla Elworthy
Founder of the Oxford Research Group and Peace Direct.
Co-Founder of Rising Women Rising World and Councillor of the World Future Council.

'This book is both a tribute to the work of Adam Curle and testimony to his living legacy. It is also a timely reminder of the importance of personal integrity and an ethical world view, to better navigate contemporary challenges of conflict, violence and the turmoil of change.'

Judith Large
Senior Research Fellow at the Conflict Analysis Research Centre (CARC)
University of Kent, Canterbury, UK.

'...an excellent introduction to the work of a pioneer of peace and conflict studies, linking Adam's family background and career path to his ideas, his activism, his humanity and his influence...'

Christopher Mitchell
Emeritus Professor of Conflict Research, School for Conflict Analysis & Resolution,
George Mason University, USA.

Adam Curle
Radical Peacemaker

Tom Woodhouse
John Paul Lederach

Hawthorn Press

Hawthorn Press

Published by Hawthorn Press, Hawthorn House,
1 Lansdown Lane, Stroud, Gloucestershire, GL5 1BJ, UK.
Tel: (01453) 757040   E-mail: info@hawthornpress.com
Website: www.hawthornpress.com

Cover design and typesetting by Lucy Guenot.
Photographs by kind permission of Deborah Curle and the authors.
Printed by Henry Ling, The Dorset Press, Dorchester.

Every effort has been made to trace the ownership of all copyrighted material. If any omission has been made, please bring this to the publisher's attention so that proper acknowledgement may be given in future editions.

The views expressed in this book are not necessarily those of the publisher.

Printed on environmentally friendly chlorine-free paper sourced from renewable forest stock.

British Library Cataloguing in Publication Data applied for.

ISBN 978-1-907359-79-8

Acknowledgments

We wish to thank all those who helped us in the making of this book, which was a creative labour of love involving many friends and colleagues. Deborah Curle has been generous in providing photographs and permissions to freely reprint Adam's work, in guiding on family history and in supporting us enthusiastically throughout. Barbara Mitchels, whose book *Love in danger* is a superb study of Adam's work on trauma, therapy and peacebuilding, produced the comprehensive bibliography of Adam's publications, which appears in Part 4. Barbara also provided the photograph of Adam at home in London, in Chapter 1. Alison Cullingford and Martin Levy in Special Collections at the J.B. Priestley Library of the University of Bradford, which holds the Adam Curle Papers, were unfailingly helpful with access and advice. Tim Woodhouse worked tirelessly as our scanning techie, while Jen Woodhouse, Gill Redfearn and Jean Redfearn read, commented, fed, watered and mopped the occasionally overheated brow. Tony Chapman provided a keen, if pedantic, eye on photographic history. Special thanks to Hawthorn Press – Judith and Martin Large for taking this on so positively and professionally, and Claire Percival for her expertise in steering the book into production. Thanks also to colleagues and friends Oliver Ramsbotham and Hugh Miall, and to Hugh especially for encouraging a series of rewrites in order to breathe life into what might have been a dull academic text. Derek McAuley generously allowed permission to reprint *Peace and love: the violin and the oboe* which was delivered as the Essex Hall Lecture of the Unitarian Church in 1977.

Thanks to the Joseph Rowntree Charitable Trust for their generous support of this publication.

Images: Thanks to Esperando La Paz and Carlín Díaz for the cover design. Thanks also to Linda Murgatroyd for permission to use her poster design of Adam Curle.

Contents

Image in memory of Adam Curle by Linda Murgatroyd

Foreword

Adam Curle was a scholar, a Quaker mediator, a peace activist and a Buddhist. He lived a remarkable life and touched the hearts of those who knew him. He journeyed far in search of peace, physically, intellectually and spiritually, and left behind a rich legacy of writing that still speaks to our condition today. Tom Woodhouse, who worked closely with Adam Curle, has done a great service by bringing together a selection of his most important thinking in this excellent edited book, together with the insightful commentary by John Paul Lederach.

Adam Curle is celebrated as the first Professor of Peace Studies at Bradford University and as a pioneer in the field. But he came to peace studies quite late in life, as Tom's admirable biographical introduction shows. Having studied history, anthropology and psychology, he moved from the Anthropology Department at Oxford, via wartime service in the British Army, to a Lectureship in Social Psychology at Oxford, a Chair in Education and Psychology at Exeter, a role as adviser to the government of Pakistan, a Chair in Education in Ghana and a Chair in Education and Development at Harvard. He was already 57 when he moved to the Bradford School of Peace Studies, via a year in the Richardson Institute for Conflict and Peace Research in London. Yet everything he had done up to that point prepared him to be the kind of peace scholar he was to become. Out of his wide experience and his interdisciplinary interests, he forged an original and coherent synthesis of ideas about peace and peacemaking.

If we try to assess Adam's legacy to peace studies, three defining contributions stand out for me. First, he had a distinctive understanding of peace, and peace-making, which guided his own work and is still a beacon for the field. This was his idea of transforming 'unpeaceful' into 'peaceful' relationships, the centrepiece of his book *Making Peace*. He agreed with Johan Galtung that peace must be defined in positive terms and that it must incorporate justice and development as well as the absence of violence. But by putting the emphasis on peaceful relationships, he made task of peace building seem immediate and feasible. His own contribution to thinking about moving from unbalanced and violent to balanced and peaceful relationships has been the basis for a theory of conflict transformation, further developed by Diana Francis and John Paul Lederach. His concept also gave Adam a way of defining the scope for peace studies. It was to work out, through research and practice, how to transform unpeaceful into peaceful relationships. By peaceful relationships he meant ones that were friendly, cooperative, involved mutual understanding and made development possible. Over time he thought of this increasingly in affective and spiritual terms. Peaceful relationships have the qualities of 'mutual respect, toleration, cooperation and above all, love.' Love forms the bridge to inner peace, a peace which also has an outer dimension. Love and peace ultimately reflect our 'deep longing for a union which transcends the painful limitations of our constricting individualities'. Not many peace researchers have gone so far in this direction, but Adam's contribution deserves fresh attention, especially now that there is a new turn in peace studies towards defining positive indicators of peace.

A second important contribution, linked to the first, was the emphasis Adam placed on the psychological dimension of peace and conflict. At the centre of all conflicts, he saw anger, fear, hatred and ambition. The roots of any quarrel lie not in the past, where they would be inaccessible, but in the minds of the conflictants. This was not to exclude the significance of unbalanced social structures and power relations – Adam was acutely conscious of these. But he always put the emphasis on reaching the psychological roots of conflict, and on the importance of awareness in making peaceful relationships possible. Like Lewis Fry Richardson and the early psychotherapists, he saw these psychological forces as operating at the collective as well as the individual level. He sometimes used the image of a collective mind, which could have positive or malign consequences. On the one hand, collective waves of fear and hatred arising from unpeaceful relationships, which he saw as a Hydra or a Black Cloud, could sweep people to disaster. But the collective mind could also take the form of a creative, unifying awareness that could constitute a state of peace. This thinking again went ahead of the field. Some social psychologists of conflict, like Kelman, Morton Deutsch and Bar-Tal, have pursued these ideas, but they still set an important challenge and agenda.

The third contribution, which follows from the first two, was Adam's belief that we can make peace, individually and collectively, by engaging deeply with others. For Adam, this meant meeting the full person, giving them full attention, listening deeply and creating a friendly and deep bond through which fears and prejudices could be brought to the surface and situations seen in a new light. This book describes how Adam brought this quality of deep engagement to bear when he was a mediator and when he was supporting peace activists in Croatia. I experienced it myself when I interviewed Adam and I am sure many will treasure the openness, depth, humour and lightness Adam brought to his encounters. He set a remarkable example of how to be a peace practitioner, combining academic insights from all the fields he had mastered with a deeply engaged personal response to whatever situation he was in. John Paul Lederach, himself a leading 'pracademic', acknowledges this quality when he writes of the 'radical humility' Adam practised during his 'intrepid journey into the inner world of peacemaking.'

There is still much to be learned from reading Adam's work. We can be grateful that Tom Woodhouse and John Paul Lederach have given us such an accessible and inspiring account of the work of this truly radical peacemaker.

Hugh Miall, Emeritus Professor of International Relations,
University of Kent.

Preface

It has been a privilege to have been involved in the preparation of this book 10 years on from my father's death and on the 100th anniversary of his birth. Tom refers in the first chapter to what Elise Boulding called the '200-year present', the understanding that the past affects us in the present, and that how we are in the present moment will affect the future. This has felt very relevant when looking back at the family story and how it shaped Adam, the clearest example probably being the bereavement of his mother who lost three brothers to war, which led to her abiding hatred of war.

As a child, I experienced my father as a dad who helped with homework, went to the office, told me stories, taught me how to do things and occasionally had to tell me off. Yet I was also aware of, and probably took for granted, the visionary and innovative nature of much of his work. He was often deep in thought and busy writing. I remember his absences when away on missions, particularly during the Biafran war when I was very young, and realising that he was involved in something important and dangerous. So, at an early stage, I was aware of him being engaged in both reflection and in practical action.

Adulthood brought increased appreciation of his work and ideas and the enjoyment of knowing him on a different level, and on occasion of working with him, as in the project in Zupanja, Croatia in the mid-1990s. As well as being deeply concerned with the problems of the world, he loved life and was great fun. He was a wonderful raconteur and mimic and could easily reduce us to fits of laughter. He and my mother loved entertaining and were famous for their hospitality. His ability to balance seriousness with levity and joy rendered even the most trying situations bearable and helped give much-needed perspective, something I try to hold onto.

As well as focusing on different aspects of Adam's life and work, this book brings out the connections between past, present and future, between inner and outer worlds, the mystical and the practical, and a sense of the interdependency of all things – Indra's net – of which he had such a deep awareness.

He always wanted to be useful to the world. After his death in 2006 the letters and tributes that poured in showed what a huge impact he had had on so many people, as well as confirming the appreciation of his contribution to peacemaking. I felt sad that he could not read them (although I could imagine his self-deprecating chuckle if he had done so!). I am very pleased that this book is now consolidating his work to play a part in our continued journey into the future, in which he is still contributing.

Deborah Curle, London, May 2016.

CHAPTER I

Introduction

ADAM'S STORY – PEACE EDUCATOR AND PEACEMAKER

A true teacher is one who, keeping the past alive, is also able to understand the present.   Confucius

We are all of us linked, our ancestors and ourselves, just as all living human beings and indeed all living things are linked and interdependent. The better we understand this, the richer our lives will be.
                                                                                Adam Curle

'...you will have to fly on one of the rebel arms-carrying planes which my fighter aircraft have orders to shoot down. I am afraid I could not make any arrangements for the safety of your particular flight.' We assured him that we would be tactful in our dealings with Ojukwu and we were prepared to risk the possible dangers of the flight.

Two of us agreed to transport $57,000 in cash (a formidable amount in 1968), which had been raised to help the centres which had been established for starving people driven by war from their homes in Biafra. It was a rather hectic journey – as we spiralled down at night to the Uli airstrip, a mere widened roadway, incessant flashes from the battle down below us lit up the jungle, and the tracer curled up towards us.[1]

Adam Curle was deeply and directly engaged in armed conflict and its transformation in a lifetime of working for peace. His experience as a peacemaker is vividly evoked in the quotation above, which is an account of his mediation in the Nigerian Civil War from 1968-1970. Even in this most brutal of conflicts, which took the lives of over three million people, he was prepared to put his own life at risk and engage in a mission to conciliate, inform, communicate and befriend the protagonists, General Yakubu Gowan, leader of the Federal Military Government of Nigeria, and Colonel Odumegwu-Ojukwu, who led the secession of the Eastern Region of Nigeria (Biafra) in May 1967.

From such experiences, Adam will have known that making peace is indeed harder than making war. This chapter tells the story of why he was prepared to undertake such hazardous but rewarding work and how, in his life as a radical peacemaker, he has left a rich legacy which inspires peacemakers today. This book commemorates the 100th anniversary of Adam's birth (in 1916), and was launched during another celebratory event, the conference on Peaceful Relations and the Transformation of the World: An Academic-Practitioner Dialogue on Peace in the 21st Century, held at the University of Bradford in September 2016. It is organized in four parts: an introduction, Adam's Story, by Tom Woodhouse, provides an overview of his life and influence as a peace thinker and pacifist. Part 1, Making Peace presents extracts in five chapters from key publications which define his seminal work of peace and conflict studies, from *Making Peace* in 1971 to his inaugural lecture, the *Scope and dilemmas of peace studies*. The selections in Part 2, Tools for Transformation, are presented in four chapters and reveal his role as an academic/practitioner, working as a mediator, peace educator, and facilitator or partner in citizen peacemaking. Part 3, The Fragile Voice of Love, contains four chapters exploring in more depth the values which guided him. Part 4 is a bibliographic listing of his published and unpublished work, most of which is available in the JB Priestly Library of the University of Bradford in the UK.

The concluding chapter, 'Remembering Forward: The Visionary Practical Scholarship of Adam Curle', by John Paul Lederach, is a reminder that this book is concerned with the future as much as the past. While Adam's life connects us to the past, his work has permeated our lives today and informs our thinking about how to navigate our futures.

ADAM'S STORY

The Fishers and the Curles

If we are to understand Adam's journey to peacemaking the best place to start is with his family and the society in which they lived. Charles Thomas William Curle was born on 4th July 1916 in the town of L'Isle-Adam, an island on the banks of the River Oise, about 25 kilometres to the north of Paris. The circumstances of his birth were as unconventional as his life and academic career. His mother was Cordelia Fisher, his father Richard Curle. Adam, as he was known all his life, was not his birth name.

When Cordelia became pregnant in 1915, she did something remarkably at odds with the instincts one would imagine an expectant mother to have. In the midst of the First World War she moved to France so that the baby could be born there, partly to show solidarity with the French and to be near her brother Edwin (known in the family as Tom), who was fighting in the trenches, and also to feel closer to her other brothers William and Charles, who were in the Navy. He was given the name Adam after his birthplace, when another uncle, Edmund, wrote to Cordelia to say how happy he was to think of 'little Adam on his island'. From then

Charles Fisher

on, 'Charles Thomas William' became 'Adam' Curle. Edmund, a highly respected architect, also served in the war with the Royal Field Artillery, fought at Ypres, and like his brother Charles, became a victim of the war. Charles, an eminent historian at Christ Church College Oxford, was killed in action in the Battle of Jutland in May 1916 when the battleship, HMS Invincible, was sunk with a loss of 1,026 men. Another brother, Arthur, was killed in the Boer War in 1902. Adam recalled how the deaths of Arthur, Charles and Edmund devastated Cordelia.

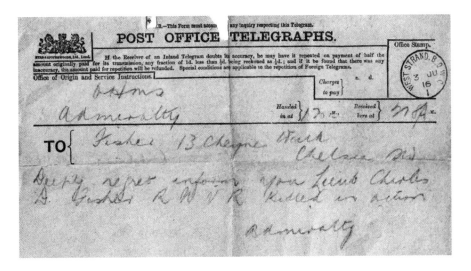

Telegram from the Admiralty, informing the family of the death of Charles. It reads:
'Date 3 Jul 1916. To: Fisher, 13 Cheyne Walk Chelsea SW.
Deeply regret inform you Lieut. Charles D. Fisher RNVR killed in action'

Ralph Vaughan Williams, the musician and composer, was Cordelia's brother-in-law, married to her sister Adeline. Vaughan Williams had finished one of his major works, The Sea Symphony, in 1909, seven years before the death of Charles. The symphony was performed at the Leeds Festival in 1910 and is one of the first to include a choir in every movement, with words from the American humanist poet Walt Whitman's *Leaves of grass*. The centenary of the Battle of Jutland is also the centenary of Adam's birth, and it is indeed remarkable that when, in June 2016, the London Concert Choir performed The Sea Symphony in London to commemorate the battle, Adam's daughter Deborah was a member of the choir. In The Sea Symphony, the choir and the orchestra 'pay tribute, in the poetry of Whitman, to the seafarers of 'all seas, all ships and all nations' whom the sea unites in life, or death.'

Adam was born into a family that was widely and deeply rooted in all that was great in the life of Victorian and Edwardian England, influential in the world of art, scholarship, and liberal politics. His mother Cordelia was the 10th of 11 children (seven brothers and four sisters). As previously mentioned, Adeline married Ralph Vaughan Williams. Another sister, Emmeline, married one of Vaughan Williams pupils, the composer R.O. Morris. The eldest sister, Florence, married the medieval historian F.W. Maitland and then, following his death, Francis Darwin, the son of Charles

Darwin. His uncles included Herbert (HAL) Fisher, historian and member of Lloyd George's coalition government from 1916-1922, when he served as President of the Board of Education. Herbert Fisher was the architect of the Education Act of 1918, which made education compulsory up to the age of fourteen. Adam found Herbert to be the most remote and austere of his uncles and one wonders if he perhaps had this image somewhere at the back of his mind when just over 50 years later, he wrote *Education for Liberation*, which argued for a much more radical mode of education than that institutionalized by his uncle Herbert. Another of Adam's uncles, Admiral Sir William Wordsworth Fisher, was Commander-in-Chief of the Mediterranean and Home Fleets of the Royal Navy. The youngest of Cordelia's brothers, Edwin (Tom), became chairman of Barclay's Bank.

There was a remarkably strong creative literary and artistic trait in the family. Julia Margaret Cameron, Cordelia's great aunt, transformed Victorian photography in the 1850s, when it was largely dominated by men. She introduced the soft focus style, pioneering the idea of photography as art rather than merely as technique. It is a fitting coincidence that the Julia Margaret Cameron Society celebrated the bicentenary of her birth in 2015, an event marked also by a major exhibition of her work at the Victoria and Albert Museum in London. The novelist and feminist Virginia Woolf, and the artist Vanessa Bell were also related on his mother's side, and brought the Bloomsbury Group into the network of connections of family and friends.

These creative independent and innovative women provided Adam with powerful and positive role models. Cordelia planted the seed which eventually led to his pacifism, his decision to become a Quaker in 1959 and his leap of faith in 1973 to leave his comfortable post at Harvard to travel to the north of England to set up a peace studies department. As he recalled in a memoir of Cordelia: 'She hated war, to which she had lost three of her beloved brothers, and was determined that she would instil her loathing of it in me as well. To this end as soon as she could after the end of the First World War, she took me off to France to see what it had done to the country .... I remember well ... walking along the deep trenches in which there were still fragments of clothing, and staying overnight in shattered towns.' It is not surprising that when he began to develop his work in peacemaking he acknowledged his debt to women peacemakers. In *To tame the Hydra*, published in 1999, he acknowledged the 'splendid vanguard' of women peacemakers: 'the collective wisdom, the steadfast courage, and the imaginative fire of all these women have put the brakes

Richard Curle   *Adam with his mother, Cordelia. Early 1930s*

on the juggernaut of war. Their love for humanity, expressed in countless ways, as mediators, negotiators, healers, leaders and mothers, has weakened the world's violence and strengthened the culture of peace'.[2] He described his aunt Adeline as the linchpin of the family. Of significance to his future development, she also opened up the Vaughan Williams household to him, and he spent much of his family life in the company of the man recognized at the time as the greatest figure in English music, igniting in Adam a love of music and the arts. This, as we shall see, had an abiding and creative impact on him.

Art, music, the creative muse, literature and love of family and friends all came easily and naturally to Adam, although his father Richard Curle did not feature much in his early years. Adam described him as 'a fascinating, enigmatic, tormented, brilliant man – erudite, and wildly funny, he was totally unsuited to family life'. After four years of marriage he disappeared first to South Africa and then to Singapore, where he became editor of the *Singapore Times*. 'He was a wanderer and only settled down (in hotels in Somerset) during the last 25 years of his life,' wrote Adam. 'I – his only child, did not meet him until I was three.' They became closer in later life, on a man-to-man basis, having, as Adam reflected, missed out on the 'father-son' phase. A novelist and writer as well as a journalist, Richard Curle was a close friend of the novelist Joseph Conrad and wrote a number of books about him, but he had himself published widely, including volumes of literary criticism on Dostoyevsky and George Meredith. As Adam recalled, he shared with Conrad 'a profound sense of the inwardness of things, of mystery, of the strange hidden behind the banal'. Richard Curle had in common with Conrad a fascination with the use of words to describe nuances of feeling and atmosphere. Adam absorbed much of this fascination with words, feeling and atmosphere, the love of travel, the sense of the inwardness of things. He also had his father's sense of humour and gregariousness: 'He was incredibly good company, having tricks for a child ... and for the adult a wealth of information on bizarre topics from genealogy to molluscs. Best of all ... was his ribald sense of the ludicrous. Give him a prosaic topic like a vicarage tea party and he would weave around it a scurrilous fantasy which was incredibly funny.'

Those of us who were privileged to be friends of Adam will know that he was, like his father, a great spinner of stories and anecdotes. Cordelia too was an inventive storyteller, endlessly entertaining her grand-daughter Deborah. What he also learned from his father was the importance of wisely navigating the inner journey. Richard Curle also had a darker side to his nature. He was subject to melancholy, and tormented by inner fears and anguish. There may not be any direct relationship, but it is nevertheless significant that Adam's thinking on the inner and outer dimensions of peace, the search for stillness, happiness, moral courage and balanced personhood was beginning to take shape more explicitly in the late 1960s. Richard Curle died in 1968, his final years unhappy and haunted by a sense of failure.[3]

Adam's childhood with the mildly eccentric Cordelia was idyllic in many ways. On their return from France, they lived in an old Rectory in a tiny hamlet, Wheatfield, near Oxford, surrounded by animals including a dog, Julius, and a tame badger, Wadge. Soon after the move to Wheatfield, from about the age of five, he describes a feeling 'of the prison walls closing in.' This marked the beginning of institutionalized schooling including time at Charterhouse, which he hated, although he claimed this was true of the place but not the people. His grandfather had been headmaster there, and his uncle Ralph Vaughan Williams had also been a pupil. In one of his last books (*To tame the Hydra*), he referred to it, echoing novelist William Makepeace Thackery who had also been a pupil there, as 'Charnelhouse.' Although he liked and respected many of the teachers and his fellow pupils there, for Adam life in this society was completely unnatural. Its values were to me at best ridiculous, at worst savagely cruel and inhuman'.

So how, out of this varied and also privileged background, did the character of the peacemaker eventually evolve? There was no clear role model for pacifism or nonviolence in the family – an uncle who was Commander-in-Chief of the Royal Navy in the Mediterranean, another who became Chairman of Barclays bank, an absent father who was a man of letters, a journalist and a generous socialite but, as Adam recalled, beset by inner demons. Yet the family and the world they lived in so comfortably as members of the British elite was also composed of intellectuals, academics, artists, musicians and innovators. They were patriotic but not jingoistic, at ease in all levels of society, urbanely agnostic in the sense of being open minded and creative. We have noted already Adam's acknowledgment of the positive examples of women peacemakers. His mother Cordelia was not a pacifist in any political sense, but she was viscerally anti-war because of its effects on her personal world and because she had lost three of her brothers to war. She gave Adam the quality of character that explains much of what he became as a man:

> She was a great influence on my life. It was not that she taught me what to think and believe – she never indoctrinated me in the slightest. But she gave me unconditional love, she helped me in every way and for as long as possible. She thought I was wonderful and she believed in me. This, I hope ... gave me the self-confidence to take important or risky chances which someone without this psychological advantage might have avoided doing. Some people have said that this self-assurance was to do with class. Partly, maybe, but class without Cork would have been of very little use.[4]

This reflection by Adam on the role of his mother and the nature of his social world highlights the power and importance of childhood socialisation, something Adam realized as he grew as an academic, as a person and as a father. Elise Boulding wrote a lot about the neglected role of the family, mothers and children in peacemaking and in transmitting peaceful values. Her writing helps to explain Adam's evolution as a peace educator and peacemaker. In *The Child and Nonviolent Social Change*, she reviewed the literature on childhood socialisation in order to understand 'how some children come to perceive themselves as creators of alternative futures, and can remain unthreatened and nonviolent in the face of changes and tensions that bring out aggression or withdrawal in others.' She identified a number of factors that facilitated a peaceful world view, including – 'optimal opportunities as a child for development of emotional, cognitive and intuitive capacities in home, school and community, in settings that allow for maximum expression of a wide range of innate behavioral repertoires; substantial exposure to events in the larger society, and the knowledge stock of that society ...'[5]

Adam was surrounded by these influences and opportunities, re-enforced by Cordelia, Vaughan Williams, Herbert Fisher, his father and the cultural and intellectual circles he moved in. He had the confidence, self-belief and creative open-minded world view that enabled him to take risks, to change and innovate, and to develop his capacities to their fullest extent. This development of capacity in fact became his definition of 'peaceableness' – the ability to become fully human, to make peace and to live peacefully.

The journey to peacemaking; early steps
Oxford and war 1935–1945

In 1935 he went from Charterhouse to New College Oxford, initially to read history on the advice of his uncle Herbert, also an eminent historian. In the free atmosphere of the university his interest in wider systems of thinking intensified. He was fascinated by the *philosophia perennia* – a term he used to mean 'the reality behind the formal statements of all religions and systems of belief.' He absorbed the early ideas of psychology and psycho-analysis as well as the ideas of the mystics and of the Sufis, related to self-awareness and self-knowledge.

In a memoir written for the family he recalled: 'In my early twenties while at Oxford I first met people who influenced me in this direction. They were pupils of an extraordinarily remarkable man who, it seems, although he was never precise about his journeys, had travelled in Tibet and learned much from the Lamas, and from the Sufi masters (Muslim mystics) in the Middle East. He taught a startling and original form of psychology. He said that we misuse our potential by, for example, using the intellect for what is emotional, and the emotions for what should be automatic. Thus we diminish our true humanity and instead become more like machines without real freedom of choice or decision. The way of escape was through increased awareness, consciousness of our own being'.[6]

A brief introduction to the idea of mysticism is helpful here if we are to understand fully the evolution of Adam's ideas about peace and peace-making later on. Once again the influence of family and family friends was decisive. Amongst the group of intellectuals and writers associated with Adam's father was Alfred Orage, a schoolteacher from Leeds, who founded the Leeds Arts Club and subsequently, after his move to London in 1905, became the editor of *The New Age*, a magazine which was influential in ex-ploring the connections between art, spiritualism, philosophy and politics.[7] The Leeds Arts Club and *The New Age* were focal points for the expression of modernist ideas, advancing the view that human beings were the agents and not the objects of social change. The ideas of modernism called for people to reshape their world through progressive innovations in the arts, technology, science and politics. Orage came under the influence of three key philosopher-mystics: Dimitrje Mitrinovic, George Gurdjieff and Peter Ouspensky. The work of these men was popularised in England through Orage's *New Age*.

As a teenager at school and in his time as a student at Oxford, Adam grew up absorbing these ideas. They stimulated his later interest in inner and outer peacemaking, and his notion of the collective conscious or uni-versal mind, which became a guiding motif in his attempt to understand the essence of peace. Although there were differences between them, Mi-trinovic, Ouspensky and Gurdjieff shared the same quest to understand the modalities of progressive human transformation in an intellectual cli-mate itself transformed by scientific theory, not least by Einstein's theory of relativity, formulated in 1915. Gurdjieff espoused a method of transcending normal consciousness to reach a higher state in which human potential could be fully realized.

His friend Mitrinovic wanted to establish ways of envisioning utopian futures and wrote about training for cosmopolitan citizenship. It is another remarkable coincidence that his personal papers and archives have, like Adam Curle's, come to be located at the University of Bradford's Special Collections library. Ouspensky, a mathematician, developed with Gurdjieff the idea of the fourth way and the fourth dimension as a means of achiev-ing self-development and enlightenment. He endorsed the idea that this could be done not by withdrawing from the world but by living in every-day life and observing it. The fourth way entails an aspiration to a higher level of consciousness which may be achieved when people learn to work in harmony with the body, the emotions and the mind. The belief that a fourth way could be reached was linked to another idea, that there was a fourth dimension, a new concept of space and time which was defined in 1907 by the Russian born German-Jewish mathematician Hermann Minkowski. Minkowski added time to the three dimensions of space, and this 'Minkowski spacetime' formed at least the basis of Einstein's theory of relativity. Ouspensky wanted to develop philosophy to represent these revolutions in theories about the natural world, so that the new concept of four dimensional space in physics made it possible to believe that human consciousness as experienced in everyday life was incomplete and that there are ways of comprehending a new or fourth dimension of consciousness, a higher *collective* consciousness – the universal mind envisaged by Adam in *The Hydra* and in *Fragile Voice*.

When we add to this Gurdjieff's idea, passed on to Ouspensky, of 'self-remembering' and 'self-observation', whereby knowledge and understanding is gained by being aware not only of the external world but also of the internal, we can see precisely how Adam came to use this thinking in his work on peace. It is no coincidence then that when he did come to write about peace, one of his first books was entitled *Mystics and Militants*; nor that the idea of self-awareness permeates all of his writing on peace and peacemaking. This preoccupation with the inner journey and the search for the essential or universal mind became more pronounced especially in his later work. Some of the work of these mystics went beyond what Adam would have recognised as helpful, descending at times into personality cults and an obsession with the occult. As with other influences on his thinking, he remained reflective and critical and took those parts of the thinking that allowed him to build his relational and person-centered pedagogy and practice of peacemaking.[8] In so far as he ever became a follower, it was expressed by membership of the Society of Friends and by engaging with the teachings of the Dalai Lama, but even here he saw Quaker and Buddhist beliefs as ways of also reflecting on human relations, not as strict dogmas.

All these ideas influenced his move out of history and into the new subject of anthropology, which he believed was a more revealing source of knowledge about human behaviour and social systems than history was capable of providing. Anthropology enabled him to combine the study of societies in the process of change and to combine this with the chance of

Adam in Egypt, 1938   *Adam in uniform, 1939*

travel to interesting locations. In 1937 he travelled to study the Sami peoples in northern Scandinavia, obtaining a Diploma in Anthropology for this work. Following the award of the diploma and still at Oxford he was taken under the wing of Professor Edward Evans Pritchard, a pioneer of social anthropology, and travelled with him in Upper Egypt, living among and studying the Nuer people who inhabit the Nile Valley. This fieldwork resulted in Evans Pritchard's classic trilogy on Nuer culture and religion, and his book on the political anthropology of Africa. This experience of travelling and working with Evans Pritchard was a point of transformation for Adam: 'in some places and in some circumstances the mysteries within us and the mysteries outside us open up to each other. These are points of growth'.[9]

Adam returned from Egypt in the summer of 1939 and with the outbreak of war in September 1939 his point of growth was interrupted. He spent six years, from 1939 to 1945, on active service in the British Army reaching the rank of Major. He rarely spoke about his wartime experience and wrote very little about it, but acknowledged that despite the efforts of his mother to educate him about the horrors of war, he did not consider becoming a conscientious objector because his convictions were not strong enough at the time.

Just after war broke out and at the age of 23 he married the Oxford academic Pamela Hobson. They had two children, Tina and Anna. The marriage ended in divorce in the mid-1950s.

The emergence of the academic-practitioner 1945–1973 Oxford, Tavistock, Exeter, Pakistan, Ghana and Harvard

We can see the emergence of another turning point when Adam came out of the war and returned to his academic life. Between 1946 and 1947 he went back to Oxford and in 1947 was awarded a D.Phil. for a thesis combining the disciplines of psychology and anthropology, using earlier field experience in Northern Europe (Lapland), and the Middle East. From 1947 until 1950, he had also started to work as a member of the Tavistock Institute of Human Relations, on problems of development in rural southwest England and on rehabilitating former British prisoners of war suffering from years of traumatic experiences. This new interest through the Tavistock Institute, particularly in the approach to the socio-psychological problems of post-war reconstruction, was a strong influence on his thinking. The damage caused by conflict and war on human communities, on their culture and psychological health, remained a constant concern. His first academic publication was for the journal *Human Relations* and described the specific problems encountered by prisoners of war as they adapted to the strains of returning to everyday life.

In 1950 he was appointed as a lecturer in social psychology at the University of Oxford. During this time he became interested in the link between social psychology and education policy, 'believing that if we could educate our children in the right way, the sort of psycho-social problems I had been trying to cope with would be much less prevalent'. Knowing 'nothing about education apart from my own unhappy experience of being at the receiving end of it, ... I rapidly wrote three articles on education and psychology', and, as he put it in his memoir, 'got the job'. In 1952, at the remarkably young age of 36, he was appointed Chair of Education and Psychology at the University of Exeter, where he served until 1956.

During this time between 1947 and 1956, from his work at the Tavistock Institute and then at the University of Exeter, he published over 30 journal articles, reports and policy papers, one of the earliest with E.L. Trist in 1948, ('Transitional communities and social reconnection'. *Human Relations.* 1:74).[10] While at Oxford he had carried out a number of short-term

Adam with daughters Tina and Anna, mid 1950s

assignments for the United Nations, and as a result of this he resigned from Exeter in 1956 to take up a new post as Advisor on Social Affairs to the Government of Pakistan. This marked a further turning point, from a domestic and English focus towards international development policy and research into the relationship between education and development. The post was organized through Harvard University and funded by the Ford Foundation, a connection that was to lead to another watershed in the future. Much of the work he conducted in Pakistan was published some years later, when he took up a new post at Harvard in 1961, which will be looked at below.

It was also in Pakistan that he met Anne Edie, a health worker from New Zealand who had been based in the Palestinian refugee camps in Jordan, and then moved on to serve in a Quaker centre in the slums of Dhaka. Adam met Anne in East Pakistan/Dhaka and they married in 1958.

Before Harvard came another overseas posting and another step closer to his shift from education psychology and development to peace education and peacemaking. In 1959 he was appointed Professor of Education at the University of Ghana. It was here that Adam and Anne joined the Society of Friends (Quakers), and their daughter Deborah was born. Becoming a Quaker was a hugely significant and influential step in his life and lifestyle.

He recorded the experience in an unpublished memoir:

> Another important personal happening (in Ghana) was that we
> joined the Quakers. This is a small religious body something
> over three hundred years old. It's distinctive because it doesn't
> have any set of dogmas in which one has to believe (most Chris-
> tian churches expect their adherents to believe a lot of unbeliev-
> able things). There is only one central idea, which is that there is
> an element of the divine in everyone. But from that follow a lot
> of things which were important to us: that everyone is worthy of
> equal care and respect, that the violence of war or any other sort,
> is an affront to the essential goodness, however much it was
> masked, of the other; that the idea of racism and racial superior-
> ity must be opposed.

Becoming a Quaker provided him with a set of values which were not
dogmatic, which were attuned to his interest in mysticism, and which
for him were significant in his search for the principles of an underlying human unity. It also signified a commitment to engagement, to
activity in accordance with the values of the Society of Friends. On joining the small group of 25 Quakers in Accra (Africans and Europeans),
Adam and Anne immediately set about helping students whose grants
had been taken away for falling foul of politicians, and campaigning
for the provision of meals for hungry children in the capital. It was
also significant because it led him to apply another Quaker principle of
'speaking truth to power', which in turn resulted in him resigning from
his post at the University of Ghana and to involvement in the nascent
anti-apartheid struggle in South Africa. His resignation was the outcome of a disagreement with the President of the recently independent
Ghana, Kwame Nkrumah, who Adam felt was correct in his policy of
forcing out Europeans in order to 'Africanise' the education system in
the country, but who was also damaging the university by interfering
too much in its everyday affairs and teaching.

He left to take his new post at Harvard, but before going there he visited South Africa on a mission to arrange opportunities for black South
Africans to access university education abroad. The visit was organized
by the National Committee of Liberation, later the African Resistance
Movement, formed by the Liberal Party of South Africa to oppose and

dismantle the apartheid system. In the aftermath of the Sharpeville Massacre of 1960, the government regarded this organization as a threat to the security of the state and Adam found himself arrested in a night raid. He recalls a period of detention and interrogation as 'the most unpleasant month of my life'. Two of the poems in *Recognition of Reality* ('The Policeman Calls' and 'Hope and the Prisoner'), are about this arrest and another, 'Quakers', pays tribute to his Quaker values and the peace work they inspired.[11] 'The Policeman Calls' is reproduced here because it shows (in the third verse) his struggle to connect with the common core of humanity even in the most difficult and frightening of situations. 'Quakers' follows because it reveals the source of much of his conviction to believe in the existence of a universal and compassionate humanity.

The Policeman Calls

We wait for it knowing it must come
– but when? – the dreaded visitation;
at length, while we sleep uneasy,
there it is, the midnight call,
that quintessential happening of our age;
I dress slowly, fumbling, trying to gain time
to put my wits together.
The darkness standing by my bed:
'get a move on you, he's waiting'.

He, the secret policeman, gross with authority,
a mauling beast with male suspects,
capable of strangling an obstinate
prisoner in the cells barehanded,
yet somehow shifty, ill at ease with women;
thinning sandy hair, lumpy face,
spreading buttocks that overflow the chair,
blank saurian stare, bludgeoning first words:
'we know how to make you talk, professor'.

Must I give in to fear and loathing
Eventually living in the mire

of having squealed out confessions
that implicate my friends;
or manage to retain awareness that
behind the ugly mask of illusion
hides the reality, the potential for enlightenment,
the ground of all being
from which emerge, only to return
and mingle inextricably,
policeman, professor, prisoner
and the intimidating women.
If so I may be stronger to resist.

Quakers

They don't care much
For dogmas, but believe in
The essential divine goodness of
Our being, exploring its deeps
Together in their worship,
Then surface refreshed, illuminated
By the Inner Light, strengthened
For the work they see ahead.

His life's mission as a mediator and conciliator, much of it under aus-
pices of the Quakers or with Quaker support, was shaped by this experience in South Africa. This work was conducted over the course of
45 years in various hot conflicts in India and Pakistan, Nigeria, South
Africa and Zimbabwe, Northern Ireland, the Balkans, and Sri Lanka. It
is worth noting that his experience in South Africa, where there was a
large and obvious power imbalance between the apartheid regime and
black majority population, made him aware that mediation was only a
part of the broader task of peacemaking, which had to proceed along a
broader change process, addressing power imbalances and empowering
the oppressed. This comprehensive model of peaceful transformation,
which contained four processes – education, confrontation, bargaining
and conciliation/mediation – was at the core of his book *Making Peace*

(1971), and is reproduced in Chapter 2 (Making peace: peaceful and unpeaceful relationships).

Still, it would be over 10 years before all of this thinking and experience combined to direct the move to peace studies. He left South Africa for London, where the family stayed with Ursula Vaughan Williams, before sailing on the Queen Mary liner to take up his new post at Harvard, where he served as the Director of the Harvard Centre for Studies in Education and Development. Adam worked at Harvard for 12 years from 1961 to 1973. His preoccupation there was to advance understanding of development and especially the role of education in promoting development. During his time at Harvard he published a series of books and articles on this topic (in 1963, *Educational strategy for developing societies: a study of educational and sociological factors in relation to economic growth;* in 1966, *Planning for Education in Pakistan: a Personal Case Study;* in 1969, *Educational problems of developing societies with case studies of Ghana and Pakistan*). Most of this work reflected a fairly conventional approach embedded in an underlying belief in progress through economic modernisation. However, he also registered an early concern that development should not be measured only in economic terms but also through social and cultural dimensions, in particular in the emergence of a purposive society capable of fulfilling human potential in social relationships. By the late 1960s he began to have doubts about the whole underlying project of development. Above all, conflict and violence were beginning to feature in his work as subjects demanding urgent attention and especially so because of his direct experience of the Nigerian Civil War between 1967 and 1970, and the war between India and Pakistan. In Pakistan, the short war with India in 1965 (when he was sent on a mediation mission supported by US and British Quakers), and the violent events of 1971 when the country was divided, swept away the fruit of development in a tide of death, destruction and hatred. His mediation activity in Nigeria from 1967 to 1970 is the subject of *In the Middle*, and Yarrow's *Quaker Experiences in International Conciliation*.

Drawn into work as a mediator in international conflict, his experience at Harvard, the rise of student radicalism and the movement against the war in Vietnam all disturbed his self-image as an expert academic with unchallengeable knowledge. It was time for another shift in direction.

From Harvard to Bradford 1973-1978: Peace with work to do
1. Peace as reflective practice[12]

During 1969 and 1970 Adam enjoyed a sabbatical year at the Richardson Institute in London. The Institute was then under the direction of Michael Nicholson, a pioneer of peace research, and part of a small but influential network of academics who had formed the Conflict Research Society in London in 1963.[13] It was in London that Adam became aware that peace was beginning to be treated as a subject of academic enquiry and in the course of the year he wrote *Making Peace*, the book that announced his arrival in the academic world of peace research. Having heard of a Quaker concern to establish a peace studies department in a British university (there was after all a War Studies department in London), he was invited by the Quaker Peace Studies Trust in 1973 to consider taking the post of Professor and to head up the new department at the University of Bradford. Arriving in England in 1973, the fledgling School of Peace Studies was launched with its first teaching programme in autumn.

Adam's inaugural lecture at Bradford was delivered in 1974, the year in which the teaching programme started. It was republished in 1985 along with the inaugural lecture of the second professor, James O'Connell, under the title *Peace with work to do*, and is reproduced in chapter 6.

It should be clear from this account that his academic interest in peace was a product of experience through which he not only witnessed threats to development from the eruption of violent conflicts, but he had been drawn increasingly into the *practice* of peacemaking. Most importantly, during the intense and disturbing experiences of the civil war in Nigeria he felt a compelling need to understand more about why these conflicts happened. He began to see violence, conflict, the process of change especially as this affected social attitudes, and the goals of development as linked phenomena. The three major studies, published between 1971 and 1973, in which these changed perceptions are hardened into substantial analyses, are *Making Peace, Mystics and Militant* and *Education for Liberation*. *Making Peace* represents the application of ideas from peace research to his own work and experience. In this book he tackles problems of definition, looking at peaceful and unpeaceful relationships, and in a general sense at the process of peacemaking; *Mystics and Militants*, written as a sequel to *Making Peace*, looks more closely at the personal beliefs of the peacemakers themselves and at the

Peace Studies Bradford University inaugural lecture 1974 (top)

School of Peace Studies staff group and first MA students, Bradford University, 1974 (middle)

Textile sampler presented to Adam by staff at Harvard University on his departure for Bradford, 1973 (left) qualities and skills they need to build. *Education for Liberation* examines the ways in which the process and values of educational institutions and educators serve to smother and repress or to liberate the creativity necessary for making peace and living peacefully. These books have had a widespread influence on the emergence of peace studies as a coherent area of study. They established Adam as an original and innovative thinker, capable of providing a comprehensive view of the academic validity and viability of peace studies, and were a significant reason for his move to Bradford when the university there decided to add peace studies to its portfolio of new study areas. The focus on *relationships* as the subject of peace which above all distinguishes and characterises his work can be seen in the following extract:

> I prefer to define peace positively. By contrast with the absence of overt strife, a peaceful relationship would, on a personal scale, mean friendship and an understanding sufficiently strong to overcome any differences that might occur ... On a larger scale, peaceful relationships would imply active association, planned co-operation, an intelligent effort to forestall or resolve potential conflicts.[14]

Peace was concerned then not with the containment of conflict, but predominantly with building relationships: 'As I define it, the process of peacemaking consists in making changes to relationships so that they may be brought to a point where development can occur.'[15]

Peace with work to do
2. Mediation 1960s -1980s[16]

Given this approach to peace studies, which evolved slowly from his experience and academic orientation in anthropology, psychology and development education, it was natural that Adam should see peace broadly in terms of the full development of human relationships and capacities, rather than as a set of 'peace-enforcing' rules and organisations. By the end of the 1960s and increasingly during the early 1970s he became aware of the work of John Burton, Johan Galtung, and Kenneth and Elise Boulding, and realized that his work and theirs were leading to the same general goals towards an emerging field of peace research and education, especially concerned with finding new non-violent ways of dealing with violent conflicts.

The primary peacemaking tool through which Adam hoped this goal might be realized was mediation. *In the Middle* points to the importance of mediation and reconciliation themes in peace research and practice in the conflict-ridden world of the late 20th century. Adam was a pioneer of a new form of mediation, now referred to variously as track two mediation, non-official mediation, or citizens' diplomacy, to distinguish it from power based diplomacy (usually called track one mediation) as used by governments.[17] The strength of his form of mediation is that, even in conflicts that are characterised by a very clear perception of differing interests for which people are prepared to fight, the fighting creates its own dynamic where the fighting groups cannot be seen to step down from their set positions without appearing to be weak. Mediation is appropriate when the parties in a conflict are willing to at least consider, however tentatively, that third-party intervention might have benefits, and at this point skilled mediation may, through the removal of misperceptions and the calming of violent emotions, provide the window of opportunity for negotiated settlement. Adam identified four elements in his mediation process: the mediator acts first to build, maintain and improve communications; second, to provide information to and between the conflicting parties; third, to 'befriend' the conflicting parties; and fourth, to encourage what he referred to as active mediation, that is to say, to cultivate a willingness to engage in co-operative negotiation. The account at the start of this chapter about his activity in the Nigerian Civil War shows how much he was prepared to take risks and put himself in danger in pursuit of the values of peace.

Most of this track two mediation was based on the four-stage model described above – a committed but nevertheless neutral role where the mediators work to inform, communicate, befriend, and conciliate. The model applied to, and was derived from, his experiences in his mediations between India and Pakistan, in Zimbabwe, Nigeria, Northern Ireland and in parts of his work in Sri Lanka.

However, he became aware in the 1990s that the nature of warfare had changed and the narrow mediation model described in *In the Middle* needed to be revised, with a deeper version of peacemaking. As he explained:

> My work in the Balkans, in Rwanda and some of my work in Sri
> Lanka, coupled with the experience of my friends during the last
> 10 or 12 years has differed greatly, as has that of friends working in

other places, from earlier experiences. The wars have been more genocidal – between peoples rather than between governments, they have been controlled by warlords rather than statesmen, more cruel, more chaotic, completely unresponsive to international opinion or conventions. For all these reasons they are less amenable to otherwise generally accepted diplomatic approaches by the UN or any other authorities. Previously my role had mainly been that of mediator. Now there is seldom anyone with whom to mediate or who is ready to listen to a mediatory voice. During all my time in the Balkans I was only called to mediate once – between two hostile warlords. My main concern was support for a suffering community which was, despite great difficulties, radiating a sense of peace and purpose into a much wider sphere.[18]

Peace with work to do
3. Tools for transformation:
Nurturing cultures of peace 1990s -2006[19]

Adam's later work, during the decade from the mid-1990s, is characterised by a revision and broadening of his concept of mediation and its place in peacemaking. Throughout his academic career (when he retired from the Chair of Peace Studies at Bradford University) and also during the period of his retirement from the university, he had been deeply involved in the practice of peacemaking, moving more from academic/practitioner to practitioner/activist. In the 1990s much of his involvement took the form of supporting the activity of the Osijek Centre for Peace, Nonviolence and Human Rights. Osijek, a town in the Eastern Slavonia province of Croatia, was, with the adjacent town of Vukovar, the site of the most violent fighting during the Serb Croat War. This involvement with the people of Osijek, who were trying to rebuild a tolerant society while surrounded by many people consumed by enraged and embittered feelings caused by the war, prompted a considerable amount of reflection on the problems of practical peacemaking. It was apparent, for example, that the model of mediation specified in his book, *In the Middle,* and distilled from his experiences in the conflicts of the 1970s and 1980s was very difficult to apply on the ground, in the confusion and chaos of the type of conflict epitomised by the wars in former Yugoslavia in the 1990s. It was still the case that the use of mediatory techniques would be much more likely to produce the shift in attitudes and understanding necessary for a stable peace, a resolution of conflict, than the use of conventional diplomacy alone: 'Solutions reached through negotiation may be simply expedient and not imply any change of heart. And this is the crux of peace. There must be a change of heart. Without this no settlement can be considered secure.'[20] However, he realized through his involvement with the Osijek project that the range of conflict traumas and problems was so vast that the model of mediation based on the intervention of outsider-neutrals was simply not powerful or relevant enough to promote peace. He made an important revision to his peace praxis:

> Since conflict resolution by outside bodies and individuals has so far proved ineffective (in the chaotic conditions of contemporary ethnic conflict – particularly, but not exclusively, in Somalia, Eastern Europe and the former USSR), it is essential to consider the peacemaking potential within the conflicting communities themselves.[21]

He came to see the role of conflict resolution in post-cold war conflicts as providing a variety of support to local peacemakers through an advisory, consultative-facilitative role with workshops and training in a wide variety of potential fields which the local groups might identify as necessary. The challenge is to empower people of goodwill in conflict-affected communities to rebuild democratic institutions, and the starting point for this is to help in 'the development of the local peacemakers' inner resources of wisdom, courage and compassionate non-violence.'[22]

Deep peace and the long view:
Taming the Hydra and the fragile voice of love

Adam decided to retire from his post at Bradford in 1978, at the age of 62, ending a 35 year career as an academic. After his retirement, he lived with Deborah and Anne in a converted farmhouse and barn in the village of Austwick in the heart of the Yorkshire Dales, about 30 miles to the northwest of Bradford. The family moved to Dulwich in London in 1985. For the 28 years of his life after retirement, until his death on 28 September 2006 in Wimbledon, London, he continued to travel and work as a mediator-peacemaker, and to write and lecture. Between 1973 and 1978

Adam at home in Wimbledon, London, 2006

he made numerous visits to Ireland. From 1984 to 1989 he made more than 20 often lengthy trips to Sri Lanka and India as part of a Quaker mediation mission. From 1989 he was active again on behalf of the Quakers with the conflict in Zimbabwe. From 1992 he worked as a peacemaker in the Balkans, principally in Osijek and continued as a key supporter of the Centre for Peace, Nonviolence and Human Rights until his death in 2006. In 2000 he was awarded the Gandhi International Peace Award. He continued to speak at universities in the UK, the USA, Canada, Australia, New Zealand and the University of the South Pacific.

His life and work touched many people worldwide, and his academic thinking is now firmly embedded in modern peace theory. His career in peace studies spanned over 40 years. During this time he created the first Department of Peace Studies in a British university and established the credibility of peace studies as an area worthy of academic recognition. Through his publications and teaching he built up a rich theory of the nature of peace and peacemaking, and was a pioneer and practitioner of the process of tracktwo mediation, which, in his later practice, he transformed into a model of peacemaking based on the idea of peace building from below. Influenced especially by his peacemaking work during the Balkan Wars of the early 1990s, he was one of those peace intellectuals who led a revision of thinking about the process of peacemaking. This included the idea that effective and sustainable peacemaking processes must be based, not merely on the manipulation of peace agreements made by elites, but more importantly on the empowerment of communities torn apart by war to build peace from below.

Adam published over 250 written pieces – papers in academic journals, essays and commentaries in newsletters and magazines, mimeographs of talks and lectures presented to numerous peace organizations, chapters in edited books, and 14 single authored books, one of which was a book of poems. Among these 14, nine were concerned with peace and conflict. All of these publications, along with unpublished material, are listed chronologically in Part 4 of this book, and many of them are held in the University of Bradford J.B Priestley Library and in the Special Collections Archives. This anthology of his work brings together extracts from most of the nine books and other articles which together represent all of his published output on peacemaking. Despite this obviously prodigious output, and despite having held senior positions and professorships at the most prestigious universities and institutes (Tavistock, Exeter, Oxford, Ghana, Harvard and Bradford), he insisted that he was primarily a peace activist rather than an academic. In 1977, a year before he retired from Bradford, he wrote a short piece called *Reflections on working in a university*, in which he commented on the tensions between, on the one hand institutionalized scholarship and the administrative burdens that came with it, and on the other, the freedom and energy needed for peace activism. He often felt limited and frustrated by the way in which the conventions of academic writing failed to convey the full sense and realities of peacemaking. In his last two books, *To tame the Hydra* (1999) and especially in *The fragile voice of love* (2006), he largely freed his voice from the need for extensive academic references and footnotes. Here he looked forward, experientially and reflectively, to exploring in his own voice the continued evolution of a common consciousness of mind and spirit – the long view that would guide the quest for peaceful humanity. While he remained active as an engaged peacemaker in the stressful and challenging situations and places outlined above, and while these outward journeys took much of his time, he made it clear that the inner journeys were more important. This was because, he said they conditioned 'the way we feel about the outer ones, whether we meet them with joy and excitement or with worry, apprehension and fear'. Buddhism, learned from the Dalai Lama, enhanced his awareness as a Quaker, 'by the constantly repeated emphasis on generosity and kindness ... by the all-pervading sense of the unity yet ever changing character of life ... by the emphasis on nonviolence and the essential worth and interdependence of every human being in the world ... by cheerfulness and fundamental optimism despite clear sighted recognition of pain and disease and disaster ...' Yet he remained undogmatic and eclectic in his thinking and his judgement, believing that the fundamental lessons from all the systems of thought he studied are the same – that 'all people who penetrate sufficiently far below the different idioms and conventions of faith and culture, must perceive that the same universal principles ... govern our lives'.[23]

This idea of deep peace and the long view, of the challenge to create spaces to imagine peaceful social and political alternatives to the structures and cultures of violence, and the need to be visionary, was shared by many of the first generation of peace educators. Elise Boulding said that peacemaking should be understood as an evolutionary capacity, a process which must be observed not only by looking at our own decade, because 'social progress happens in bigger chunks than our present-focused minds can easily digest. We are all starving for vision...'. The use of social imagination and the idea of imaging the future was placed within the context of what she called the '200-year present', that is, the idea that we live in a social space which reaches into the past and into the future: 'It is our space, one that we can move around directly in our own lives and indirectly by touching the lives of the young and old around us.' For Elise Boulding, the next half of our '200-year present', that is, the next 100 years from the 1980s, contains within it not only the basis for a world civic culture and peaceful problem-solving among nations, but also the possibility of Armageddon.[24]

It is helpful to think of Adam Curle's life within this timeframe, which stretches back to our grandparents and forwards to our grandchildren, and to remember that celebration and commemoration form part of the vital life forces we need to inspire us. Once again Elise reminds us of the importance of the wholeness of personhood – of what it means to be human. She spoke of three modes of knowing – the cognitive/analytic, the emotional/affective, and the intuitive. In a world increasingly governed by science and technology, the cognitive/analytic mode has come to dominate and the emotional/affective and intuitive modes have become used relatively less frequently. For her it was important to find ways of 'freeing the other modes for action by developing the skills of the imagination'[25]. As we will see in the following chapters, Adam's life and work embodied this perspective – properly scholarly in the construction of knowledge but holistic in recognising the importance of imagination, creativity and the desire for happiness in peacemaking.

Adam, Deborah and Anne mid 1980s   *Adam in 2002*

PART I

MAKING PEACE

In this part we have selected extracts from the texts which represent the core of Adam's work on peace, written in a very productive three-year period, as he developed his thinking in the formation of the Bradford School of Peace Studies in the early 1970s. The extracts are presented in five chapters, Chapter 2 Making Peace, published in 1971; Chapter 3, The Practice of Peacemaking, (also from Making Peace); Chapter 4, Mystics and Militants, published in 1972; Chapter 5, Education for Liberation, published in 1973. Chapter 6 is his inaugural lecture, delivered in 1974, which defined the research and teaching agenda for peace studies at Bradford. Chapter 2, from Making Peace, presents his definitions of key concepts in the field: conflict (incompatibility); balanced and unbalanced relations of power; unpeaceful and peaceful relationships, where peace is defined as the development of the full and positive capacities of human beings. Chapter 3 is also from Making Peace and looks at the processes involved in changing un-peaceful relationships into peaceful ones, a process which combines four elements: research, conciliation, bargaining and development. Chapter 4, from *Mystics and Militants*, focuses on this discussion of the tensions between belonging identity and levels of awareness. Chapter 5, from *Education for Liberation* presents his view that peace studies should be located within what he termed affective education, that is education which recognizes as its conscious goals, the education of feelings and actions as well as thinking–education which is in fact affective or behavioural rather than solely intellectual. In Chapter 6, his inaugural lecture he defines the pedagogic approach for the new School at Bradford. His work in leading the emergence of peace research and education at Bradford, and in the definition and application of specific modes of peacemaking, is significant for a number of reasons. Firstly, the Bradford Department of Peace Studies, was one of the first full academic departments operating the complete range of peace studies, from BA through to Masters and PhD programmes, and has served as a stimulus for groups around the world seeking to establish their own centres for peace research. Secondly, in his writing and in the pedagogic tradition he established at Bradford, he validated a broad definition of what constituted legitimate peace research. He identified three main strands of activity which are relevant to peacemaking; to nurture social and economic systems which engender cooperation rather than conflict; to oppose violent, dangerous, and oppressive regimes with non-violence; and to bring about reconciliation between those who are in conflict. The first strand has been explored within Bradford in terms of a focus on critical research on weapons technologies, the arms trade, arms control, alternative security policy, resource conflicts, and institutions for international co-operation and interdependence. The second strand has been represented by work on peace theory, peace history, nonviolence and anti-war movements; and the third has focussed on mediation as a specific component of peacemaking, and it is one to which he brought his distinctive style. This third area emerged in large part because of Adam's practical involvement especially with Quaker mediation, a firm basis for track two or citizen's diplomacy. The Bradford 'tradition' has then, through Adam's initial conceptualisation, contained both the structural analyses of conflict which appears in the work of Johan Galtung and the subjective-psychological orientation which appears in Burton, Fisher and other problem solving approaches.[26]

CHAPTER 2

Making peace

PEACEFUL AND UNPEACEFUL RELATIONSHIPS[27]

S ome relationships are inherently unpeaceful. They do damage to one or more of the parties concerned, through physical violence, or in economic, social, or psychological ways. Absence of peace, in my definition, is characteristic of many situations that do not present overt conflict. Unpeacefulness is a situation in which human beings are impeded from achieving full development either because of their own internal relations or because of the types of relation that exist between themselves (as individuals or group members) and other persons or groups. Thus the internal relations within an individual may be so discordant and conflicted that his enjoyment of life is destroyed and his capacity to act is paralysed: he does not, as we say, enjoy peace of mind. Again, an unharmonious marriage in which the capacities of either partner (or both partners) cannot flower is unpeaceful; so, on a much larger scale, is the relation between the colonizer and the colonized, and that between underprivileged minorities – racial, religious, or linguistic – and the majorities responsible for their lack of privilege; so also, in some senses, is that between the world's small number of wealthy nations and its many poor ones. War is such a relationship: it epitomizes all the evils of unpeacefulness.

Conversely, in my terms, peace is a condition from which the individuals or groups concerned gain more advantage than disadvantage. Ideally, it means something even more positive: the harmonious and constructive collaboration typified by a happy marriage, for example, or an effectively run common market.

In general, books dealing with peace or its opposite are concerned with hostilities between nations, groups, or individuals, and the ways in which they may be curbed or prevented. Lack of peace is usually associated with physical harm or obviously disturbed, unhappy, or potentially violent relationships. I, however, take the view of Galtung, who maintains that violence (though I would term it unpeacefulness) exists whenever an individual's potential development, mental or physical, is held back by the conditions of a relationship.[28] It may seem peculiar to suggest that emotional, social, or educational deprivation, or a low level of health, should be regarded as symptoms of 'unpeace' if conditions are otherwise 'peaceful' and if the people concerned are satisfied with their lot. An example may show, however, that in such cases – whatever one may think of the desirability of the relationship – there is a potentiality for overt, physical violence.

The American 'Negro' ghetto communities in the 1950s were relatively peaceful in the sense that the blacks, though suffering violence, seldom responded in kind. The anger that flared in the 1960s on a large scale in many places was therefore not anticipated. But in the earlier, as in the later, decade, the black communities were underprivileged and subtly discriminated against: their educational level was lower than that of surrounding communities; their standard of nutrition was poorer; their life-expectancy was lower,[29] and many suffered from the psychological difficulties so well described by Grier and Cobbs (1968), two black psychiatrists. Yet one might go so far as to say that, despite their disadvantages, black people in the 1950s were 'satisfied': they were 'better off than their fathers', or 'knew their position', and were, therefore, at peace with the world. But it is clear that these were the conditions that led to the violence, the unpeace – which no one would objectively deny – of a few years later. Thus even if domination by one group produces the abject submission of another, the relationship (which is necessarily based on inequality) bears the seeds of rebellion. When the level of awareness rises in the dominated group, as we shall see later, the seeds germinate.

Before we are submerged in detail, I should perhaps attempt to identify my position in relation to various schools of thought on peace and conflict. Some writers, like Schelling (1960, 1966) and Etzioni (1967), are concerned with strategic studies which deal, essentially, with ways in which one unit (normally a state) can best improve its position. Others, such as Boulding (1962)[30] and Rapoport (1966), and many contributors to the *Journal of Conflict Resolution*, are largely involved with studies of conflict as a system of interaction in which, at whatever level it occurs, certain similarities can be observed. Yet again, the problems of peace and war may be approached through the study of international relations, and prominent writers in the field include Deutsch (1968)[31] and Kelman (1965). Lastly, there is the relatively new field of peace research, originating largely in Europe, and particularly associated with the name of Galtung. Although peace research is beset by controversy, it is perhaps fair to say that most workers in the area are particularly concerned with research whose results can be applied to the task of maintaining or restoring peaceful conditions. There is, naturally enough, a good deal of overlap among these branches of study and the dividing-lines are by no means well defined, but the broad differences of emphasis may be recognized. My own approach is related relatively less to strategic and conflict studies (though it is not entirely unconnected with them) than to international relations (though I also deal with interpersonal and intergroup relations) and peace research (though what I have to say results from experience and reflection rather than research and I am, in general, more practical than scholarly). But the general field is perhaps both new and broad enough for each explorer to tread out his own path. This I have tried to do.

KEY CONCEPTS

Conflict

In discussion of unpeaceful relationships it is convenient to use the idea of conflict. By conflict I mean, essentially, incompatibility. The cat, in the psychological experiment, that can reach its food only at the cost of suffering an electric shock experiences an inner conflict arising out of the incompatibility of wishing both to avoid pain and to gratify hunger. On the larger scale, conflict develops when one individual, community, nation, or even supranational block, desires something that can be obtained only at the expense of what another individual or group also desires. This is a conflict of interest, which can all too easily lead to a conflict in the sense of war or strife.

My broad conception of unpeaceful relationships introduces, however, a controversial issue into the definition of conflict, on which I should state my position before proceeding further. My position constitutes, in effect, a value. If one holds that relationships that impede human development are unpeaceful, it follows that one holds an objectivist view of conflict. In this view, conflict is a question not of perception but of fact. Thus if, in a particular social system, one group gains what another loses, there is – even if the loser does not understand what is happening – a structural conflict, which is what Galtung means (*see note 1*) by his term 'structural violence'.

Readers who hold other values will inevitably disagree with much that I have to say. They might quote the example of the benevolent master and his devoted slave: the slave does not question the rightness of his role and sees no other part for himself; the two work together in perfect harmony. This, in the subjectivist view, does not constitute a state of conflict. In the objectivist view, however, there are certain privileges and possibilities that are not open to the slave. To the extent that he is unaware of them, ignorance may be bliss, but the fact remains that his existence is narrowed by social factors rather than by his own personal qualities. Moreover, although he is unaware of any incompatibility of interest, should he wish to change his role in the master-slave relationship (and if he does not, his son or his grandson probably will) the conflict would at once become apparent. For this reason, it would be hard to deny that, in situations where conflict is absent only because of low awareness, there is at least latent or potential conflict.

In such relationships there are usually, as I have indicated, quantifiable indices of inequality. Moreover, in my experience of many oppressed peoples, happy slaves are something of a myth. They may be politically unaware, but that is not to say that they are happy, and they normally live in circumstances conducive to misery. They are, in general, angry, resentful, and embittered; if they show a grinning face, it is for self-protection.

I maintain, therefore, that it is reasonable to treat the master- slave relationship (and, of course, all relationships represented by this term) as one of conflict, which should be changed. (These points are well argued by Herman Schmid, 1968.) But what of the happy slave who doesn't want anything to be changed? By what right do we interfere? Is not our judgement of what ought to be done based on those very subjective values we claim to reject? This is correct. Ultimately, any measurement of what is best for people is based on a judgement of value. My values emphasize life and health, the development of human potential, equality of opportunity. But these things cannot be empirically demonstrated to be better than their opposites. One has heard it argued that hunger is good because it promotes spirituality; that an early death is good because one ascends sooner to heaven, having – with luck – fewer sins to be purged of; or that a slow, painful death is better than a quick, painless one because one has more time to ponder on and expiate one's faults. One's views on these matters are based on values that are not amenable to proof. I, then, hold the value that it is right to change the condition of the happy slave. If he does not want to change, it may well be that he does not know, in his present state of ignorance, that change is possible or what it might portend.

Balance and imbalance

The second concept I utilize is that of balanced and unbalanced relationships. The current convention is to refer to symmetrical and asymmetrical relationships[32] but I find this unrealistic: symmetry implies a degree of similarity that is exceptional if not unknown. By a balanced relationship I mean one in which there is a more or less equal division of power. It need not necessarily be the same sort of power: for example, in the conflict between the government and the University of Ghana, the government obviously held all the conventional power, but the University could invoke many potent sanctions – international moral indignation, the alienation of educated Ghanaians, the loss of qualified foreign staff, and so on. The government made things most uncomfortable for the University, but in the last resort failed to impose demands that would have destroyed the central core of academic autonomy. The University, to put it another way, possessed strong deterrents. Clearly, in all other senses the government was the more powerful, having wealth, armed forces, and considerable coercive capacity, but these were of little use in this particular relationship. In assessing balance, therefore, we have to consider the extent to which, in a given setting, one party to a relationship is able to dominate another. Schelling (1966)[33] argues that power is the capacity to create uncertainty; but what matters is the degree of uncertainty and the means – economic, psychological, physical (including military) – by which it is created.

The situation in South Africa permits further exploration of the concept of balance. The white population there has great power over the non-white. Its police are well armed and ruthless; its armed forces well equipped and efficient. The seeds of rebellion have hardly germinated before they are uprooted. This is not to say, however, that the black population is entirely lacking in power: the evidence for this lies, paradoxically, in the strength that the whites, in their uncertainty, have felt impelled to build up. But the power of the non-white South Africans is potential rather than actual; at present, there is very little they can do to impose their views or wishes on the whites. By contrast, the whites, having rejected world opinion and being confident in the support of powerful vested interests, can do almost anything they please. However, if the 15 million non-whites were educated and organized to mount effective opposition to the apartheid policy of the 3-5 million whites, the balance of power would shift greatly. The essence of a revolutionary struggle in South Africa, as in any case of disadvantage and social injustice, would be to mobilize the underdogs to the point where they could rival the power of the rulers. Even so, the type of power wielded by the blacks might well be of a very different order – possibly consisting of massive strikes and boycotts – from the military strength of the government.

A further instance of imbalance, subsequently discussed, is seen in relations between the rich and the poor countries. These seem to me to be, in general, unbalanced in the sense that the rich have the power (primarily economic, but backed by military power should the need arise) to impose economic and political conditions on the poor. That the latter have little redress is shown by the failure of the rest of the world to implement the policies advocated at meetings of the United Nations Conference on Trade and Development.

In the last two examples, the imbalance of power is used by the stronger partners in the relationships (South Africa, and the wealthy countries) to exploit the weaker. In fact, it may be taken as axiomatic that, since none would suffer it gladly, exploitation is in itself evidence of imbalance. But imbalance does not always entail exploitation. Although a parent may exploit a child emotionally (or, in fact, vice versa), the parent-child relation is ideally one that helps the child to mature and to grow stronger. The same might be said of relations between small-scale and large-scale organizations, such as local governments and national governments. In such cases, the power to impose self-seeking demands is subordinated to concern for nurturing the smaller unit.

It should be stressed that, just as not all unbalanced relationships are unpeaceful, so not all balanced ones are peaceful. Nations at war are often evenly matched at many stages of the conflict, as is shown by the long duration of some conflicts and the inconclusiveness of others. Indeed, sometimes the very fact that a state resorts to war instead of achieving its objectives by pressure – as did Hitler's Germany in Austria and Czechoslovakia – implies a greater degree of balance; the most powerful countries can sometimes frighten the weaker into submission. There are, of course, relatively clear cases of imbalance: Belgium, for instance, was ill-matched against Germany in 1914 – although there was a considerable degree of balance between the Allies as a whole and Germany. Then, again, there are confusing cases.

How does one assess the balance of Israel and the Arab states, the former so successful militarily, the latter so superior in manpower, and both perhaps equally well armed? Or the United States and its allies against North Vietnam and the NLF, the former strong in numbers and technology, the latter in morale and guerrilla skills? For the argument in this book, however, it is not necessary to attempt precision about the balance of power in conditions of war. If exploitative imbalance leads to an armed uprising on such a scale that it is characterized as civil war, the implication is that the imbalance has largely been corrected. In other wars, unless there is a swift victory, the implication is that neither side had a significant advantage at the outset of hostilities, though of course either may achieve one later. In every case, what each side is striving for is a superiority that will enable it to gain a more satisfactory settlement. These matters are discussed in Chapter 20, on 'Bargaining'.

In what follows, we shall be primarily considering exploitative imbalance as constituting a particularly prevalent form of un- peaceful relationship. The achievement of balance, in which the advantage no longer rests with the formerly more powerful party to the relationship, does not necessarily lead to peace. The struggle may be merely intensified, as it enters on a new phase.

Awareness of conflict

A third concept relates to the degree of perception, or awareness, of conflict. In many unpeaceful relationships, the parties are perfectly aware of the discordance of their aims. In others, however, the conflict is not clearly recognized. Thus, among colonial peoples before the independence movements, among many oppressed and ignorant people today (such as the Faqir Mishkin, who are discussed later), to some extent among students, among some segments of the black American population, and among many black South Africans, there has been little awareness of conflict. It has not been obvious to these people that their poverty, powerlessness, or subjection, or the injustices they suffered, related directly to the riches, power, and authority of the ruling group; that there was, in fact, a conflict of interests. Now that these interests have been made manifest, the conflict has become apparent to most of those concerned. The dawning awareness of our age, an awareness affecting many of the issues discussed in this book, is described by Camus:

What characterizes our times ... is the way the masses and their
wretched condition have burst upon contemporary sensibilities.
We now know that they exist, whereas we once had a tendency
to forget them. And if we are now more aware, it is not because
our aristocracy ... has become better – no, have no fear – it is because the masses have become stronger and keep people from
forgetting them.[34]

Types of unpeaceful relationship

The concepts discussed above enable us to suggest different types of
unpeaceful relationship. There are those in which the power relation is
approximately balanced and there is considerable awareness of conflict;
those in which the power relation is unbalanced and there is considerable
awareness of conflict; and those in which the power relationship is unbalanced but awareness of conflict is lower. There are also more ambiguous
relationships in which there is something approaching the appearance of
a power balance coupled with low awareness of conflict: for instance, in
the South African Bantustan, the illusion of a certain degree of independence for the non-white blunts perception of the deep conflict of interest
between black and white South Africans.

These relationships, together with a fifth category, are now described
more fully.

1. Balanced relationship: considerable awareness of conflict

A fairly clear-cut example (though few issues are as clear-cut as the lessons we would like to draw from them) of this type of conflict was what,
depending on one's point of view, one called the Nigerian civil war, the
Ibo rebellion, or the Biafran struggle for independence. To oversimplify
considerably, what the federal government of Nigeria was determined to
do was to retain the whole of the former Eastern Region, which seceded
in 1967 as Biafra, as an integral part of Nigeria, whereas the other side
wanted to be independent. The essence of this conflict was, in effect, that
what one side won the other lost. This all-or- nothing approach can lead
to extremes of violence; consequently, one of the cardinal aims of conflict

resolution is often to secure an arrangement by which both sides gain something, are satisfied with it, and so call off their hostilities. I consider the Nigerian war to have been balanced rather than unbalanced for the empirical reasons that it lasted two and a half years before the federal victory, that there were long periods of stalemate, and that the eventual losers had some significant military success. In war, one of the aims of the contestants is to build up their armed forces so that the relation between them becomes unbalanced.

The India-Pakistan war, with preceding and subsequent periods of non-violent conflict, provides a further illustration of this type of unpeaceful relationship. This example also demonstrates the point that such relationships need not necessarily be violent but are always in danger of becoming so.

2. Unbalanced relationship: considerable awareness of conflict

The essence of this type of relationship is the dominance of one party over the other, and the others consciousness of that fact. It is the relation, for example, of the landlord to his tenant in semi-feudal West Pakistan; of the colonial ruler to the 'subject people'; of the national government to the tribe that prizes its autonomy; of many American whites to the black population; of some powerful nations to some dependent weak ones. These relationships differ from the unbalanced relationship that exists between the government and the citizens in a democratic state because there, although the citizen lacks the power and authority of the government, he has had a part in electing it and his individual rights are in many respects protected – even against the government. By contrast, the type of relationship under analysis here is one between a top dog and an underdog who has very little redress. The top dog is free to withhold his resources from the underdog and devote them to his own people: thus in South Africa a minuscule proportion of the money spent on education goes to schooling and social services for the Africans (see Chapter 4).[35] The top dog makes decisions about the underdog that the latter should make for himself, and does things to or for him (including, in some cases, benevolent things) that invade his proper autonomy; for instance, again in South Africa, the servant of a white family is provided with quarters but may not bring his wife and children to live with him.

The undermining of an individual's autonomy by such means, some-times harshly crude, sometimes subtle, does much to stunt the develop-ment of normal maturity. In particular, the individual's sense of identity is impaired and his self-respect eroded. Thus, in the Portuguese colonies, the educated African, by a kind of psychological capitulation, can come to enjoy many of the advantages of the rulers. He is termed an *assimilado*, one who is assimilated into Portuguese society as a reward for betraying his own heritage; but while ceasing in a sense to be an African, he never becomes European: who is he? In a similar way, whole communities, even whole nations, may be held back economically, socially, education-ally; used and exploited; made to feel inferior; denied justice. These are conditions of unpeace as I have defined the term. Such relationships are unpeaceful for two reasons: first, they deny to many the opportunity to develop as they might in what we would like to think of as peaceful exist-ence; second, they lead to, and sometimes cannot be changed except by, the eventual outbreak of physical violence in the form of insurrection, rebellion, civil war, and even international strife.

But these are extreme and obvious examples of unbalanced relation-ships. Elements of inappropriate domination may also occur in the most egalitarian and democratic societies and for reasons that are wholly well-meaning: the case of the Firm, discussed below is an example.[36] Again, many of the ills of imbalance may occur when a government or other au-thority feels impelled, in the interest of the general good, temporarily to override the rights and ignore the feelings of a particular group: thus, in East Pakistan, the entire Chakma tribe was thrown into angry confusion and eventually displaced by a hydro-electric project that was designed to bring great advantage to the province as a whole. Moreover, time brings about changes, with the result that what seemed a reasonable relationship a generation ago no longer does so today: thus the events of the last few years show that the relationship between professor and student, at least in the eyes of many students, should be restructured. Yet again, many authorities – university administrations, governments, trustees, boards of management, etc. — and, on a personal level, spouses or parents, run the danger of cutting across the interests of others by doing what has – or what they believe has – to be done. The razor edge between constitutional and authoritarian behaviour is one on which many statesmen and many much more humble administrators, organizers, and private citizens have cut themselves, and full peace is more often jeopardized than we would like to think. In these less extreme and, in general, more benevolent circumstances, the unpeacefulness is not demonstrated by crass indices of ill health or injustice, and still less by violence. The symptoms are more subtle: lack of cooperation, self-damaging withdrawal, personal quarrels and vendettas, self-doubt, lack of trust, anxiety; and their effect may be to create circumstances in which many people fail to develop or to use their capacities to the full.

3. Unbalanced relationship: lower awareness of conflict

One example of this third type of relationship, discussed more fully below concerns the Faqir Mishkin of Chitral.[37] They constitute one of the most depressed and oppressed groups in the world, but are so dominated, miserable, and ignorant that they are unaware of the abjectness of their position: they accept and endure it as a fact of nature like the bitter winters and the annual time of hunger.

Similarly, the peasant tribesmen among whom I lived 30 years ago in the Middle East were apathetic about their landlord. This does not mean that they were indifferent to him: they loathed and feared him for his selfish wealth, for his callousness and ruthlessness. When he rode by, they cowered humbly at the side of the road, though when he had passed they followed him with hate-filled eyes. But they never considered turning him out of his fine house and taking his possessions for themselves. This was not so much because they feared the consequences of such a step as because they felt the difference in their conditions to be part of the order of things: they had always been poor, the rich had always been rich; it followed, as night follows day, that the rich oppressed the poor. By the same token, they could not change places. The peasants hated the landlord, but they did not envy him, because to envy someone is to imagine oneself in his place – and this was inconceivable.

4. Pseudo-balanced relationship: low awareness of conflict

These relationships are more common than one might suppose. They occur whenever a dominant group attempts to placate or assuage a less dominant group by creating a superficial appearance of balance. Thus the South African government, in establishing 'Bantustans', has attempted to give a sufficient impression of equality of power between black and white to resolve – at least in the minds of some Africans – the conflict of interest between the races. There is, in fact, an element of this kind of relationship in many attempts at conflict resolution where effort is devoted more to concealing conflict in the hope of avoiding disturbance than to peacemaking in the more positive sense of working towards relationships that are not conflicted. In the case of the Firm, the Amenities Committee was established at least partly with the aim of introducing democratic procedures that would satisfy the members of the community that their relationship with the directors was egalitarian, that is, balanced. But the directors did not see that this perception of them must inevitably be confused and ambiguous because they in fact exercised absolute power over key aspects of the community's life, such as the allocation of housing.

A considerable part of the work done on peace and conflict research has been devoted, in effect, to studying techniques for changing unbalanced high-awareness-of-conflict relationships into ones in which there is a pseudo-balance and a low awareness of conflict. This emphasis developed, not surprisingly, in the postwar period when interest in the expanded field was largely focused on the dangers of the Cold War. It was natural to concentrate attention on ways of controlling or cooling down tensions that might have led to nuclear war. At the same time, the other major trend of conflict research, dealing with industrial disputes and the negotiation or arbitration procedures through which they might be settled, was little concerned – naturally enough, considering the interests of industry – to effect radical changes in employer-employee relations. Most industrial disagreements were concluded by settlements which, some would maintain, did little more than paper over the cracks of an inherently un- peaceful relationship. As a result, researchers in these areas tended to act as though the absence of overt violence, or of disharmonies that might lead to violence, was an absolute value to be preserved at all costs.

5. Relationships of alienation

These constitute a fifth type of unpeaceful relationship, but one that does not fit into the pattern of the others. The salient feature here is not conflict in the sense of any objective incompatibility of interest, but the alienation of one group from another, often, but not necessarily, accompanied by a sense of grievance – even of conflict – which is completely unwarranted by the facts. In the single individual this is a condition approaching paranoia. It is illustrated at a more institutional level in the case study concerning the foreign adviser, whose plight stems from his failure to understand a situation he has come into and, to a lesser extent, from the failure of his local counterpart to appreciate what he has to offer. The relationship is unpeaceful because it involves a misuse of the adviser's talents and because it may easily result in tensions, and perhaps genuine conflicts. Thus I have known sorry instances where advisers and the local nationals with whom they should have been working in constructive harmony have been intriguing against each other and striving to undermine each other's position. The village of Thornley (see p.140)[38] provides an example of a community alienated from its surroundings for reasons that had little to do with the contemporary situation.

To conclude, relationships of alienation exist when one party to the relationship feels and acts as though he were the underdog in an un-balanced/higher-awareness relationship while the other feels and acts as though he were engaged in a peaceful relationship – or at least tries to do so. If, however, one is treated with suspicion and hostility one tends to react in kind, though probably not to the extent of changing the structure of the relationship completely.

Peaceful relations

Peaceful relations can be defined negatively in terms of absence of conflict. Absence of conflict may, however, mean little more than absence of association: there are many people with whom one does not quarrel because one does not know them well and is never placed in a position where a clash of interests or personalities could arise. But I would term this negative peace. Another form of negative peace characterizes those relationships in which violence has been avoided or reduced, without the removal of the conflict of interest, or in which the conflict has been mystified, that is to say, concealed or disguised. The latter, as I have noted, is a not uncommon outcome of industrial disputes. The workers may have a genuine grievance which, if it were to be redressed, would be very costly to the employers; the employers therefore avoid both expense and disturbance by expressing sympathy with the workers, meeting with them cordially, and making some minor but ostentatious concession to them by which they hope the workers will be dazzled. In my terms, these forms of negative peace constitute unpeaceful relationships.

I prefer to define peace positively. By contrast with the absence of overt strife, a peaceful relationship would, on a personal scale, mean friendship and understanding sufficiently strong to overcome any differences that might occur. On a larger scale, peaceful relationships would imply active association, planned cooperation, an intelligent effort to forestall or resolve potential conflicts. This aspect of peace contains a large quotient of what I term development.

If development is to occur, that is to say, if a relationship is to grow in harmony and productiveness, it is axiomatic that there must be equality and reciprocity in large measure. The mutuality of a peaceful relationship differentiates it from an unpeaceful one: mutuality in which one partner assists the other to achieve his ends and so serves his own. In peaceful relationships there is neither domination nor imposition. Instead there is mutual assistance, mutual understanding, mutual concern, and collaboration founded on this mutuality. As I define it, the process of peacemaking consists in making changes in relationships so that they may be brought to a point where development can occur. As we shall see, some of these changes may not accord with other definitions of peace. Revolutionary upheavals may be necessary if, for example, the slave seeks equality with his master. But if he achieves it – and who can say what price should be paid or danger incurred for this end – the relationship changes into one of man to man. If two men can find common ground and live together without destroying each other (and this is the next task in the quest for peace), they may then begin to learn to work with and for each other; this is the quality of development that typifies positive peace.

Peaceful relationships may be balanced or unbalanced. Examples of unbalanced peaceful relationships would be those between parent and child, family and community, provincial and federal government, small state and large state, and so on. The essence of these relationships is that the smaller or weaker partner is helped to develop his potentialities and that, in the process, he contributes to the development of the stronger. It is equally easy to think of examples where such relationships have engendered an element of conflict: many Americans, for instance, are keenly aware of conflict between the rights of individual states and the demands of the federal administration; the relationship between parent and child may be agonizingly conflicted. In these cases the potential of the smaller or weaker partner is prevented from being realized.

I would emphasize these points relating to development and to the positive definition of peace because they dominate the arguments that follow. The kind of peace we want determines our approach to peacemaking and the methods we employ.

Figure 1 Peaceful and unpeaceful relationships

	UNPEACEFUL RELATIONS		PEACEFUL RELATIONS
	Lower awareness of conflict	*Higher awareness of conflict*	*No conflict*
Balanced		*Approximately evenly matched conflict; e.g. India/Pakistan.*	*Development; e.g. the European Common Market and other peaceful and constructive associations.*
Unbalanced	*Ignorantly passive groups; negative peace; e.g. the Faqir Mishkin.*	*Revolution of the underdog; confrontation, violent or non-violent; the essential effort is to acieve a more equal relationship: e.g. the Black Americans..*	*Development; harmonious relationship of unequal partners; e.g. parent/child, state/federal government, France/Monaco.*

Figure 2 A pseudo-balanced relationship

	UNPEACEFUL RELATIONS		PEACEFUL RELATIONS
	Lower awareness of conflict	*Higher awareness of conflict*	*No conflict*
Balanced	SOUTH AFRICAN BANTUSTAN		
Unbalanced			

NOTE: *No one could assert that all South African blacks have a low perception of conflict in their society, but in many of them awareness is low and this has prevented the development of an effective resistance movement. The creation of Bantustans gives some impression of a balanced relationship and serves to maintain in many their low perception of conflict. In effect, of course, the conflict persists.*

These types of peaceful and unpeaceful relationships – except alienation, which is in a somewhat different category – are set out in Figure 1. Note that no example is given of an unpeaceful relationship in a balanced/ lower-awareness-of-conflict situation, since this combination is probably never as clear cut as the others, though there is an element of ambiguity in many. The nearest to it is a pseudo-balanced relationship coupled with a low awareness of conflict, as shown in Figure 2.

The case studies

The case studies presented in Part I of this volume illustrate the five types of unpeaceful relationship outlined above and cover a very varied field. I have drawn my examples from different countries and on different scales: they include the alienation of individuals and of nations at war; small-scale group relations; relations between the wealthier nations and the poorer; and very violent and completely non-violent relationships.

The choice of these case studies itself indicates the book's purpose and nature. I have gone far beyond what might be considered the conventional topics of peace and conflict studies because I believe that unpeaceful relations are to be found at all levels of human interaction and that, since they possess common features, they should be described as a totality. A large number of my instances derive from the poorer areas of the world. This reflects a dominant concern as well as much of my relevant experience. I should stress, however, that an extremely high proportion of the world's unpeaceful relationships are in what is often termed the Third World. This is largely a result, in my opinion, of its relationship with the affluent world, whether communist or capitalist, which has made its own demands and attempted to impose its own standards and values upon it.

I should also observe that both in the case studies and in Part II I draw upon my own experience where it seems suitable. I did this in an earlier work (Curle, 1966) and was accused by some critic of writing a gossipy travelogue rather than a serious textbook. But the purpose, then and now, is highly serious. In the 1966 study I wished to illustrate the problems and limitations of the foreign adviser (some of whose experiences are included in one of the case studies below), and felt I could most cogently do so through personal examples. In this book I am discussing relationships, that is, systems of interaction between two or more people or groups. Anyone, such as a conciliator, who tries to influence a relationship becomes, in some degree, part of that system. To pretend that he is an impersonal outside observer is dishonest. It is better to say as openly as possible what he did and how he felt.

Despite their diversity, most of the cases can be categorized fairly readily according to the framework of Figures 1 and 2. That is to say, they describe unpeaceful relationships which are either balanced or unbalanced, and in which there is either a relatively high or a relatively low awareness of the conflict of interest; or relationships in which there is some ambiguity concerning balance and awareness, as exemplified in Figure 2. Some of the cases illustrate relationships of alienation, in which the perception of conflict is one-sided and not justifiable objectively.

The art of peacemaking is to move the relationship out of one of the unpeaceful categories into a peaceful one. I shall not, however, deal with the transformation of unbalanced unpeaceful relationships into unbalanced peaceful ones. This is, of course, perfectly possible. In certain circumstances, as for example between parents and children or between national and local governments, unpeaceful unbalanced relations can become peaceful unbalanced relations, and very often the same processes are involved as when peaceful balance is achieved. In particular there is likely to be some element of confrontation involving a certain redistribution of power and the acceptance, after bargaining, of safeguards that render the imbalance advantageous to both parties, or at least not harmful to either. In many circumstances, however, such a resolution more closely approximates the pseudo-balanced/ low-awareness relationship of the South African Bantustan shown in Figure 2. For this reason we shall be mainly concerned with what may be done to change the various types of unpeaceful relationship, including relationships of alienation, into ones that are more balanced and in which there is no conflict of interest.

In some of the vignettes of unpeaceful relationships that comprise Part I there are accounts of peacemaking approaches.[39] For example, in 'Returned Prisoners of War and their Society' I have described the therapeutic role of the Civil Resettlement Units; in 'Employers and Employees: the Firm I have outlined my work as an intermediary; in 'Pakistani Villages and the Government' I have written about the essentially conciliatory part of the Village AID organization. However, in 'Colonialism and Neo-colonialism', 'Two Wars', and 'Adamzadas and Faqir Mishkin: Chitral', no specific peacemaking activity is advocated. These may simply be taken as descriptions of different types of conflict and the reader may divert himself with speculation as to how they might be rendered more peaceful.

In Part I peacemaking is related specifically to individual cases and is not discussed. In Part II, 'The Practice of Peacemaking', there is an attempt to generalize. Six components of peacemaking are identified, and in the context of these there is wider discussion of the work described in Part I. The six components are:

1. Research, through which the would-be peacemaker acquires enough knowledge of the situation to work effectively.

2. Conciliation, through which he lays the psychological foundation – the changed perceptions, the heightened awareness, the reduced tension – necessary for rational discussion and negotiation.

3. Bargaining, in which the two parties to a quarrel try to reach agreement without making excessive concessions.

4. Development, in which a formerly unpeaceful relationship is restructured along peaceful lines.

5. Education, through which the weaker party in a low-awareness/ unbalanced relationship gains awareness of its situation and so attempts to change it.

6. Confrontation, through which the weaker party to an unbalanced relationship asserts itself in the hope of gaining a position of parity, and hence the possibility of reaching a settlement that will lead to a restructuring of the relationship. Confrontation may have many forms, ranging from revolution to non-violent protest.

In the case studies, most of the peacemaking described is in the form of conciliation or, to a lesser extent, of development, as in the example of the Pakistani villages. Research, though referred to only a couple of times, is to some extent a component of most cases. There is an element of confrontation in 'Employers and Employees: the Firm', and of bargaining in 'The University and the Government: Ghana'. Suggestions are made, however, concerning other peacemaking techniques – education, for example – which might have been applied in these and comparable cases.

Finally, I should apologize for the completely non-quantitative nature of the case studies and their discussion. The small size of the sample precludes statistical treatment. However, wider experience and a greater refinement of method may make it possible to test the validity of some of the ideas and approaches put forward by 'harder' techniques than I have been able to apply. In the meantime, I hope that the case method, which has proved its usefulness at the beginning stages of many studies that have subsequently become more empirical and more quantifiable, may illustrate the themes I am interested in, promote argument, and encourage further – and more precise – inquiries.

Revolution

It will have become obvious from what has been said above that I consider it essential, in many cases, for relationships to undergo radical change if they are to be made peaceful. I have referred to the awkward case of the happy slave and to confrontation as a peacemaking technique. But what is involved is close to, and may become, revolution – a prospect that poses a fearful dilemma for a student of conflict who may have been drawn to the subject out of sincerely pacifist idealism. The following brief discussion of revolution does not attempt to resolve the basic problem but to present some of the issues that will be expanded in the chapter on 'Confrontation'.[40]

In all revolutions there must, at some stage, have been a movement from lower to higher awareness of the situation, followed by a striving for greater balance. The resultant rebellions have been either put down, in which case there may have been another uprising later, or successful, when they have led to a greater degree of balance between the parties. Most colonial wars of liberation have resulted in the independence of the colonies and, despite the impositions of neo-colonialism, in a much greater balance in their relationship with the former rulers. Likewise, in many European countries, political evolution (as in France), through which oligarchies have in general given way to democracies, has reduced or blurred differences of class or birth: the conflict of interest, though perhaps in places never entirely resolved, has usually shifted its focus from hereditary to achieved position and has become much less sharp. It is tenable (though I would not fully agree) that, with some qualifications and exceptions, the various social and economic groups that comprise a modern democratic state (or, for that matter, one of the Eastern socialist states) are not in conflict with each other and may jointly contribute to the good of the nation in what I term the stage of development.

There are other revolutions, however, that do not stop at the point of balance. They continue until the power structure is entirely reversed and the former rulers are annihilated or rendered completely impotent. Such were the revolutions of Russia, China, and Cuba. Such, there is little doubt, will be the revolutions in any nation where the entrenched ruling group is located within the country and stands to lose all if the underdogs attain power. It is hard, for example, to imagine any compromise, any agreement to share equal power, between black and white in South Africa, or between the guerrilla bands of Latin America and the oligarchies they oppose.

There can certainly be no peaceful relationships while such oligarchies remain in power, and if the power cannot be held in common one may argue that peace can be achieved only by eliminating them. But the idea jars. If peace can be won only by turning the top dogs into underdogs (or perhaps dead dogs), can it be said to be peace? There has simply been a reversal of the power position. Although the oligarchy may have been small in number and its rule odious, it was composed of human beings who should be fitted equitably into the new system. If they are brutalized, or continue to exist as a resentful or disadvantaged minority, peaceful relationships can hardly be said to have been fully established.

For this reason, revolution must be accompanied by conversion (this, as we shall see, is part of the purpose of confrontation). The revolutionaries must win not only the power but also the minds of their opponents. Rather than just defeat them, they must change them to a point where they reject their own past and are prepared to take an equal part in the future.

Oligarchies, admittedly, are not easy to convert. Unless revolutionary tactics are used against them with intelligence, consistency, and courage, their self-assurance is unlikely to waver. But the smaller the amount of violence employed, the greater the eventual likelihood of harmony. Once the killing begins, bitterness and anger burn deeply into the human spirit, often precluding real accord for generations.

The problem, moreover, is not only what to do with the top dogs but what to do with the roles of the top dogs. In those cases where the top dogs are evicted, as from a former colony that acquires independence, the general tendency has been to retain an administrative structure very similar to that of the colonial power, though, of course, with the jobs filled by natives of the country. The latter, then, have all too often begun to behave towards their subordinates in the same way as did their colonial predecessors; this, indeed, is a form of unconscious concealed neo-colonialism. Only in countries such as Tanzania, and in the revolutionary movements in Portuguese Guinea and Vietnam, has this danger been appreciated. Revolutions are not achieved merely by putting new people into old positions; the social system must also be changed. It is not enough to kill our opponents and to retain the social system that they – and with frightening frequency we also – support. It is more important to change the structure of society, and in order to do this we may first have to change ourselves. In the wisdom we may acquire in so doing we may learn also how to carry our enemies with us – as friends.

Sequences of peacemaking

In the extensive discussion of peacemaking in Part II it will become apparent that some techniques are more appropriate than others to particular forms of conflict, or rather, to particular stages in the transformation of unpeaceful into peaceful relationships, and an appropriate sequence of peacemaking methods related to stages of conflict is described. The implied corollary is that techniques in themselves valid are useless or harmful when applied at the wrong juncture. There is little point, for example, in attempting to conciliate the top dog in an unbalanced relationship. The structure of the relationship will not thereby be changed and he may well be confirmed in his sense of power and authority by our approaches; at best he will, at his pleasure, treat us with condescending indulgence; at worst he will be convinced that he can go to any lengths without reprisal. Such, perhaps, was the mistake of Neville Chamberlain at Munich.

Conciliation and bargaining are of very little use in revolutionary situations, or in situations that cannot be changed without a revolutionary adjustment of relationships. These methods will lead only to a false solution in which the conflict is obscured and the underdogs are fobbed off with some illusion of improvement or concession. Yet much peace research has been devoted to techniques for applying them more efficiently. In fact, one purpose of this book is to show that, although the methods of conciliation and bargaining are vital at the right juncture, there are more limitations on their effective use than is generally believed. By the same token, I hope to present an extended range and variety of activities relevant to the complex process of peacemaking. This may perhaps help those involved in unpeaceful relationships to analyse their circumstances more constructively.

Conclusion

Finally, I should stress that there is nothing sacred – or, for that matter, diabolical – about relationships except in so far as they affect human beings. It is arid to talk of peace and peaceful relations only in terms of structures and organizations. They are only means to human ends, and if we forget this our quest for peace may be corrupted, becoming an empty search for ideal forms which cannot of themselves confer warmth or creativity. Peaceful relationships constitute a desirable, perhaps a necessary, but certainly not a sufficient, condition for human developments that could advance and complete the developmental work we have already considered.

For these human developments to flower in the context of peaceful relationships we need a new, or perhaps rediscovered, understanding of man's nature and potentialities. For too long the Christian and later the Freudian view of man's nature, in an unnatural alliance, have persuaded us of our wickedness and our limitations; and to the extent that we have believed them, we have been emotionally, intellectually, and morally stunted. However, if we derive our norm not from the failures, as has been common in a psychology based on the psychopathological, but from the successes, our view of man's potential is much more encouraging. He may even have the capacity to build and preserve a world of truly peaceful relationships. There is evidence – much of it, paradoxically, from both Christian and psychiatric sources – which suggests that man's nature is richer, his capacity for joy, creativity, intellectual effort, altruistic service, spontaneity, courage, and love far greater, than we commonly suppose; that he is more complete, more consistent, gayer, and stronger.[41] Alas, we have a long way to go before our potentialities are widely realized. Our political, social, economic, and educational institutions have evolved very largely in accordance with a drab philosophy of human nature. The traces of this philosophy are all around us. Indeed it would have been unnecessary to write much of this book but for the existence of degrading and dehumanizing institutions such as colonialism and the imperialism of race or class. No one can give conscious support to such systems, and many do, without tacitly accepting the indignity of man – both oppressor and oppressed. And, by a sad irony, those who are oppressed the more easily accept the oppressors' evaluation of them. In general, suffering is not good for people.

I am not suggesting that we have first to make peaceful relationships and then engage in the more delicate task of raising the human condition. On the contrary, it may be impossible to make peace unless we all become more fully human. Indeed, the two tasks are interdependent, and must always remain interwoven. If I have written about peacemaking in the sense, ultimately, of restructuring relationships it is because I have been largely involved with this approach, not because I give it priority.

Because the extension of development in the peacemaking sense merges with development in the sense of individual growth, it is vital to avoid a contradiction between what we do in the name of peacemaking and what we do in the name of human beings. As the reader has seen, I have become convinced of the necessity for revolutionary change. Unfortunately, much of this is likely to come through a dehumanizing violence. One of mankind's most urgent challenges is, then, to find ways of eliminating unpeaceful relationships without eliminating people, to help people to change their perceptions and enlarge their understanding, not to destroy them.

CHAPTER 3

Making peace

THE PRACTICE OF PEACEMAKING[42]

Elements in peacemaking

The terms conflict management and conflict resolution are commonly used to describe the processes involved in changing unpeaceful relationships into peaceful ones. I hold that these terms are certainly appropriate for the stage of bargaining or negotiating that must normally be a part of the business of reaching a settlement and achieving better relations, but that other terms are required to differentiate other stages that commonly occur. I identify the following approaches to, or components in, peacemaking:

Research

By this I mean simply the investigations and researches any would-be peacemaker must pursue in order to master the facts of the particular unpeaceful relationship. If one gets involved with delicate and complex issues without understanding the specifics (however good one may be on the theory) one's ignorance will quickly become apparent; it is then unlikely that one will get very far.

Conciliation

This is activity aimed at bringing about an alteration of perception – the other side is not as bad as we thought, we have misinterpreted their actions, etc. – that will lead to an alteration of attitude and, eventually, to an alteration of behaviour. Conciliation has to be carried out by someone who is not caught up in the turmoil of emotions that usually besets the participating parties to a quarrel; the conciliator normally has to be a third party. His task may be thought of as the psychological aspect of peacemaking, for he will be concerned as much with creating an atmosphere in which a settlement can be reached as with the terms of that settlement. His job is to lower the temperature, to provide a moment of calm in which reason can reassert itself, and to present a different interpretation, another point of view, a possible way out of an impasse, a face-saving device that will enable an unpopular thing to be done. Conciliation oils the machinery of negotiation with trust and prevents the tragedy and loss that occur when one nation bludgeons another into submission and then imposes terms which sow the seeds of a future confrontation, as in the case of Germany after World War I.

Bargaining

This is the process of negotiation, or 'horse-trading' as it is commonly termed, through which two conflicting groups try to reach a settlement in which each gives as little as possible and gains as much as possible. When the parties are unbalanced it is likely that the settlement will be correspondingly lopsided and so perpetuate the unpeacefulness of the relationship. In a more balanced situation, however, successful bargaining can lead to circumstances in which both sides can live without mutual impairment. Successful bargaining leads essentially to a resolution of conflict and to the establishment of a peaceful relationship, that is to say, a balanced relationship in which the advantages of one side are not gained at the expense of the other.

Development

I use this word to represent a phase in peacemaking that is characterized by a restructuring of unpeaceful relations to create a situation, a society or a community in which individuals are enabled to develop and use to the full their capacities for creativity, service and enjoyment. Unless development in this sense can take place, no settlement will lead to a secure and lasting peace.

I have deliberately employed the term development in order to link this stage in peacemaking intrinsically to development in economic, social and political spheres. Since much of my experience has been with 'developing' nations, I am particularly concerned with the persisting conflict and turmoil so many of these nations display. Such conflict is attributed by some to a lack of development (in economic and political terms), but I believe it is also a product of faulty development, which has created unpeaceful relations rather than healed them. For in the 'developed' world, too, a development of relationships as defined above is obviously required. Thus there is a clear need for a restructuring of the relations between the black and white communities in the United States; and indeed of the relations between the rich and the poor in that and many other countries.

I must make it clear that by a restructuring of relations I do not mean bringing about subjective changes of attitude among the poor and weak which might make their condition more acceptable to them. Nor do I mean effecting superficial improvements in their circumstances which might be sufficient to divert their attention from the deeper conflict of interest. On the contrary, when I talk of a restructuring of relations between the rich and the poor, for example, an essential first step would be the bringing about of a progressive reduction of the gap between the two until something like parity, or at least the political equivalent of it, had been achieved.

The process of bringing about a balance of power – in economic, political and other spheres – is usually part of what I refer to as confrontation (see below). Development, in the sense of a restructuring of relations, is essentially a later phase. When confrontation, by reducing the disparity of power, has led to successful bargaining, then development can take place. It is the consolidation of a peaceful relationship through collaboration and cooperation, and the mutual adjustments these demand.

To these four processes of peacemaking I would add education and confrontation as making a contribution that is in some ways even more important to the eventual establishment of peaceful relationships.

Education

Among communities of 'ignorant slaves', such as the Faqir Mishkin[43], no change will occur, no move away from passive unpeacefulness, until there is an increase in the level of awareness of the fundamental conflict of interest. This will come about through, in the widest sense of the word, education.

Confrontation

This term is used to cover all the techniques by means of which the weaker groups in unbalanced relationships attempt to change the character of those relationships, specifically to make them more balanced. Ghandian non-violence, civil disobedience, protest, sabotage, the various non-violent alternatives to war and confrontation as practised by the students of today and by the black Americans – all are included. Revolution is, of course, the classic mode of confrontation. It may seem strange that a study of peacemaking should include such violent or potentially violent methods. It is not my intention, in fact, to prescribe violent solutions. Nevertheless, we are concerned with methods of changing relations, and one way of attempting to do so is by violence.

The possible interrelations of these different elements of peacemaking are discussed in, 'The sequence of peacemaking' (see p. 69).

It may seem that values intrude unduly in what follows. Indeed, this whole essay is based on a value that I term peace: that is, a condition in which the relations between nations, and between groups within nations, and between individuals, and perhaps in the future between planets, are such that no unnecessary violence, physical or psychological, is done either actively or passively through a failure to do what might have prevented it. This admittedly is a value, but one with which I imagine few would disagree. If it is accepted, then much that is subsequently advocated will be seen, I believe, to follow logically.

Note on conciliation and bargaining

In the chapters on conciliation and bargaining I may be criticized for ignoring or dealing inadequately with a large number of well-tried peacemaking approaches. In fact, the greater part of conflict-resolution theory is concerned with this area and includes, for example, studies of mediation and arbitration, the role of the United Nations and the International Court of Justice, games theory and simulation, arms control and escalation strategies. But I have not intended to summarize, still less to supplant, the enormous amount of work done in those fields. All I have tried to do is to suggest that in the movement of a relationship from a condition of conflict to one of peace there is a stage when the functions of conciliation and bargaining are essential.

Let us take conciliation first. Whether we are concerned with a precarious marriage, uneasy labour relations, groups at odds with each other or international disputes, the problem of improving bad relations is sharpened by suspicion, distrust, faulty perceptions, poor communications – what in a later section I refer to as the mask-mirage phenomenon. The deterioration of relations is accompanied by a worsening of the psychological ambience to a point where, especially in times of war, perceptions are so distorted that peace initiatives are doomed to failure almost before they are launched. Conciliation is essentially an applied psychological tactic aimed at correcting perceptions, reducing unreasonable fears, and improving communications to an extent that permits reasonable discussion to take place, and, in fact, makes rational bargaining possible. (It does not always follow, of course, that a bargain will be struck because objective difficulties may remain even if all the subjective obstacles have been removed.)

Conciliation is a function that may operate within any peacemaking context. It is a psychological technique, or rather the rudiments of one, which I believe may be refined and developed as a therapeutic technique. Any negotiator, to the extent that he is successful, and whether he is working on a large scale or a small scale, whether he is an arbitrator, an intermediary or a mediator, whether he represents a government, an international agency, an organization, a profession or simply himself, is also engaged in conciliation. I do not discount any of the many approaches to achieving settlement of disputes; I merely suggest that unless they include an element of conciliation they are unlikely to be successful.

Conciliation involves individuals, both those who conciliate and those who are conciliated. Governments can exert influence and apply pressure, but only individuals can carry out the delicate task of helping other individuals to see more clearly the agonizing and confusing issues on which they must make decisions. It is my belief, in fact, that the fewer ties an individual has with a government (which is always seen as a potential exerter of pressure) the more effective he will be as a conciliator; hence, the section on private diplomacy (page 225) (*NB The section on private diplomacy is not included in this extract*). In practice, of course, in the majority of cases the conciliator has some public position, and there are also, as we shall consider, certain advantages in this.

It need hardly be said that conciliation is a third-party activity. Only in exceptional circumstances can individuals involved in a quarrel be sufficiently detached to view the attitudes of both their enemies and their own side with objectivity. If they could, moreover, they would probably be suspected, for different reasons, by both friends and foes.

The chapter on conciliation, though fairly long, does not pretend to do more than give examples of what this function of peacemaking might imply, and try to show some of its psychological roots.

Conciliation and bargaining, more often than not, are overlapping and inextricably interwoven. It may also happen that the sequence is reversed so that bargaining comes first and conciliation second (or rather, successful bargaining – unsuccessful bargaining often precedes conciliation). For example, an unpopular solution may be imposed on two conflicting groups by powerful external forces, but the parties to the quarrel, now that the grounds for their dispute have been largely removed, may begin to lose their fear of each other and move gradually forward to the stage of development. It is for these reasons, perhaps, that most writers treat the two stages as though they were one. The following differences, however, may be noted:

1. Conciliation deals primarily with subjective phenomena; bargaining with objective.
2. Conciliation tends to be carried out at an individual level; bargaining is more a matter for organizations (governments, unions, etc.).
3. Conciliation is a third-party function; bargaining is more likely to be carried out by the principles in the dispute.
4. Conciliation is the beginning of a psychological settlement; bargaining leads to a material settlement.

Bargaining is the stage usually reached by the parties to an unpeaceful relationship after they have been brought together somewhat through conciliation. But bargaining itself may be divided into two phases. First comes the rather desperate haggling, the proposals and counter-proposals through which, in times of crisis, each side jockeys for position either before or during the early stages of negotiation.

During this phase many of the psychological themes carry over from the stage of conciliation (which means in effect that conciliation must continue). Throughout the process of crisis bargaining, in fact, fear and distortion are overriding elements of the situation – conciliation has reduced them merely to the point where it may be possible to begin discussions, however wary and hostile. Nevertheless there is a shift of emphasis; there is some common attempt to consider rational solutions to joint problems. And a cooler atmosphere may be created in which solutions that were previously rejected, because they were perceived differently, can be accepted.

The second type of bargaining is more rational. It may still be dominated by fear that the other side will try to cheat, but this is a not unreasonable fear which might, so to speak, be computerized. The stress is more on the long-term struggle for advantage or for maintaining balance, which might be exemplified by the negotiations for Britain's entry to the European Economic Community or by the USA/USSR.

Strategic arms limitation talks

I have dealt almost entirely with the first phase of bargaining because I am particularly concerned with the question of how contestants can be brought to the bargaining table in a spirit of constructive compromise. This is by far the most important step in the transition to peace.

I might perhaps have dealt with the second phase of bargaining with the sorts of arrangements that are arrived at and the sorts of stratagems that are employed to reach them – but was held back by several considerations.

First, to do so would have meant opening up the whole vast issue of how governments regulate their relationships. This is not an area of which I have any particular knowledge while it is, on the other hand, one that has been most extensively documented.

Second, my subject is unpeaceful relationships, whereas a great deal of second-phase bargaining takes place in the course of normal international relations. Even in cases of serious conflict much of the venom must have been drawn from the situation before such bargaining can occur.

Third, in my opinion the truly critical phase in changing an unpeaceful relationship into a peaceful one occurs during the preliminary exchanges, through which the contestants to the dispute are brought to the point of negotiations genuinely aimed at settling it.

Fourth, most conflicts in the world today are on a relatively small scale in the poor countries. On the other hand, a great deal of work on conflict theory refers almost exclusively to relations between the great powers and to the cold-war situation. I have not dealt with these at all in this book, and the unpeaceful relationships with which I have been concerned are on a smaller scale.

The actual solution adopted, the actual bargain accepted, depends upon circumstances too varied to permit of generalization. I would stress only that, in the context of my arguments, a valid settlement must be one that is based on, and maintains, a relatively balanced relationship. Any other solution will push the relationship back to a previous stage of unpeacefulness, leading to a subsequent second round of hostilities. A related general point is that the effectiveness of conciliation and bargaining as peacemaking techniques depends upon the stage at which they are applied. They are appropriate to conflict situations only when there is a balance of power; for if the discontented slave is brought by conciliation to be contented with his lot, conciliation has in this case merely prolonged an essentially unpeaceful relationship.

It is important to note at this point that conciliation may fail or bargains may be broken because of factors quite outside the control of the peacemaker. Thus changes in the domestic or military situation may lead to the repudiation of agreements reached in an earlier context; or the influence of external powers may prevent a settlement between two contestants (or perhaps promote an unsuitable one). Indeed, in any quarrel more are embroiled than the two principals. In the Nigerian civil war, for example, the complex calculations of interests that determined the giving of support by the United Kingdom, the USSR, France, Portugal, South Africa and other countries, and the withholding of it by the USA, greatly affected the course of the conflict and, at various stages, the chances of settlement.

Finally, I should re-emphasize the difference between bargaining and development. The former creates conditions in which two groups are prepared to coexist without overt hostility. The latter implies a much more positive collaboration for mutual benefit. Although bargaining continues at the stage of development (just as does conciliation at the stage of bargaining), many other functions, institutions and types of individuals are now involved.

Types of Peacemaker

We are accustomed to think of the peacemaker as someone who, through wisdom, experience, and goodwill, brings warring nations to the conference table. This is, indeed, an important peacemaking role, but many additional modes of peacemaking are outlined in this volume, and it is very unlikely that one individual could be concerned with, let alone responsible for, more than one or two of them. It is not a single Promethean human being who guides the slave from ignorant apathetic subservience to awareness and revolt, leading to equality and – by way of subtle bargaining – to constructive collaboration. The educator in awareness is a revolutionary. The man who stages the confrontation in which the slave, newly aware of his position and identity, faces his master, is likewise a revolutionary. The conciliator who attempts to change the perceptions of warring groups about each other is an outsider to the dispute whose skills are grounded in the social sciences and in psychology. The bargainer who arranges the settlement once the conciliator has done his work may be a politician or an administrator (though a dash of social science will help him), and he will probably be a member of one of the parties to the quarrel (unlike the third-party conciliator, though their roles overlap). The man concerned with development may be almost anything, since it involves such a broad and varied field; essentially, perhaps, he will be a politically wise statesman, but any number of specialists will be concerned with the details – economists, educationists, political scientists and many others.

Many of these peacemakers, if it is proper to lump together so many different people with so many diverse functions, will be activists. They will take the initiative in changing relationships, just as did Fidel Castro and Che Guevara in the Cuban revolution when they stirred the rural population to take control of its political destiny. Those concerned with the development stage will be politicians and planners attempting to implement their ideas. The bargainer will be a tactician trying to get the best deal. Only the conciliator will be ideologically neutral, and that only to a relative degree. His role can perhaps be likened to that of the psychoanalyst in that his task can be carried out better by listening and interpreting than by taking the initiative; but he is not committed to passivity and in the interest of reaching a settlement he may find many ways of exerting pressure.

The sequence of peacemaking[44]

We are now in a position to draw tentative conclusions concerning the relationship between type of conflict and type or types of peacemaking approach.

Much of the literature on conflict resolution deals, in effect, with what I have termed bargaining, a process that is important, but not exclusively so, in establishing peaceful relations between states or between employers and employees, these being the fields in which most work has been done. I believe, as stated above, that there are three additional processes, the four together forming a sequence: research, conciliation, bargaining, development. Some of these processes will be less crucial than others and there may also be some overlapping, but there tends to be at least a shift in emphasis from research to conciliation and then to bargaining and then to development. This progression applies principally, however, to conflict situations that are relatively balanced and in which there is some awareness of conflict.

Where the conflict situation comprises an unbalanced relationship, the peacemaking sequence is less predictable, and the techniques of education and confrontation will be required to stimulate awareness and to achieve the degree of balance without which conciliation and bargaining can be used by the powerful as tools of pacification. In cases where the strong partner in the relationship takes the initiative in peacemaking (as did the Pakistan government with regard to the villages, through the agency of Village AID and the Basic Democracy system) the element of bargaining becomes much less important. Research is still necessary, but now much greater emphasis is placed on conciliation, both to solve the practical problems and to take the relationship a stage further. By these means the relationship gradually changes into one that is more balanced: the people can express their will, they elect their own representatives, they have the relative degree of freedom enjoyed by the people of a democratic society who can, in the last resort, overthrow the government and choose a new one.

A very different situation prevails in cases where the strong partner not only does not help, but actively opposes attempts by the weak one to redress the balance. Top-dog intransigence must lead, eventually, to underdog militancy. At this stage the only peacemaking technique open to the underdog may be confrontation. The rulers, whoever they may be – the rich nations, the tyrannical or insensitive government, the professors, the whites, the landlords – must be forced to look at the underdog, to change their perception of him and hence their behaviour towards him, and ultimately to make the relationship more balanced. The actual technique employed may be violent or non-violent, but the principle remains the same. The masters, faced with potential (or indeed actual) revolution, have two alternatives. Either they can try to crush it, rooting out the ringleaders, imprisoning or killing them, and intimidating the rank and file; or they can attempt to use the tools of conciliation and bargaining. In the latter case they try to avoid trouble by making concessions which will assuage the people's hunger for freedom without actually giving it to them. They attempt to produce the appearance of balance without the substance. This technique might be called sweeping conflict under the carpet.

Many studies of conflict have been concerned with the preservation of negative peace, in the sense of the simple absence of violence. Fewer have been concerned with positive peace: the building of creative and cooperative associations between groups and nations. To conceal conflict not only does not contribute to positive peace, but makes it harder to attain. It falsifies the position in a fashion that makes it more difficult to put right. Moreover, it militates against the condition of 'peace' it aims to promote; it merely postpones the eventual explosion, which is likely to be all the more violent for the suppression and the delay.

It can be seen, then, that the combined techniques of research, conciliation, bargaining and development are appropriate to conflict situations in which the two parties have a balanced relationship and can in fact negotiate because one of them does not have a preponderance of power. The various techniques of confrontation are appropriate to the weaker party in an unbalanced relationship because he is trying to reach a greater degree of parity. Once he has achieved this he will become able, through the conciliatory efforts of a third party, to enter into rational discussion of the situation, or he will be in a position to bargain – but he cannot do these things while he is weak. His overtures would be rejected, or he would be unable to strike a fair bargain.

The strong party who engages in bargaining holds all the best cards. In particular, he is usually strong enough to do a great deal of damage if he wants to. He can also offer some attractive propositions which may well be accepted with relief by people who, though angered by injustice, fear the consequences of opposition and are ready to accept compromise.

Thus, from the point of view of the government or employer wanting a quiet life, it seems to be sensible policy to apply to one sort of conflict the peacekeeping technique suitable to another. In fact, such a policy prolongs the conflict; it might be termed a technique of non-resolution which postpones open violence, but it may be felt to be justified if the violence is postponed for a long enough time.

What we have just been considering applies to unbalanced relationships in which there is some awareness of conflict. When awareness is low, the situation is different. This is negative peace in the sense of passivity or submission; it is apathetic acquiescence in crippling, inhibiting, degrading and limiting circumstances. Revolutionary governments of peoples unaware of their miserable conditions have, of course, tried both to change these conditions and to raise the level of awareness through community education and other methods of information and propaganda. But where continued ignorance is in the interest of the rulers, the education must be carried out by anyone who has sufficient nerve. The purpose of such education is to move the conflict into the stage of awareness; and at that stage the object of the weaker party is to move it into a stage of greater balance; and thereafter it is to be moved into the stage of development.[45]

This progression is shown in Figure 4.

Figure 4 Peacemaking approaches appropriate for different sorts of conflict[46]

	UNPEACEFUL RELATIONS		PEACEFUL RELATIONS
	Lower awareness of conflict	*Higher awareness of conflict*	*No conflict*
Balanced		3. Techniques of conciliation and bargaining applied to end the open conflict, agree a settlement, and permit development.	4. Development and restructuring of the formerly unpeaceful relations.
Unbalanced	1. Various forms of education, to increase awareness to the point of confrontation.	2. Various techniques of confrontation aimed at reducing the imbalance and enabling the under-dogs to negotiate (conciliation and bargaining) on a basis of greater equality.	

NOTES:
(a) The peacemaking sequence may, of course, begin at any of the stages of conflict.
(b) The broken arrow would illustrate, for example, that a minority group, having striven for greater equality, is satisfied with a measure of self-govern-ment short of independence; even so, the relationship would clearly be more peaceful than it was previously, with an acceptable degree of imbalance.

Among the case studies, only that of the Firm[47] demonstrates anything approximating the complete change from an unbalanced relationship with low awareness of conflict to a peaceful relationship of development, but the shifts were somewhat blurred and inconclusive. Moreover, the people involved, far from being ignorant peasants or *Lumpenproletariat*, included a large number of educated and sophisticated persons. Nevertheless, their circumstances were such that few of them had articulated to themselves the conflict in which they were engaged. My discussions with them, though consisting mainly of their answers to my questions, did have an educative effect as a result of which they formulated the issues. They became more aware of their situation and more intent on doing something to change it. Some of the subsequent meetings with the directors had, indeed, the character of confrontations. These, because of the goodwill and understanding of the directors, led to a process of conciliation and bargaining in which the directors tried to ensure that their interests would not be damaged by any concessions they might make. Finally, there was a restructuring of the relationship between the employers and the employees, and various steps were taken to ensure harmonious growth in the future.

Figure 5 shows a different progression. It illustrates graphically the technique of pseudo-resolution by which an appearance of balance is created. It will be noted that this involves applying methods suitable for the resolution of one type of unpeaceful relationship to the resolution of another.[48] The end-result of the sequence shown here is the Bantustan, as depicted in Figure 2. Other examples of pseudo-resolution are the integration movement in the USA and the privileges granted to the Angolan *assimilado*. In the American case those who promoted integration were certainly well intentioned, but they succeeded in blurring the conflict; it is for this reason that the blacks have turned so bitterly against the white liberals.

Figure 5 Negative peacemaking by obscuring conflict

| | UNPEACEFUL RELATIONS | | PEACEFUL RELATIONS |
	Lower awareness of conflict	*Higher awareness of conflict*	*No conflict*
Balanced	2. *the Bantustan situation: pseudo-balance and generally low perception of conflict.*		
Unbalanced		1. *Conciliation and bargaining (inappropriately applied in a situation of imbalance) stifle confrontation and lead to* ———	

The only way in which the unpeaceful relationship shown in Figure 5 can be transformed into a peaceful one is by a reversal of the process: the pseudo-balance must be recognized as imbalance; there must then be confrontation; this, if successful, will lead to conciliation and bargaining – and thence to development. It will be noted that the conciliation-bargaining techniques are pushed up into their proper case.

Figure 6 Reversal of negative peacemaking

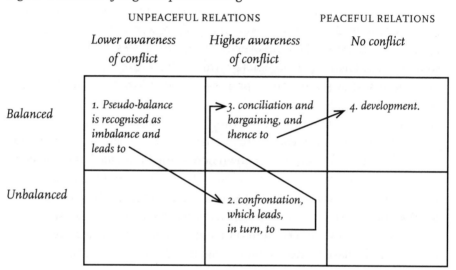

	UNPEACEFUL RELATIONS		PEACEFUL RELATIONS
	Lower awareness of conflict	*Higher awareness of conflict*	*No conflict*
Balanced	1. Pseudo-balance is recognised as imbalance and leads to	3. conciliation and bargaining, and thence to	4. development.
Unbalanced		2. confrontation, which leads, in turn, to	

In relationships of alienation, the most useful peacemaking technique is conciliation. This aspect of peacemaking is largely psychological and it is appropriate to situations in which, to a greater extent than is normal, one-sided misperceptions are dominant. In addition, however, some developmental reordering of the relationship might be needed to prevent relapse into this form of social paranoia. Thus it might be advisable to devise a charter for advisers, elaborating and confirming the nature of their relationship with their counterparts.

The most important conclusions to which our discussions have led us are these: peace means more than the absence of open strife; to reach the phase of development, the ultimate stage of peacemaking, it may be necessary to pass through the stage of confrontation which may, although there are alternatives, be violent; our understanding of the nature of peace determines our approach to peacemaking.

CHAPTER 4

Mystics and militants

CHANGING AWARENESS LEVELS
AND MAKERS OF PEACE AND VIOLENCE[49]

L evel of awareness is a key element in life. When awareness is low it is associated with the belonging-identity,[50] which is the source of competitive materialism and all the bitterness and violence that flow therefrom. When it is higher it generates attempts to change the situation through the militant or mystic mode and, ultimately, through a fusion of both. It is important, therefore, to consider how the levels are altered.

Awareness-reducing agents

We can daily watch the lowering of our own level of awareness. We can see the obliteration of those moments of relatively high self-consciousness, calmness, self-observation, detachment; moments when we have a feeling of strength and wholeness, a clear, warm, and objective view of others. Or rather, we ought to be able to watch this process of change, but the elements involved in it take away our capacity to perceive ourselves objectively. Without realizing it we are suddenly different. How did it happen? Can it be prevented?

Much can no doubt be explained in terms of neurology and psychopathology. The shifting patterns of cortical activity touch associations of anxiety or guilt, with the result that a different, negative feeling seeps into the central position, dominating our mood. Freud's *Psychopathology of Everyday Life* (1901) demonstrates both lucidly and entertainingly how all-pervasive are such mechanisms, how unaware we are of them, and what wide ramifications they have in the psychic structure.

If these relatively benign manifestations of psychopathology can distort memory, speech and feeling, the clinically more serious ones will have a far greater impact on awareness. Severe anxiety conditions, depressions, paranoid feelings and the like are prolongations and intensifications of the negative emotional states which, in the experience of us all, temporarily reduce awareness to almost nothing. In these cases the first need is psychotherapy, which imparts to the individual some insight into his condition and thus to some extent raises awareness.

I am concerned, however, not so much with clinically pathological states as with awareness-reducing elements in everyday life. Even those who, by psychiatric standards, have the best mental health are susceptible to these. They are the minor fears and anxieties that plague us all: the pomps and prides with which we hedge our self-doubt, envy, resentment of the success of others, self-pity, the urge to show ourselves (to ourselves and to others) in the most flattering light, peevishness, jealousy, self-indulgent laziness, depression, anger. This sounds like a list of deadly sins and indeed, apart from any theological implications, they are responsible for damaging the awareness on which our ultimate human usefulness depends.

It is interesting that many of these feelings are associated with the belonging-identity. Pride and vanity, for example, build up the self-image. Resentment, jealousy, envy and anxiety are responses to a threat to the identity. Depression and self-pity result from injury to it. It is, of course, perfectly possible to experience pity (not self-pity) or anger or grief in an objective sense. What might be called 'pure' emotions, that is to say, those that are not servants of identity but are aroused by suffering, or by corruption or exploitation, feel very different. They are strengthening rather than weakening. Unfortunately, even the purest emotions can easily become negative. We may be genuinely sorry at a friend's misfortune, but imperceptibly the clarity of the emotion is clouded: we feel smug that it did not happen to us; or anxiously self-pitying lest it might; or proud self-satisfaction that we feel so keenly for another's hurt.

It is not at all easy to control these shifts. The principal reason is that they erase the awareness that would signal us to try to do so. Thus they either creep upon us so quietly that we do not recognize what is happening, or they take us by storm, as when we are 'carried away' by 'blind rage' which makes us 'beside ourselves'. These common terms significantly illustrate the effects of negative emotions on awareness and autonomy. We are not, however, completely impotent. Even when 'transported' by violent feeling we can sometimes remember who we are and what we are doing and make a purposeful effort to change the direction of our feelings. Old wives' advice is that we should count a hundred, look in the mirror or hold our breath when in the grip of strong negative emotion. The main point of such procedures (though breath regulation may effect some helpful change in body chemistry) is to stop the automatic sequence of feeling, to effect a pause in which self-observation can be practised.

One great difficulty is, however, that we enjoy our negative emotions. If we are feeling sorry for ourselves we do not want to stop. If we are angry we do not want to be assuaged. When we are not in the grip of these feelings it is hard for us to remember how absorbing they were. It is as though we *become* our emotion; we personify – as it is said – self-satisfaction, greed, jealousy, or whatever it may be. We do not want to abandon what has become our temporary self.

A vicious circle revolves here. To oppose negative emotions with awareness demands an effort of a particular kind; but negative emotions weaken the capacity to make the effort. Indeed, they enervate us generally. Who has not felt 'shaky' after an outburst of anger, or physically debilitated during a fit of depression?

In general, then, people who are being constantly affected by negative emotions – and some are clearly more susceptible than others to anxiety or depression, for example – must find it difficult to generate the strength either to work on themselves or indeed to do many other things requiring sustained or creative effort. On the other hand, people who are not constantly drained by negative emotions should have, as both cause and effect, a higher awareness and a recognizable energy which enable them to deal effectively with their lives and their work.

Thus, in the terms of my schema, level of awareness is particularly threatened in two situations. The first is when our awareness is relatively low, and our belonging-identity is jeopardized. We then spring to its defence with all the weapons at our disposal. Say, for example, that I am a fairly liberal and tolerant white man whose identity is largely built up through my position in the community. This position and the very nature of the community are then threatened with change by the introduction of a group of coloured immigrants. My liberal ideas are rapidly flushed away. I become extremely hostile to the newcomers, not only because they disturb the pattern of my belonging-identity, but also because *by placing myself in polar opposition to them I am helping to define and reinforce that identity.* My awareness has diminished because I unthinkingly abandon my principles and resort to any intellectual trick to rationalize my fear and hostility.

The second situation occurs at various points along the line of rising awareness and weakening belonging-identity. At this stage it frequently happens that anxiety caused by separation from the specious security of belonging clouds awareness. Indeed, the configuration higher awareness/weak identity is unstable for this reason. It is only when the autonomy of awareness-identity is achieved that belonging identity ceases to influence us, and to have extreme attraction when we are for whatever reason made to feel uneasy or insecure. In most people, of course, the level of awareness fluctuates, but for some people the pressures are such that the capacity for higher awareness they have previously manifested is more or less permanently dulled. We then meet people who continue to behave like militants or mystics, but who have lost awareness of those roles as techniques of change. Their activities have been subtly transformed into foci of belonging – to the commune, to the movement, to the revolutionary group, to the hippie culture and so on. Many people continue to play parts although they are no longer aware of their fundamental purpose. These are the real zombies.

Ways of raising awareness

Up to a certain point, by nature or circumstances, we may be endowed with a higher-than-average capacity for awareness. This, so to speak, is given. But to raise it beyond this level requires a deliberate effort, and various types of effort can be made.

The method with which we are most familiar, perhaps, is to undergo some kind of psychotherapy. The first step here is to acknowledge that we need therapy. Many people who are sick by accepted clinical standards resist this knowledge. They reject the idea of treatment because to accept it would either damage their self-esteem – it is still easier to accept the need for an appendectomy than for psychoanalysis – or expose them more closely to sides of their nature they would prefer to keep in the background of consciousness. The admission that we are in need of treatment implies some degree of self-insight, but it may merely be that we are aware of being troubled by a symptom. There is hope, however, that during the course of therapy a more general awareness will develop, but unless it becomes what I have termed self-conscious awareness, little more may be achieved than the unravelling of a minor psychic knot.

Awareness may also be raised by completely fortuitous circumstances. We may be thrust into situations which, so to speak, jolt us awake. I often advise my students, who, being young, lack material commitments and are in a good position to take chances, to visit strange places, do unusual things, throw themselves into movements, take risks. To experience danger, the suffering of others, hardships, the challenge of extraordinary conditions, may draw the scales from our inner eyes. Being forced to take a new sort of heed of what lies around us, we also become more aware of ourselves. By our response to these circumstances we become conscious of new sides of our own nature. But this is a chancy, haphazard business and can hardly be recommended as a systematic approach to the raising of awareness levels.

The essential incentive is a realization that one is deficient in awareness, not that one has a psychological problem as such or that one wants a more exciting life. Most of us, most of the time, have no such thoughts, and the older we grow the less we have them. But occasionally, in middle age, we have the sense of standing at the edge of a mystery, of almost grasping something very important, but being held back by some lack of capacity within ourselves to perceive.

Young people today, being more perceptive than those of my generation, are more aware, if this is not a contradiction, of deficiencies in their awareness. They are prone to blame these deficiencies on certain facets of contemporary civilization, in particular competitive materialism, which not only promotes a lust of belonging but in a sense technologizes everything – including the human spirit. They are of course right, but other ages have had their particular faults. What is constant is the magnetic attraction and the easiness of belonging-identity, coupled with the difficulty of achieving higher awareness. Nevertheless, though today's young people may perhaps exonerate themselves too much, they do recognize the vital necessity for awareness.

Many of the ways by which they seek it are, seemingly, dead ends. For instance, there are innumerable small cults and groups, completely without guidance, which are likely to lead only to disillusion and to a giving up of the search for higher awareness. They are particularly likely to fail when they are attempting, as most of them are, to reach awareness of a supraliminal kind. One reason for this is that the ideas they employ are mainly Oriental, and are thus not only very alien to Western civilization but were intended to be applied or elaborated in special circumstances, such as the relationship of pupil to master. Unfortunately, we have few genuine gurus.

Far more successful, but in a sense more limited, in my experience, are attempts to achieve self-conscious awareness through T-groups, sensitivity training and the work of organizations such as the Esalen Institute.[51] These are largely based on the group therapy techniques devised by Bion (1961) and others in the 1940s and have an acceptable foundation of well-tried method and concept, but many of them have made a creative and imaginative leap forwards to a point where there is a fusion of science, art and warm human feelings. Some have leapt too far into absurdity and meaninglessness, but this is only to be expected. However, many people have been helped by them to make a genuine advance in awareness. This is what one T-group participant said:

> 'It was quite extraordinary how conscious I became both of myself and of others. At first, there we all were, locked in our little boxes and really terrified that someone might have the key to open us up. Faced with all these strange people in this extraordinary situation in which none of us had a clue as to what was expected of us, of what we were supposed to do, I got into a sort of panic and wished I had never come. But by the end of the workshop, only ten days, the most amazing change had taken place in, I think, about all of us. Just because we couldn't act out the parts we had learnt to play [note that what he is mainly talking about here is escaping from the belonging-identity] we all began to be very much more ourselves, whatever that means. We weren't a lot of dummies trying to one-up each other; we were human beings engaged in a common effort to be aware of each other and ourselves. It was so difficult, painful and, yes, frightening, to start with. It was so rewarding at the end – we all loved each other. I felt these were some of the very few real relationships I'd had in my life: as the barriers came down in myself and I saw myself as I had never done before, so the barriers came down between me and the others.'

Accounts like this, and there are many of them, are encouraging. But what next? Is high awareness a quality which, once achieved, will persist and perhaps even grow? I tend to think that it is like many garden flowers which, if left to seed themselves, gradually revert to something like the wild state. Awareness needs cultivation. The forces counteracting awareness – belonging-identity, the stress of separation from it, the enervation of negative emotions, apathy – are so strong that unless we struggle to maintain it we, too, will revert. This, of course, applies to all, irrespective of their individual approaches to awareness of different sorts.

I am convinced that the key factor in striving and continuing to strive for awareness is the recognition of how little we have, of how much this impairs our capacities, and of the extent of the damage done by the collective low awareness of the world. We resist this realization emotionally even if we admit it intellectually, but it is not until we are forced to acknowledge it fully that we can begin to accept the arduous work that is involved in raising awareness. Our resistance stems from a combination of laziness and a refusal to admit that we are less autonomous than we would like to think. Sometimes we are impelled to act only when faced with the disastrous effects of our low awareness: a friend is hurt because of our uncontrolled impulse to speak cruelly, or because of a damaging habit we cannot abandon; a job is lost through our inability to concentrate. Sometimes it is the cumulative impact of many minor evidences of our low awareness that makes us want to do better. A simple experiment will demonstrate the low level of our awareness and reinforce our determination to raise it. Let us try to empty our minds of thought for a minute; we will be lucky if we have enough control to prevent stray ideas from sliding into consciousness after less than half that time. I am reminded of a story about Saint Francis. He was journeying with his donkey and entered into a discussion with a fellow traveller about concentration and prayer. Saint Francis maintained that it was hard; the other, that it was easy. Saint Francis then said that if this man could recite the Lord's Prayer with complete attention, he would give him his donkey. The Saint's companion laughed. 'The donkey is as good as mine', he said, and began to recite, 'Our Father, Who art in Heaven, Thy Kingdom come, Thy Will be done on earth as it is in Heaven – and will you give me the saddle as well?'

Two points should be emphasized about efforts to raise awareness: namely, that they require both self-discipline and the help of others.

Unless we work on ourselves regularly we will achieve little and will gradually backslide into inactivity. Most religions are, in basic purpose, though seldom as practised or understood by most of their adherents, systems for raising awareness; most of them advocate regular observances such as weekly churchgoing and evening prayers. Even such completely non-spiritual practices as eating fish on Fridays (who would not prefer lobster or salmon to the average meat dish?) serve as *aides-memoire* to remind us of our religious obligations.

Second, it is very hard to be disciplined on our own. There are bound to be occasions when we are lazy, tired or preoccupied, and it becomes progressively easier for us to forget ourselves. But the companionship of like-minded people makes things better. If one has a fit of lassitude, the others will spur one on. Moreover, joining with others is helpful in itself, as most religions have indicated by their emphasis on communal worship, and as sensitivity training demonstrates in another context.

There are many channels to higher awareness and certainly I would not wish to recommend any single system or nonsystem more than another. The important thing is that it should be followed seriously but without fanatical exclusiveness. I have known people of many faiths and many kinds of lack of faith who have achieved high awareness, because the question of awareness underlies all major religions and psycho-philosophical systems.

Another way in which we are helped to maintain a higher level of awareness may be mentioned. This is that, as we struggle towards increased awareness, we distil values from our deeper perceptions. These we objectify as specific goals, moral, philosophical or social, which persist even though our awareness may fluctuate downwards. They remain then like pitons thrust into the rocks of uncertainty by which we may draw ourselves upwards again.

But however we set about raising the level of our awareness, there is one essential thing: *we must at all times try to remember who we are.* This is the fundamental exercise in awareness. We must look at ourselves, feel ourselves as we act in various ways or talk or move or even think. We must try to see ourselves as part of a network of human beings who comprise our family, our friends, community, associates; we must, in a sense, locate ourselves in the universe.

As with most things, of course, it is infinitely easier to say what needs to be done than to do it. It is true that there are a few tricks that may help: it even contributes to awareness to say one's name ('I am Adam Curle') and try to recognize the fact, or to look in a mirror and realize that this is I. We soon find, however, that it is incredibly hard to persist in such efforts. It is almost as though they were impeded by a perverse natural force. This may in a sense be true: for awareness can bring pain and uncertainty, impelling us to make uncomfortable changes in our life. I suspect, though, that there is another and more deep-seated reason. The psychological pressures of existence militate against awareness: they drive us to identify with the things, situations and emotions that blind us to an objective appreciation of ourselves. We become too easily involved with our anger or fear, caught up in our hopes, absorbed in our interests. We become these things and, however good, altruistic or creative they may be, in doing so we lose ourselves.

To gain awareness is like swimming upstream. It is intensely hard work and if we relax for a moment we are swept backwards to a point below where we started. Such systems as Zen, the various forms of yoga, Sufi practice and some aspects of Christian mysticism are all directed to achieving increasing awareness. But apparently they all demand enormous efforts with no guarantee of success; the world has a large number of what might be termed failed mystics. For this reason we should perhaps approach the problem of awareness with greater relaxation and receptivity. Intense effort can defeat its own end. If we can point ourselves in the direction of what we perceive as the good, and accept thankfully what happens, we may come nearer to awareness than if we strive grimly to achieve it.

What this further awareness, if cultivated, will eventually reveal can in no way be specified.

In conclusion, it is hard to become aware and many catastrophes can occur on the way. But nevertheless I am not completely pessimistic. Throughout the world, it seems to me, there has taken place in the last quarter of a century an extraordinary awakening of awareness, almost a revolution of awareness.[52] I noticed this first in the Third World. Then it seemed to spread (at least in my limited experience) to the young, especially the educated young, of America and Europe, and to the black people of the USA. I am astonished that so many men and women less than half my age have an awareness of themselves and the world which is so much sharper than mine and of a completely different order from that which I had at their age. Admittedly, many fall by the wayside, for the pressures are great, but I cannot help feeling that, even so, something very remarkable is happening. I may be wrong about the generality of this awakening, but, if I am not, is it too fanciful to suggest that humanity is reacting to the appalling dangers to which we have been brought by materialistic greed and rapacity? Have we perhaps responded to our critical situation by producing a new psychic mutation?

It may in fact be that our awareness of the need to change was stimulated by the very changes against which we are reacting – the extraordinarily rapid changes wrought by technological developments. These have not only incited man's cupidity, thus intensifying injustices and dangers to liberty, but have shaken the foundations of his belief. When the blinkers of traditionalism are removed, letting in a glimpse of a new vision, man can more readily tolerate the confusions and ambiguities that must simultaneously arise; or he can reject them all the more violently and fiercely because the old assurances are partly gone. The greater the volume of awareness, therefore, the greater the probable opposition to it.

Makers of peace and violence

The conclusions I reach in this chapter will not come as a surprise to the reader. Although the core of this book, everything since Chapter 1, has been devoted to elaborating a system, the implications of that system for my original purpose – if I have expressed myself with any clarity – must be obvious. In the first chapter I defined the processes of peacemaking and placed some emphasis on what I called the revolutionary stages by which the underdog in an unpeaceful relationship achieves, or is helped to achieve, equality with the top dog. These are the stages I termed education and confrontation: unpeaceful relationships of inequality and injustice, which are to be changed by them, are far more prevalent than any others.

Moreover, it is on this sort of unpeaceful relationship that the awareness of today's younger generation, and of a growing number of their elders, is focused. Dissent from and protest against the exploitative network and the spirit of competitive materialism are everywhere evident. The world's students have, as it were almost overnight, become a political force to be taken into account. They have shaken many governments and toppled some – for example, in South Korea and Turkey; they almost succeeded in France. At the same time they are active in the social field, and service to the poorer or underprivileged communities is as much a part of the scene, though less salient, as political work. The political and economic thinking of the New Left, disorganized as it still is, exemplifies this group at an intellectual level. Then again, concern over (or desperation about) the state of affairs has driven many away from involvement in the social system and into communes aimed at establishing the counter-culture or into various forms of mysticism.

The people concerned, both the militants and the mystics (except for the various counterfeits I have mentioned), are in Configuration 3, characterized by higher awareness and weak identity (both modes). Their instability, their difficulties, failures and backslidings – especially as they grow older – stem from their weak identity; and this is the corollary of their higher awareness, which has largely invalidated their earlier belonging-identity. It is probably true to say that unless, by the time they are established in their careers, they have built a much stronger awareness-identity, they will mostly revert to a belonging-identity, with concomitantly lower awareness.

Those whom they oppose, whose opinions they want to change, whose way of living they challenge, whose hold over the poor (when they are rich) they hope to break, or whose acceptance or even ignorance of that hold (when they are poor) they try to shake, are men and women in Configuration 2 (low awareness/strong belonging-identity). There is a mass of stability, inertia and resistance to significant changes in this group. Despite much instability round the edges where it merges with Configuration 1 (people of low awareness and weak identity) and Configuration 3 (those beginning to be troubled by awakening awareness), the core is almost immovable. There is too much vested interest, emotional and material, in the *status quo*, and the two reinforce each other. I should reemphasize that these people are no more the wealthy than the impoverished. Both equally resist any threat to their identity with ridicule, anger and violence. Remember the attack by 'hard hat' construction workers on marchers protesting against the American invasion of Cambodia.[53] This resulted from long pent-up anger against the types of people who, they had been led to believe, were undermining the 'American way of life.'

Let me dwell on this case for a minute: it is complex and illustrative. The construction workers are, as a group, neither particularly well off nor very poor. Their version of the American way of life cannot be very lavish. Like most other workers in a capitalist society they have plenty to complain of, particularly the lack of equality. But they love their chains. They do not see that the American dream of golden opportunity for all has faded and that they are stuck where they are. Are they not all now members of the middle class? Resentments and fears they have, of course, about losing their jobs, about sickness and doctors' bills, about not being able to keep up the payments on the colour TV. But when things go wrong, it's not the system, it's not America that is at fault. To admit that would be dangerous to their identity. It's the long-haired students, the blacks, the commies: apart from them everything would be fine. So, when they have an excuse to bash them, all their anger boils up and they bash them good. They'll feel better afterwards, their identity will be strengthened and confirmed, and the conservatives will be reinforced – except for a few waverers on the fringe who will be alienated by their brutality.

One of the war cries of low awareness/strong belonging-identity is for law and order, and it would be hard to complain of this if law and order did not, in effect, mean – very often – going far beyond what was either legal or orderly in order to suppress groups working for radical reform, and thus ensuring further violent confrontations in the future. Nor should it be taken to mean that people within this configuration are all good, law-abiding citizens. The majority, I suppose, are. But a strong belonging-identity in no way precludes crime. The court records are full of cases in which the criminals were excellent members of their communities, displayed the flag on all appropriate occasions, hated those they considered their country's enemies and manifested other hallmarks of this configuration – but also embezzled, accepted bribes, practised fraudulent conversion and were vicious and violent.

These are the opponents of the peacemakers and they are both powerful and, when challenged, ruthless. The peacemakers are, of course, strengthened, indeed inspired, by a higher level of awareness, but they are weakened and rendered unstable by their deficient sense of identity. It is only when awareness is raised to the point where awareness identity emerges that real stability is established. It is my fear, however, that awareness-identity is something that comes with age. I know few of the young who have come near, so far as I can judge, to achieving it fully, and none of the very young, however sensitive their awareness. The danger is that, before they can develop a stable awareness identity, their anxieties will have impelled them to revert to the belonging system. The hope is in numbers. The more aware young people there are, the more they will together be able to withstand the formidable pressures upon them.

The other peacemaking techniques, conciliation, bargaining and development, are applied outside a revolutionary situation when two more or less equal parties to a conflict are reconciled to the point where they can discuss, and with luck resolve, the conflict of interest between them, and finally move forward together in a positive relationship from which each derives benefit.

The situations that require these methods range from the interpersonal (in which the services of, say, a marriage guidance counsellor might be most useful) to the international (where a mediator appointed by the United Nations might be necessary). Every mature human being is, of course, called upon in the course of his ordinary life to act on countless occasions in roles equivalent to those of conciliator, bargainer and developer, usually in unpeaceful situations involving family members, friends, neighbours, work associates and so on. But for many interpersonal problems, and many conflict situations involving larger groups or nations, a professional is called for. The conciliator or bargainer will be, for example, a social worker, a psychiatrist, a lawyer practised in mediation, a professional diplomat, an international civil servant. Those concerned with development (that is, with establishing a collaborative relationship and a form of society that makes such collaboration possible and fruitful) will be specialists from a wide range of fields, such as city planners, social workers, lawyers, politicians and political scientists, economists and educationists. How, if at all, do the people carrying out these jobs fit into the categories we have discussed?

In the first place, these are not revolutionary tasks as such: development in particular is evolutionary. Second, the emphasis is on technology rather than ideology. Third, the work tends to demand people with fairly advanced professional qualifications. I find myself asking, then, whether there is a complete break in type between the first revolutionary group of people engaged in changing unpeaceful relationships and the second group who are concerned with the later stages of peacemaking.

My own opinion is that there may be, but that if this is so it is undesirable and could simply lead to a recrudescence of the old unpeaceful relationships. The effective third-party mediator, whether his role is primarily that of conciliator or bargainer, must have, in addition to his professional qualifications, a sensitive awareness of the people on both sides: he must be aware of the strains they are undergoing and the distortions that desperation has wrought on their perceptions, and must have a capacity to understand what they are trying to express even though they are prevented from saying it openly for fear of losing face. He must be able to avoid being sucked into the vortex of strong feelings and thus losing his impartiality, his genuine sympathy for the agonies of both sides, his clear consciousness of the actors and the situations. Unless he is able to do this he will be ineffective. Either he will not contribute to the reaching of a settlement, or – worse – he will be instrumental in fabricating one that is unjust to one or other of the parties.

The tasks of development similarly demand a high level of awareness as well as professional competence. This is vital if the errors of the past are to be prevented, if we are not to slide back into the materialistic rivalries, the chauvinism (that epitome of belonging), the inequalities, the feudal relationships of the past which in fact spawned the conflict.

Thus men and women of high awareness are essential at every stage in the building and maintenance of a peaceful society. The difference between those who practise the skills of revolutionary peacemaking and the others may lie, therefore, not so much in level of awareness and mode of perception of society, as in professional specialization and competence and, probably, age. I am not inferring that the younger activists lack training – many are highly qualified – but their lack of seniority and of extensive practical experience may make them less appropriate for some of the tasks of conciliation, bargaining and development. (Not that age and experience always count: it is more that people think they do.) It is at these stages, perhaps, that people of my age-group come in – though I hasten to add that this should not preclude us from playing a more militant part should occasion arise.

In *Making Peace* I noted that we live in a most complex web of relationships, large scale and small scale, peaceful and at all stages of unpeacefulness. The scope of peacemaking is unlimited and the contexts within which it can be carried out are immensely various. Some demand opposition to evil and inhuman establishments. Others, particularly those that are primarily developmental, require work within systems. We must be always aware of the multiplicity of tasks and the variety of ways by which they may be tackled.

Awareness and awareness-identity are in eternal conflict, in us and around us, with belonging-identity. Awareness is uncomfortable and insecure. It takes away the pleasant certainties of life, the fixed values, the easy answers to insoluble questions. It pricks the sluggish conscience, inducing us to take a stand when we would prefer to go happily with the herd. It even drives us to undignified and anonymous death for lost causes. It makes us dissatisfied with our lives: our achievements turn sour, and our possessions and position, once highly treasured, are as ashes in our mouths. We fight the implications of awareness. We envy those with what is called 'simple faith' whether it be in God or country or a way of life. How lucky they are – in a sense.

Those whose awareness is high are a constant threat to people whose security depends on a belonging-identity. They threaten either to make them, too, feel uncomfortable and dissatisfied, or actually to disrupt their protective systems of belonging. Throughout history the aware have been ridiculed, disowned, hated, tortured and killed by those who feared them. The persecution and crucifixion of Jesus is just one example. But they are hated so much precisely because they are also attractive. Few people are so blind that they do not feel the compelling force of awareness and with part of their hearts yearn for it. Thus our attacks on the more aware are violent because contact with awareness has aroused doubts in ourselves. We hate those who force us to question ourselves and we escape from having to answer by attacking. We project our inner struggle outwards and many suffer or die or kill because we will not acknowledge our blindness or try to regain our sight.

CHAPTER 5

Education for liberation

AFFECTIVE EDUCATION[54]

At this point I must take a side step to examine briefly and inadequately the vast, incoherent and overlapping fields of work known as affective education, psychological education, humanistic education, fulfilment education, education of concerns and a number of other comparable terms.[55] This is education which recognizes as its conscious goals, as Paul Nash (1971) puts it, the education of feelings and actions as well as thinking, education which is in fact affective or behavioural rather than solely intellectual. No education is, of course, purely intellectual; on the contrary, much of it has a devastating emotional impact, but this is a side effect, not consciously planned, of cognitive education. It has this effect because the exponents of affective etc. education would say it only takes into account part of the human being.

It is naturally no new idea that education should do more than train the intellect. The English public schools, under the inspiration of Dr Arnold, aimed to produce God-fearing and loyal Christian gentlemen, while much further back Spartan schooling was an education in stoic courage. Recently, however, there has been a spate of writing on new ways in education. Much of it is clustered around two centres. One is represented by a group of men and women, mostly teachers, many young, who are angered by the mindlessness, the dehumanizing quality, the subtly obnoxious hidden curriculum, and the intellectually worthless education prevailing in the schools for failure and most of Xville High. They have attempted to discover ways in which education can be made more real, more interesting, more exciting, even in one case, more ecstatic. This movement has exposed many evils, made useful propaganda, and from time to time produced extremely valuable teaching manuals. Outstanding among, but representative of, these are Kohl's *Open classroom: a practical guide to a new type of teaching* (1969) and Terry Borton's *Reach, touch and teach* (1970). Their approach to the process of education is humane, intelligent and deft. They do not ignore the intellectual aspect; on the contrary, as their examples show, their students make great progress in their capacity to write with creativity and feeling, to analyse problems, to make mature judgements, and to appreciate music or literature. This is only possible, however, because the teacher values them as individuals and creates a social setting (primarily a relationship with them) in which they are not made to feel stupid or inferior, in which they are not subjected to pointless and humiliating regulations, and in which their interests and capacities – untouched by rough impersonal instruction – are delicately uncovered and stimulated.

So far so good. The important question for me is how far excellent teaching of this sort will contribute towards achieving the objectives I have set for education: the raising of awareness, the reduction of competitive materialism and the establishment of a peaceful society. This sort of teaching I take to be the pedagogical groundwork for these other developments. Unless children in school are released from fear, the sense of failure and the prevalent meaningless futility, they will be stunted both intellectually and emotionally, and incapable of tackling the formidable tasks of social transformation – the peaceful society will not be born without pain and effort.

On the other hand, what the fortunate pupils of Kohl or Borton are experiencing is not new to the boys at Winton, who have high intellectual competence, interests and abilities, which are stimulated and developed, and are emotionally secure. How far this results from their education and how far from the fortunate circumstances of their birth and background it is hard to say, but it is reasonable to suppose at least that the latter are reinforced by the former. It is certainly true that in almost equally aristocratic but less educationally-advanced schools there is less versatile virtuosity on the scholastic side while socially there is the same sense of superiority, but more narrow and intolerant.

What is lacking is awareness. True, the feelings are released from constricting cocoons of convention, prejudice and fear of seeming 'weak', 'soft' or 'odd'. This is certainly a step forward, but strong feelings can be as blinding as lack of affect – or indeed, as an ill-disciplined or illogical intellect. Awareness, as I have tried to define it, is the total sense of self that lies behind the often distracting activities of mind and emotion. Intellectual activity refined to the point where it spins out ideas about ideas about ideas (as, for example, in some literary criticism) is of no help in tackling the intellectual problems of living effectively, let alone the emotional ones. Emotions, the marvellous capacity to love each other and to experience wonder, joy and mirth, compassion and grief, can also be readily transmuted into fear, self-pity, jealousy, depression, anxiety, anger, envy and a dozen other debilitating forms which sap the energy which we need to achieve our evolution. Someone whose emotions are 'educated' can merely be a person who allows his feelings to bubble to the surface, whether they are constructive and positive, or what has been termed negative emotions. One might argue that the more expression of feelings is inhibited, the more likely they are in fact to be negative.[56] But this is in any case a very normal tendency. A few minutes of introspection will reveal how little control we have over the flow of our emotions. They flicker across the screen of consciousness or semi-consciousness, touching chords of association, bringing now a moment of self-satisfaction; now a vaguely unpleasant feeling which – should we catch and pin it to the dissecting board – will turn out to be a sense of guilt or inadequacy; now calmness, now anxiety, now elation, now a minor, unidentified depression. The pure emotions, those which are based upon direct perception or relationship rather than fantasy, and which do not leave us with a slight feeling of enervation, easily become corroded. Suppose, for example, that we are genuinely moved to compassion by a friend's adversity; almost at once, however, we begin to feel smugness that the disaster did not happen to us, fear lest it might, and self-satisfaction that we are so sensitive to another's misfortune: the flavour of the original emotion will long since have disappeared.

To be aware is to be in touch with what lies behind our thoughts and feelings, the self from which they originate and which they serve, but often badly. The education of the servants is not education of the self, though if the servants are strong and disciplined, the self will be more powerful. The second group of persons, inevitably overlapping in ideology considerably with the first, whose writings are directly or indirectly relevant to education, are psychologists and psychiatrists. These belong to the loose-knit school which includes Allport (1955), Fromm (1956), Maslow (1970), Perls (1951) and Rogers (1961 and 1969). They are related by their general belief in the possibility of man's self-realization, self-actualization, his possibility of regeneration through peak experiences or whatever comparable terminology they employ. Unlike an older, and indeed current psychological generation, they hold in common that man is not an essentially bad and destructive creature who is only held in check by social conditioning, but that he has sublime potentialities. It is the work of the therapists and the teachers to supply first the conditions in which these potentialities can develop, and second, the stimulus for them to do so.

In their examination of man's possible modes of development, they bring into the realm of psychology what was previously in the realm of religion. It is unimportant that some of these psychologists have apparently not believed in a god who created the universe for particular purposes (Maslow), while others apparently did (Allport). What does matter is that for the first time since William James (1902)[57] a reputable body of psychologists has considered that religious experience is a legitimate field for inquiry — Fromm (1960) actually collaborated on a book on Zen – and so have elected to study a range of phenomena which most of their predecessors had considered to be fanciful or irrelevant or the symptoms of neurosis.

If these phenomena could be captured in a single phrase, one might perhaps speak of expanded consciousness. Traditionally the task of psychology has been to discover principles of mental function, perception, cognition, motivation and the like. This meant to establish norms, to discover statistical validities, to systematize data. Thus we develop concepts of average behaviour which we tend to view as normal, natural or healthy behaviour. But mystical experiences are not normal, in the sense that few people have them very often. They do not fit into the psychological system except as aberrations. What Maslow, Allport and others have done, however, is to affirm that they are not only part of the system, but the most important part. Not only are they far from being aberrations, but they represent man's optimum condition and functioning, and to strive for an expanded consciousness is neither a fantasy nor a sickness but a potentiality realized. Moreover, it may be a relatively common part of our existence – 'The sacred is in the ordinary', says Maslow (1970, p. x), but we fail to recognize it because we are trained to distrust and apologize for these apparently aberrant types of feeling. I can perhaps best convey their flavour by quoting Maslow (1970, pp 61–3) on what he terms peak experiences.

> 'In the peak experiences, we become more detached, more objective, and are more able to perceive the world as if it were independent not only of the perceiver but even of human beings in general. The perceiver can more readily look upon nature as if it were there in itself and for itself, not simply as if it were

a human playground put there for human purposes. He can more easily refrain from projecting human purposes upon it. In a word, we can see it in its own Being (as an end in itself) rather than as something to be used or something to be afraid of or something to wish for or to be reacted to in some other personal, human, self-centred way... This is a little like talking about god-like perception, super-human perception. The peak experience seems to lift us to greater than normal heights so that we can see and perceive in a higher than usual way. We become larger, greater, stronger, higher, taller people and tend to perceive accordingly... To say this in a different way, perception in the peak experiences can be relatively ego-transcending, self-forgetful, egoless, unselfish. It can come closer to being unmotivated, impersonal, desire-less, detached, not needing or wishing... In the peak experience there is a very characteristic disorientation in time and space, or even the lack of consciousness of time and space. Phrased positively, this is like experiencing universality and eternity... The person in the peak experience may feel a day passing as if it were minutes, or also a minute so intensely lived that it might feel like a day or a year or an eternity even. He may also lose his consciousness of being located in a particular place... The world seen in the peak experience is seen only as beautiful, good, desirable, worthwhile, etc. and is never experienced as evil or undesirable. The world is accepted. People will say that then they understand it. Most important of all for comparison with religious thinking is that somehow they become reconciled to evil. Evil itself is accepted and understood and seen in its proper place in the whole, as belonging there, as unavoidable, as necessary and, therefore, proper.'

In the beginning of the section from which these quotations were taken, Maslow says (page 59), 'practically everything that happens in the peak experiences, naturalistic though they are, could be listed under the headings of religious happenings, or indeed have been in the past considered to be only religious experiences'. There is little to differentiate the peak experiences from what Rudolph Otto (1958) has defined as the characteristics of religious experiences: sense of veneration, of awe, of worship, of smallness before mystery, of sublime exaltation, of the powerlessness of the individual, of the unity of creation, of the desire to kneel in worship. Maslow believes that these sensibilities derive from heeding the delicate voices of our own central inner humanness; the deist would maintain that they came from God. It seems to me unnecessary to argue which is right.

In my *Militants and mystics* (1972) I attempt to elaborate a theory of awareness and identity and to relate these two things to social action. As the general level of awareness rises, that is to say, as individuals become increasingly conscious of themselves, they also become increasingly conscious of what is around themselves. The consciousness is, moreover, the full awareness which includes as an inescapable component the need to act upon it. I have found that the type, rather than the level, of heightened awareness, differs. It may on the one hand be what I term natural or self-consciousness, that is to say spontaneous or achieved purposely, as through therapy, T-groups and the like, or it may be supraliminal. By supraliminal I mean what might otherwise be called consciousness-expanding or mystical; it is achieved less by psycho-analysis or sensitivity training than by the practice of Zen, yoga, or indeed many other cults or religions (or rather people attempt to reach it by these means: whether they succeed and to what degree and whether the results differ from others more orthodox is a matter for speculation). On the whole, natural or self-conscious awareness tends to be more prosaic, to represent the well-functioning mind uncluttered by anxieties and prejudices; supraliminal awareness (to the extent that it is achieved) has more the spiritual quality of Maslow's peak experiences. There is, of course, considerable overlap, but those whose mode of awareness tends to be more natural than supraliminal are likely to be militant in their social action. That is to say, their approach to social evils is to eradicate them by changing the institutions which produce them. On the other hand, those whose awareness is supraliminal rather than natural feel that the institutions are evil and that they themselves are also in part responsible for this evil. Moreover, if what was bad is to become good through their agency, it is first necessary for them to perfect themselves. Whereas the militant and the mystic both wish to change society, the former tries to do so by direct intervention, the latter through self-purification.

At a higher level of development, the mystic and the militant modes merge in the persons of such men as Gandhi. I believe that this coming together of the outward and inward activist is of supreme importance in moving society towards peace. Institutions may certainly be changed through many types of revolutionary action, but without the mystical element the old ills are likely to recur under any new dispensation. Unless the actors are relatively free of negative emotion, and the particular manifestations of it associated with the belonging-identity and competitive materialism, fresh institutional arrangements alone cannot afford protection against rapacity and exploitation. And without militant action of some sort the spiritual evolution of the mystics is not able to bring about the material changes necessary to peace. My concept of awareness includes as an inseparable element the sense of social involvement, sensitivity to social injustice, empathy with suffering, and in general the capacity to relate warmly to other people. This, I believe, is not inconsistent with what Maslow, Fromm and others are saying. (In the Appendix, I compare my approach to that of a different type of psychologist – B. F. Skinner.) I may simply be outlining aspects of the situation which, because of my basic concern with peace, is of greater interest to me than to them.

According to Maslow, there is a hierarchy of human needs: the satisfaction of basic bodily wants; safety, including protection, shelter, sufficient income and other forms of security; social needs for companionship and friendship; ego needs for recognition, status and esteem; and only when these have been satisfied come the higher needs for creativity and self-actualization. Thus the good teacher would be one who to the greatest possible extent ensured for the children in his charge the satisfaction of needs up to and including ego needs so that they would be ready to take off on original and exciting learning experiences. I find it hard to follow Maslow fully on this point. Many of the people of high awareness whom I have known could not be neatly categorized as having all their lower wants satisfied; on the contrary, some have been needy persons facing extraordinary difficulties. Maslow makes it sound rather middle class and this is precisely what awareness, as I know it, is not. It is a wandering and erratic flame but one which, once we have sighted it, we long to capture and, in the striving, do in part make our own.

However, I believe that the conditions for satisfying the ego needs correspond to a second vitally important tenet which the psychologists, though in varying degrees of strength and specificity, hold in common. This might be termed belief in the value of freedom. It is significant that Carl Rogers entitles the book in which he applies his psychological understanding to problems of identification, *Freedom to learn* (1969). What this means, briefly put, is that when human beings are constrained to learn subjects which are uninteresting or unreal and are, moreover, merely passive recipients of instruction (which in fact tends to make most topics boring and void) they not only fail to learn but also to develop in other ways as well. However, when there is some give and take in the learning process, when there is dialogue rather than monologue, when they have some initiative in following their own interests and arranging their own studies, they not only learn more, but also mature as human beings. The encounter group is one technique for breaking down the emotional adhesions created by what Rogers (1969, p. viii) terms 'the most traditional, conservative, rigid, bureaucratic institution of our time', (namely the educational system) and enabling this freer, happier, and more efficient form of learning to take place.

From our point of view, the right type of freedom in education has two important implications. In the first place it eliminates what is unpeaceful in the relationship of the teacher and the taught, the all too easily intrusive element of exploitation and manipulation. Thus the learning relationship can serve as a good model for relationships in the wider world, one in which understanding, nurturing and care replace the impassable barriers of hierarchy. Second, the process of developing freedom in learning and the flexible relationship on which it depends involves, in various ways, a re-learning of the self. One becomes less of a machine, no longer behaving entirely according to rule, learning to respond to elements in one's surroundings and in one's self which are intrinsic to one's nature. In this one does, in Maslow's terms, experience the gratification of ego needs. I would maintain, however, that our subsequent development does not occur because one is then liberated from these needs, but rather because the process through which incidentally, they are gratified, may be one which increases awareness.

There are, of course, many aspects of affective education upon which I have not touched. Moreover, I fear that in my references to Rogers and especially to Maslow I have, to make my point, given undue emphasis to particular aspects of their rich philosophies. I have perhaps given the impression that they are in one camp, with Borton, Kohl and other teachers in a different one. But of course there is much sharing and cross-fertilization and a common basic conception to lend light, lightness and feeling to education, all too often a dark and heavy factory of frequently meaningless knowledge.

Within the many approaches to affective, etc. education, some separate, many interlocking or overlapping, there is much which is relevant to education for liberation. It certainly provides a part of the foundation upon which the peaceful society must be built. What is lacking, I believe, is a coherent philosophy of the relationship of education to society which would make it possible for the real strength of affective education to be directed towards transforming the social setting which neutralizes so much good contemporary work in education.

CHAPTER 6

Peace studies at Bradford
THE SCOPE AND DILEMMAS OF PEACE STUDIES[58]

Introduction

Since I shall be dealing with what is, for many, a little-known and perhaps mysterious or nebulous subject, I have felt it necessary to cover a wider field than is necessary in most inaugural lectures, where the speaker wishes to deal with a particular facet of a subject whose lineaments are in general well-known. For the sake of clarity, I have divided my talk into several sections dealing with different aspects of the field. I shall first attempt to locate peace studies in the wider range of related studies. Next, I shall attempt to define what is an admittedly, but I think healthily, diverse subject — but then so are many others more strongly established. From this act of reportage I shall outline my own approach to peace studies. Then I move on to a discussion of how all these ideas are woven into a teaching programme, and what sorts of career our students may reasonably hope to follow after graduation. This leads to a rather difficult consideration of the moral and practical dilemmas in which the student of peace may be placed. I end on a note of optimism that this university is setting a progressive pattern for others to follow.

The study of peace and related subjects

It is, perhaps, wise to begin with an attempt to identify the position of peace studies within the framework of other academic studies and disciplines.

I am sometimes asked whether peace studies constitutes a separate discipline and, if so, what body of knowledge it is founded upon. Let me deal with the second point later, for during the course of my lecture I shall be attempting to define the types of knowledge which I think may be thought of as comprising peace studies. With regard to the first question, as to whether or not peace studies be thought of as a discipline, I have to admit that I am more interested in problems, both intellectual and practical, than in defining disciplines.

These, it seems to me, were created not by nature but by academics in order to demarcate spheres of intellectual interest, and are now institutionalized in the form of departments, faculties and so on. This, of course, has been necessary in order to prevent chaos but we have to be flexible. As knowledge advances, and as we are presented with fresh problems, we put together what had previously been separate, hence biochemistry or social psychology, or we separate out of previously unitary subjects certain specialisms, such as genetics or molecular biology, which have evolved to the status of virtually distinct branches of study. In order to deal with the needs and difficulties of the day, many of which in their complexity cut across a number of these useful if artificial disciplinary boundaries, we have such subjects as environmental sciences, management, international relations, planning, human purposes and the like, many of which are taught in this university. These branches of study have arisen because existing disciplines, as defined and taught, were not quite able to encompass them. Thus, international relations evolved a few decades ago because history, politics, international law and economics could not individually throw sufficient light on issues which were widely recognised to be of great importance. All of them were relevant, but new ways of combining them in focusing on particular issues had to be sought. Much the same could, I think, be said of peace studies. Whether or not, however, any particular field of intellectual endeavour qualifies as a discipline strikes me as relatively unimportant, provided that it is carried out with intellectual rigor, offers new and valid insights and generalisations, and has some practical significance.

Peace studies is, in fact, only the newest among a range of related studies. These comprise, among others, international relations (to which I have just referred), conflict research, war studies and strategic studies, not to speak of the less easily defined work of the members of the various peace movements which, as for example in the case of Mahatma Gandhi, Martin Luther King and Dom Helder Camara, have had a considerable intellectual content.

A few rough definitions may assist us in understanding this mosaic of relationships. War studies (apart from the more specific techniques of war making studied in staff colleges or defence colleges) involves the examination of how wars arise, how in general they are conducted, how they may be brought to an end and their impact on the social and economic fabric.

Strategic studies are concerned with many of the same issues as war studies, but with the emphasis on wider strategic issues; geopolitics, the balance of power, economic warfare and the use of strategic weapons.

In conflict studies the stress is on the mutual reaction of people and groups in conflict situations, and how this may be modified. It is definitely not confined to international conflict but deals equally with industrial, social, racial, and other sorts of conflict. Conflict studies have been developed by some with great statistical sophistication, and various aspects of game theory are often employed. In general, conflict studies emphasize only one stage of what I term (as I shall shortly explain) peacemaking: the stage of negotiation or bargaining.

International relations deal, obviously, with the relationships between states, with diplomacy, international law, with the international order and the way in which it is maintained and, of course, with international conflict and the processes of international peacemaking.

The separation of these fields from each other and from peace studies is not precise and all of them — at least in certain aspects — are facets of or are connected with each other. Peace studies and conflict studies are perhaps particularly close (for example, as illustrated by the name of the Richardson Institute for Conflict and Peace Research in which, so far as I am aware, no precise effort is made to separate these functions).

Peace studies, at least as I define the field, differs from these others in various ways. The focus is, as the term implies, upon peace, that is to say upon a relationship between individuals, groups, nations or even larger units, which is based on cooperation. It analyses those conditions in which, instead of cooperation, there is mutual hostility and violence, and seeks to discover techniques by which these relationships may be changed into peaceful ones.

However, before proceeding further with an examination of the nature of peace studies I would like to define what, in my opinion, the field does not include. Some would perhaps disagree with me and this illustrates that fact that there is some confusion about the word 'peace'. This theme will recur during my lecture, so I will only deal with it briefly at this point. To my mind the study of peace is not the study of pacification, of suppressing dissent, of maintaining the status quo however painful it may be to the less privileged. Some would maintain that peace was simply the absence of overt violence, which can do as much harm as more open sorts and which may, on occasion, be employed in the name of maintaining peace or law and order. Nor, on the other hand, do I believe that peace studies can be based on a kind of sentimental attempt to make everyone be friends, without correcting genuine injustices or conflicts of interest between them. The student of peace, for example, would not attempt to reconcile the master and the slave without having first worked to abolish the practice of slavery.

Nor do I include in my definition of peace studies approaches which are mainly philosophical or psychological. I admit that in doing this I am putting up one of those artificial barriers which circumscribe all disciplines or fields of study, but I believe that in this case, at this stage, it is necessary, in order that we can grapple effectively with a field which is already very diverse and complex. It has been put to me by serious people that the only peace is the peace of God, that that is indeed a peace, as it is stated in the gospels, which passes all understanding and which, although some of us may believe in it personally, it would be impossible to introduce into the form of academic enquiry suggested by our principal foci of interest. Somewhat in the same vein, a young man asked me recently whether there could be any peace, unless individuals had peace of mind. This is indeed an interesting, but ambiguous and complex question: some of the most saintly and committed persons have been tormented inwardly while, on the other hand, I have known of people who are reputed to have enjoyed great peace after having committed some atrocious act of sadism or revenge. This is not to deny the importance of the concept of peace of mind, but simply to say that its study would take us into unexplored avenues which might lead us away from what I conceive as our main problems and purposes.

Diversities and contradictions in peace studies

Those who tend to think of themselves as being involved in peace studies or peace research — the terms are often used interchangeably, though perhaps we should learn to differentiate them — can be divided along two lines: functional and ideological. The functional division is between those who are interested in scholarship and those who are interested in action: the latter may also be interested in research, but as a prelude to efficient action. Peace researchers, who may be drawn from any academic background, are concerned with a great diversity of fields. This diversity may be judged by anyone who cares to look through the table of contents of, for example, the *Journal of Peace Research*. I give a few titles chosen at random from recent issues: The Marxist theory of war and peace; The place of international law in peace research; Military spending and senate voting in the United States; Domestic and foreign conflict behaviour of nations; Developmental tension and political instability; Twenty-five years of local wars; Freedom and civilization: a quantitative conflict model; Structural and direct violence; Social inequality; Another mother for peace campaign; Peaceful co-existence; The role of ILO standards in the global integration process; Peace research and developing countries; Divided Berlin — one past and three futures; Divided nations as a process: the case of Korea; Imperialism: the dynamics of colonial violence; Ghetto riots; miscalculations in deterrent policy; Religion, war and the institutional dilemma; Children's developing orientations to international politics; Economic and power frustrations as predictors of industrial and political conflict strategies; Perceptions of foreign news; Middle East and the theory of conflict; Human resource cost of war, and so on and so on...

You may rightly feel that many of these titles might have been published in journals dealing not necessarily with peace but with conflict, war, international relations or indeed other social sciences. That they were not, perhaps indicates something more about the motivation and interests of the authors than the nature of the topic. Students of peace studies also usually have other more orthodox labels such as economist, sociologist, political scientist, biologist and so on. It is the use to which they habitually put their discipline which differentiates them from their colleagues. I might add, however, that the application of the concepts and methods of one discipline to a particular range of problems, in this case those dealing with peace, may also influence those concepts and methods. Thus, while the student of peace may well be recognised as a distinguished social scientist, he will probably be a somewhat unorthodox one.

The activists are represented, for example, by many of those who have over the years, been associated with War Resisters International or *Peace News*. I am not suggesting that there are not able scholars among these who contribute also to the various learned journals. Bertrand Russell, after all, was one such. Indeed, many are interested in both academic work and action. Nevertheless, there is a cleavage. The activists are concerned to change situations which they conceive to be liable to lead to war and violence, and if they do carry out research it is in order that they may be better informed and so act more efficiently. The 'pure' researchers tend to feel that it is enough to obtain the facts, that if only we were adequately informed we would avoid wars and violence. To which the activists reply: 'Who makes the decisions? Who uses your research results? They may be as useful to the Pentagon' — I use this word as a symbol for the war machine — 'as in promoting harmony and peace'. They would further maintain that as well as offering information it is necessary to acquire the capacity or the influence to use it to achieve the right action. This functional split is often a temperamental and often in part an ideological one.

But the chief ideological division between those who are involved with peace studies involves their interpretation of peace. To some, but I think now fewer and fewer, peace is simply the antithesis of war: war may be the most fearful expression of an unpeaceful situation but I think that most people would include in their field of interest peaceful and unpeaceful situations in such areas as industry, race relations, community and even family relations. The main difference, however, is between those who see peace, on whatever scale, as the absence of overt violence, and those who would equate it rather with social justice. The former would be in favour of maintaining the status quo on the grounds that while there is no open violence things are not so bad, but any attempt at change, particularly unconstitutional change, might lead to dangerous disturbances of the existing order. The latter would maintain that often, as in South Africa, the relatively 'peaceful' status quo is maintained by injustice and that, in fact, a masked violence is constantly done to the rights and indeed the lives of human beings. This, they would say, is actually a condition of unpeacefulness which must be changed. Those who feel like this would themselves be divided among some who believed that this form of what has been termed 'structural violence' (Galtung) can only be overthrown by militancy, involving if necessary counter-violence, and others who believe in non-violent techniques of social change.

Around all these issues there is considerable debate, often acrimony. I do not, however, find this divisiveness to be unhealthy or undesirable. There is a ferment of concern, often very well informed, on questions profoundly affecting human survival. Moreover, some approaches to peace studies have elucidated the links between war and violence on the one hand, and on the other such perils to humanity as massive poverty and hunger in the Third World, ecological damage and the danger of depletion of irreplaceable resources. Thus important links, theoretical and practical, are forged.

A personal interpretation

With all this diversity it is, however, important to attempt to develop a central core of ideas which, while permitting wide variations of interests and diversity of opinion on many topics will, nevertheless, permit some orderly growth, a greater degree of consensus. Many of us have tried to do this, and during the last few years I, too, have grappled with the problem, both in my writings, and latterly in my attempts to build up the School of Peace Studies at Bradford University. It may perhaps help if I give a brief account of how my own approach evolved.

Having spent many years concerned with Third World problems and being much moved by the violence and suffering I saw, I attempted to understand its origins. Then, over a period of four or five years, I was directly involved in mediation efforts in wars in Africa and Asia, and my rudimentary ideas on peace and violence began to focus on problems of international negotiation. However, even as I developed my conclusions, I realized that my approach was too narrow. A skilful negotiator might ease a particular situation, but the circumstances, the rivalries, the oppression, the scarcity of resources — which had given rise to it — remained. Moreover, even if wars are brought to an end, many of the conditions associated with war continue throughout large areas of the world: people are driven from their homes, unjustly imprisoned, separated from their families, flung into detention camps, virtually enslaved, exploited by landlords, victimised by the police, oppressed by the government, starved and malnourished because of official neglect or official policies; they are humiliated and have their perceptions distorted by propaganda; many in fact die because of these conditions. Circumstances such as these inflict such damage on human life, health, capacity for creative and happy existence and work, and for the development of potential, that I find it impossible to refer to them as peaceful: they inflict upon human beings, though in a less direct and concentrated form, many of the same destructive horrors as does war.

From my perception of these circumstances I drew three conclusions. First, the study of peace should not be confined to the analysis of means of preventing or terminating wars.

Second, because many of these circumstances were internal — rather than international — the study of peace should not be considered as exclusively on the international level.

Third, and for the same reason, I came to believe that support for a *status quo* which permitted or encouraged such unpeaceful conditions could in no sense be considered as the promotion of peace: on the contrary, it was the tacit condoning of violence.

The concept of peace I found, however, to be unsatisfactory. It was both too vague, too emotive, and too manipulative. I therefore developed an approach based on what I termed peaceful and unpeaceful relations — between individuals, groups or nations. This concept enables us to analyse our interaction in a number of dimensions — psychological, economic, political and indeed human — in terms of which individuals are adversely affected. I defined peaceful relationships as those in which individuals or groups are enabled to achieve together goals which they could not have reached separately, or at least do not impede each other (but neutrality of interaction is, in my experience, rare). Unpeaceful relationships are those in which the units concerned damage each other so that in fact they achieve less than they could have done independently, and in one way or another harm each other's capacity for growth, maturation or fulfilment; or they are relationships in which one party suffers in this fashion even if the other does not and may gain advantage through his conquest.

The first task of peace in my opinion is, then, to identify and analyse these relationships. I say 'identify' because they may not always be obvious. I look back on my own youth where to most Englishmen, the colonial relationship seemed not only legitimate and natural, but also beneficent whereas, in fact — although there were many wise and humane colonial administrators — it was socially, psychologically, culturally and economically damaging to the colonised. And I say 'analyse' because such relationships can be complex even if, as in the case of war, they are not hard to identify.

This leads directly to the next function of peace studies, which is to use this information in order to devise means of changing unpeaceful into peaceful relationships. Here theory and practice may become closely related. I am concerned with an attempt to define the scope of peace studies rather than to elaborate my own ideas in detail and will therefore not try to describe the various stages by which I believe that unpeaceful relationships may be transformed into peaceful ones; I will merely suggest that there must be certain key variables to take into account. One is the relative degree of power (or perceived power) of the parties in the unpeaceful relationship. Let me suggest in very simple terms the sort of thing I mean. Contrast a row between a small weak boy and a much stronger bully who intends to steal the small boy's pocket money, with a quarrel between two boys of equal size and strength. The small boy's options are different from those of the two equal contestants. He may back down and try to placate the bully, or to match his strength, for example, by arming himself with a stick or getting a friend to help him or by finding some psychological way of intimidation: in the absence of one or more of these the bully will not be deterred. The equal contestants can either fight it out or negotiate, or fight and then negotiate, or fight and part still enemies. But the weak boy cannot either engage in a straightforward fight, nor can he negotiate because he has nothing with which to bargain. If, however, he gains the advantage of a stick, an ally, or whatever, he then has the same options as the other pair.

Another variable is the perception of the situation. Let us take the boys again. The small boy may have been brought up in a society in which it is customary for bigger boys to exact tribute of the smaller ones. The latter do not like it, but accept it as part of the natural order and their acquiescence is partially self-protective. There are many groups whose inadequate perception of the situation prevents them from taking effective action. In the case of the two other boys there may be no real conflict of interest whatsoever, they may simply have quarrelled because one misunderstood what the other said. In this case a tactful third party may reconcile them before blows are struck.

These examples have several implications. First, that the quarrel (or some other form of unpeaceful relationship) can be resolved (or made into a peaceful relationship or at least moved in that direction) through changes in perceptions (growing awareness, in my terms) or changes in the power structure of the relationship (or at least the perceived power structure), or both.Second, that faulty perceptions and less apparent power tend to be associated.Third, that negotiations between the strong and the weak generally mean that the weak give in to the strong.Fourth, that negotiations in the sense of bargaining are only likely to be mutually satisfactory if both parties are more or less equally strong.

From these examples I derive two principles for peace studies. There must be concern for changing perceptions, for enlarging awareness of social reality: and there must be concern for changing the balance of power where strength is being employed to enhance or maintain the strong at the expense of the weak. These will have very different implications for both analysis and action in different settings, but in all cases they involve a purposeful alteration of the existing situation.

Thus, certain unpeaceful relations can only move towards a peaceful character after a period of change, even turmoil, in which, paradoxically, peace studies — as I perceive it — must be implicated. But if this sounds strange one can only point to the alternative of permitting the unpeacefulness to persist. It does, however, indicate a further role for peace studies: that of seeking non-violent approaches towards changing the status quo, for it would seem to me inconsistent to repay one sort of violence with another. Here we may gain guidance from a number of approaches to non-violence, some of which have been systematically and even officially developed under the title of civilian defence.

I have referred in passing to negotiation and it is clearly a task of peace studies to examine this process very carefully, determining not only how to carry it out but in what circumstances it is appropriate in that it may lead to a genuine settlement and not a formula for submission. It is part of the process which is normally a major preoccupation of conflict research.

It is now time to mention a characteristic of peace studies which differentiates the field from the others referred to earlier: its possible qualities. Most of those involved in the area do not think of peace as being the mere end of hostility or conflict but, as I have already suggested, a more purposive eventual coming together for mutual advantage.

Thus, peace studies must be concerned with approaches to reshaping society and the world order in such a way that not only is violence, overt and covert, eliminated, but harmony and cooperation are established and maintained. For this reason, a further dimension is added: the study of the future and possible alternatives to the existing system.

Given these very complex and varied tasks it will be appreciated that peace studies must be a large and diverse enterprise. It will call for the contribution of persons from very different academic backgrounds, possessing varied personal qualities and capacities. I believe, however, that it is possible to construct a framework into which these different efforts can fit constructively and thus be applied to the common good of humanity. The framework is essentially the study of relationships; the determination of what renders some destructive mutually or unilaterally, and what makes others constructive; the attempt to discover, and in some cases to practise, the methods by which the unpeaceful may be changed into peaceful relationships; and finally the imaginative effort to envisage a more peaceful world order.

Teaching peace studies

Those of you who have listened to me up to this point and even perhaps found my definition of peace studies acceptable, may still be asking the sort of questions which I admit to having asked myself when I first began thinking about how to construct an academic programme of peace studies. Would our students end up with a body of knowledge which was well-structured, significant and useful? Or conversely, would they end the course with a hodge-podge of miscellaneous information which it would be very hard for them to apply, and which would lead to no recognisable opportunities for employment? And, indeed, what forms of employment might a graduate in peace studies hope to obtain?

To begin with, let me briefly sum up what we hope to do in our teaching programme. First, to engage in a study, made systematic by the analysis of relationships, of important issues, both contemporary and historical; second, to attempt to apply analysis to practice; third, to offer what I hope will be a good general education and a useful method of approach to some of the world's most urgent problems.

I can perhaps illustrate the way in which we hope to achieve our purpose and, at the same time, provide an answer to some of the questions by looking at one particular field of enquiry. You would not, I know, wish me to go into tedious details concerning the curricula. These have already been published, but I find that formal descriptions of programmes in university catalogues give very little indication as to their real substance and quality. So let me give you some illustrative details of a part of the programme which do not appear in the catalogue. Rather than spread ourselves too widely we have decided that in our teaching on the international level we shall concentrate on the Middle East. One reason for this is that several of us have had direct experience of this area, but it is perhaps more important that it represents a number of themes which are crucial to the understanding of peaceful and unpeaceful relationships throughout the world, and even those of us who do not know the Middle East have studied these themes in other settings and can apply them to the Middle Eastern situation. This troubled area of the world is the scene of great power rivalry; it illustrates the extraordinary significance of an important natural resource — oil; it provides us with many examples of third-party intervention, both official and unofficial; of the role of United Nations peacekeeping forces and, in general, of the scope and limitations of UN involvement in international disturbances; it illustrates the part of deep-seated historical, religious and national elements in conflict; it provides interesting comparison with other recent or current conflicts with which some of us have also been involved — those of the Indian subcontinent, the Nigerian Civil War, Southern Africa and the agonising problems of Northern Ireland; it illuminates questions of socioeconomic development and of the relationship of the rich and the poor nations which are also bound up in the Middle Eastern situation; it provides classic instances of conflict situations and of the impact of war and war mobilisation upon several very different societies. And, finally, it offers an example of how like-minded groups may struggle for peaceful aims across the barriers of conflict.

I am not suggesting that the Middle East should be used as a case study. I hope to imply something more profound and more universal. We shall be looking at the relationship between many of these other elements I have mentioned — development and underdevelopment, colonialism, the distortions of perceptions which come with hostility, and the dangerous games of global strategy played by the great powers. These and the other things I have referred to are, of course, topics in themselves, but by being purposively focused on the concrete issues of a particular part of the world, over a particular period of time, they will, I hope, impart an understanding of the totality of life, and also enable both our students and ourselves to identify the separate strands out of which is woven the tapestry of human experience. You may complain that inevitably knowledge in any single one of these interrelated fields is bound to be fragmentary, but this depends upon the perspective. In my opinion it is more important to understand interactions than to have an intensive knowledge of one of the interacting elements at the cost of ignorance of the others. I recall my experience some years ago as so-called adviser on social affairs to the Planning Commission of Pakistan. A considerable number of my colleagues were economists and there were also specialists in agriculture, irrigation, mineral extraction, communication, housing and a number of other fields. I think it was a fairly common experience amongst us all that initially we found our own expertise of very little value because we had no understanding of the complex interaction of other factors in which it had to be applied. We also found, however, that we could fairly easily learn enough about the skills of our colleagues to ask the right questions, to go to the right sources for information, and to adjust our own specialised approach to the broad purposes of the group as a whole. And, I should add, in so doing to learn something unexpected about our own particular expertise. Thus, while I would not expect that our students would become experts in all the various interrelated fields, or even in any of them, I would anticipate that they would become, as it were, specialists in disentangling relationships, or, to put it perhaps in a more positive way, in fitting things together. Returning for a moment to my own experience, I soon found that I learnt enough of economic development theory to guide me in my own noneconomic contribution to a plan for economic development, and even to say things about development which were relevant to the thinking of my economist colleagues.

This, I hope, will illustrate the way in which we aim to achieve the first and third objectives of which I recently spoke, namely to study important issues and to provide a good general education. I have said nothing as yet about the second one which was to apply analysis to practice. We would not, of course, normally expect our students, more particularly our undergraduate ones during their third year, which will be spent in employment away from Bradford, to get themselves involved in the Middle East or some other trouble spot. This could be perilous both for themselves and for others. Our aims are much less grandiose. For those who are particularly interested in international affairs we would try to arrange for some attachment to an appropriate agency overseas; for those who are more concerned with situations within our own society (which would be approached from the same comprehensive point of view as I have described for the Middle East) there will be opportunities of working with suitable community agencies. I certainly do not envisage that this work will, in any sense, be dramatic. On the other hand, the world is made up of a great web of relationships many of which have their unpeaceful elements, if we only learn how to recognise them, and I hope that during their practical work our students will be able to perceive these relationships and, under wise guidance, perhaps learn some of the approaches by which they may be changed.

As for employment, I find it hard to think ahead for four years to the time when our first undergraduates will be looking for jobs. I will, however, attempt a little crystal-gazing. But first, let me refer to our postgraduate students. A considerable proportion of these are likely to be somewhat older people who have already been involved in the affairs of the world and are taking what might be called a 'sabbatical in reverse' in order to come to intellectual grips with problems which they have been facing at the practical level for some time previously. For younger people it will, of course, be somewhat different. I imagine that for a proportion of them our course will simply provide a good general critical education with focus on important problems, and that the openings available to them would be as wide or as narrow as for many students with a good liberal education in, for example, history or geography. But I also envisage that many will be involved in different aspects of community work or race relations, or will seek jobs in labour organisations. Some who specialised in the international field may join agencies such as the International Labour Office, the United Nations Institute of Training and Research, and World Council of Churches, or Oxfam, or, if they are from overseas, the Organisation of African Unity. Or they may return to grapple with the problems of their own countries. Some may very appropriately go on to professional careers such as the law, practising it according to some of the principles which they have learned through peace studies. A number may go into education, emphasising current or international affairs, or into the field of peace education, now very vigorous in America and beginning to spread over here, and I trust we will be able to help the growth in this country. But it has been my experience in other parts of the world that as people are trained in new skills and new understanding so, perhaps after some lapse of time, new types of employment become available, either created through their efforts or for them. I am inclined to think that we are entering a very troubled period of the world's history, not necessarily one of major wars but of confusion and change, and that roles which we can hardly envisage at the moment may open up for students of peace studies who have both the skill and the motivation to try to alter things a little bit for the better.

Moral and practical dilemmas

This reference to the possible difficulties which lie ahead induces me to shift gear from the somewhat abstract and academic tenor of my lecture to discuss briefly what I hope will be the hypothetical implications of what

I have been talking about. Let us assume that in a period of economic and social confusion an abhorrent regime were imposed upon this country by a powerful minority, that democratic procedures were abandoned, that those who were not of pure Anglo-Saxon descent were butchered or put into concentration camps, dissidents were brutally punished, education was corrupted with racism, censorship imposed and so on. (The same thing could, of course, happen through invasion, and might have done 35 years ago, but is now, I think, a less likely contingency.) The country would be manifestly dominated, in my terminology, by unpeaceful relationships. How should we, and I mean of course particularly those who are involved in peace studies and should be specifically concerned with such things, respond to this situation? There are several alternatives:

1. We are as pleasant as possible to our new rulers, hoping to gain their favour and then influence them to change their evil ways. I have personally refused to be implicated in such efforts elsewhere, believing them to be worse than useless.

2. We keep as quiet as possible, trying not to attract attention, and waiting for the time when the regime falls and we can once more wage peace. This is a kind of cowardice which Gandhi called worse than violence.

3. We can take up arms, join guerrilla bands and sabotage groups, as many have done, including Catholic clergy in Latin America, who felt that the only way to extirpate violence was through counter-violence. Others would feel, however, that the exigencies of the struggle would force us to develop the same type of oppressive bureaucratic structure as our oppressors: that we might become so like them that when we won we merely replaced one terror by another.

4. Or we may take part in a non-violent struggle. The political objective of this is the same as for the previous type of action. We do not, however, do to our enemy what he has done to us: that is, damage his potential as a human being. Our weapons are the massive withholding of labour, boycotting, non-lethal sabotage, making intentional mistakes in every official operation, civil disobedience of every sort eventually bringing the machinery of the state grinding to a standstill. Such a non-violent campaign requires, as indeed does a violent one, organisation, courage, determination and persistence of a heroic type.

It is not my purpose to argue the advantages and disadvantages of these different approaches, although I have already suggested that the first two do not appeal to me. Whether we feel impelled to employ violent or non-violent techniques of resistance to an obnoxious regime or indeed to a foreign invader, depends upon considerations which are, on the one hand, moral, and on the other tactical and strategic. I would only emphasize that I am not advocating pacifism of the traditional sort which a noted Quaker scholar (who is, in fact, Reader in War Studies at the University of London) referred to as the 'intellectual ghetto of pacifism', though I do recommend that we should take serious account of the tough and tough-minded approaches to non-violence as described by such writers as Adam Roberts, Gene Sharp, George Lakey, and Boserup and Mack. My main purpose is, however, to indicate that our commitment to peace and peaceful relationships, as I have tried to define them, may logically lead us to situations which are exceptionally uncomfortable and to decisions which could be all the more agonising because our choice may be seen by some to contradict the principles which we profess.

I trust the circumstances will not arise in which my colleagues or I, whether in peace studies or not, are faced with such stark alternatives. We must not forget, nevertheless, that we must always be prepared to practise the principles which we preach, and that in large ways or small the practice may make us unpopular with 'those who have the capacity to make life uncomfortable for us'.

Conclusion

I have attempted to define the scope, nature and problems of the field in somewhat intellectual terms. But I believe that most of my colleagues and I have come to this work for reasons which are not primarily intellectual. We have come to it, often with pain and suffering, because we cannot resist the obligations imposed upon us by our experiences in this darkening world. 'I have a dream', said Martin Luther King in a famous sermon. I, too, have a dream. In this sad age I have a dream which I shall not see come true, but which — if we do not seek now to realize it — our grandchildren will not see, either. I dream of a world in which we are not separated from each other by fear, suspicion, prejudice or hatred; in which we are free and equal, considerate and loving with each other.

By establishing peace studies at an intellectual and practical level we may in some measure help this world to be born. Here lies our motive. But it cannot come into being if we who comprise it are inwardly riven by guilt, self-loathing, greedy ambition or despair. Let us, then, do all we can in the world and in our minds, but above all cherish the humanity in ourselves and in each other, not least in those from whom we are separated by the more superficial barriers of ideology or religion or race. Until we can recognise that our common nature and our common destiny are more important than the things which divide us, the shadows will continue to lengthen until night irrevocably falls.

Part 2

Tools for Transformation

Part 2 contains four chapters which focus on the practice of peacemaking and the way in which Adam's experience as a practitioner evolved over time. The first piece, *In the middle: non-official mediation in violent situations* (Chapter 7) was published in 1986 and draws on a set of reflections based on his role as a Quaker mediator in the Nigerian Civil War of 1967–70. He presents a classic model of track two diplomacy or informal mediation, based on four components of the mediator's task: to build, maintain and improve communications; to provide information to and between the conflict parties; to 'befriend'; and to encourage active mediation – a willingness to engage in co-operative negotiation. The approach is very much based on engaged commitment where the mediator is neutral and outside the conflict, providing the knowledge and expertise to facilitate a willingness to make peace. It differs from track one or formal mediation in that the mediator has no power over the conflict parties and no personal or strategic interest in the outcome beyond the will to lessen suffering and move the parties towards a ceasefire or peace agreement. This was the model of mediation, and the preferred peacemaking tool, used by Adam in the 1970s and 1980s.[59]

The second piece, *Another way: positive response to contemporary violence* (Chapter 8) shows how Adam's thinking and practice developed radically in the early 1990s, in common with that of other innovative scholar-practitioners who responded to the changed dynamics and nature of post-Cold War conflict. In Adams's case much of this change of outlook developed from his engagement with the Osijek Centre for Peace, Nonviolence and Human Rights. Osijek, a town in the Eastern Slavonia province of Croatia, was, with the adjacent town of Vukovar, the site of the most violent fighting of the Serb Croat War from 1992. Early in 1992 Adam and Anne attended a meeting of the Helsinki Citizens Assembly, the non-official arm of the Conference on Security and Cooperation in Europe (now the Organisation for Security and Cooperation in Europe (OSCE), where they met Vesna Terselic, from Zagreb, a peace activist who had set up the Anti War Campaign – Anti Rama Kampgne (ARK), who told them that a small group of people in Osijek, in particular Katarina Kruhonja (a medical doctor) and Krunoslav Sukic (a social philosopher) were planning to establish a branch of ARK.

This involvement with the people of Osijek[60], who were trying to rebuild a tolerant society while surrounded by the enraged and embittered feelings caused by the war, caused a considerable amount of reflection by Adam about the problems of practical peacemaking. It was apparent that the model of mediation described in *In the middle* was very difficult to apply on the ground in the confusion and chaos of the type of conflict epitomised by the wars in former Yugoslavia. It was still the case that the use of mediatory techniques would be much more likely to produce the shift in attitudes and understanding necessary for a stable peace, a resolution of conflict, than the use of conventional diplomacy alone: 'Solutions reached through negotiation may be simply expedient and not imply any change of heart. And this is the crux of peace. There must be a change of heart. Without this no settlement can be considered secure.' This search for peacemaking as a deeper quest not only for tools but values required to guide and inform the cultivation of a deeper culture of peace is developed more in *Another way* (extracts here in Chapter 8), and was originally published in 1994, two years after the formation of the Osijek Centre, and presents Adam's move beyond mediation as a tool to this quest for the deeper universal values to sustain peace. He realized through his involvement with the Osijek project that the range of conflict traumas and problems were so vast that the model of mediation, based on the intervention of outsider-neutrals, was simply not powerful or relevant enough to promote peace. He made two important revisions to his peace praxis. First, the work of outside bodies and individuals had so far proved ineffective (in the chaotic conditions of contemporary ethnic conflict – particularly, but not exclusively, in Somalia, Eastern Europe and the former USSR), that it was essential to consider the peacemaking potential within the conflicting communities themselves. Second, the starting point for this was to help in 'the development of the local peacemakers'

inner resources of wisdom, courage and compassionate non-violence."
At around the same time John Paul Lederach, working as a scholar-practi-
tioner within a Mennonite tradition which shares many of the values and
ideas of the Quakers, also highlighted the importance of this approach,
which he calls indigenous empowerment, in two books that redefined the
course of peace and conflict studies – *Building peace: sustainable reconciliation in divided societies* in 1994, and *Preparing for peace: conflict transformation across cultures*, in 1995.

> The principle of indigenous empowerment suggests that con-
> flict transformation must actively envision, include, respect and
> promote the human and cultural resources from within a given
> setting. This involves a new set of lenses through which we do
> not primarily 'see' the setting and the people in it as the 'prob-
> lem' and the outsider as the 'answer'. Rather, we understand the
> long-term goal of transformation as validating and building on
> people and resources within the setting.[61]

Responding to the immense suffering of people on all sides caught up
in these conflicts became a central priority for Adam. The relationship
between trauma therapy and conflict and the importance of compassion
and counselling in social healing had been a part of his early practice,
indeed his first connection with what later became peace studies, in his
work with the Tavistock Institute at the end of the Second World War. At
this time over 120,000 soldiers returned home having been prisoners of
war (POWs), and having suffered loss of various kinds – whether peace
of mind, a beloved person, a community, a country, a way of life, happiness. He wrote about this in *Tools for transformation* in 1990 and indeed
his very first publications in the years after 1945 described the work of the
Civil Resettlement Units (CRUs) set up to help traumatised POWs to re-
settle in normal civilian life. His first published piece, 'Transitional communities and social reconnection' was co-authored with E.L. Trist, and
published in the journal *Human relations* in 1948. Conflict created post
traumatic stress disorder (CPTSD) and the need to assist traumatized
children, adults and communities affected by it is now widely recognized
as one of the greatest challenges facing peacebuilders and peacemakers.
Adam wrote about the central and continued relevance of this work more
recently in *Social healing of the wounds of war* (Chapter 9) in 2001, and his

conviction that in order to engage effectively with psycho-social healing of conflict trauma, it was more necessary than ever to turn to the inner dimension of peace, to discover the inner resources of wisdom, courage and compassionate nonviolence. Barbara Mitchels worked with Adam in Osijek and has provided an excellent account of the importance of trauma counselling, therapy and social healing based on this experience, in her book *Love in danger: trauma therapy and conflict explored through the life and work of Adam Curle* (2006). She pointed out in this study that the activists in the Osijek Peace Centre themselves knew the crucial importance of Adam's view that 'peace is an inward state evidenced by outer actions'. For this reason, we include as the final chapter in Part 2 *Peace-making – public and private*, originally delivered as a lecture in 1978.

CHAPTER 7

In the middle

NON-VIOLENT MEDIATION IN VIOLENT SITUATIONS[62]

Mediation

M ediators, as the word implies, are in the middle. This is true in two senses. First, they are neither on one side nor the other; second, they are in the centre of the conflict, deeply involved in it because they are trying to find a satisfactory way out of it.

Although mediation is considered here in the special context of violent conflict, it is a universal human role. All of us, perhaps even the most intractably aggressive, have practised it occasionally. We may not have called it that when we tried to persuade members of our family or friends or colleagues to see each other's point of view and stop bickering about some trivial issue. But mediation it was: we were the people in between those who had fallen out, on fairly good terms with both, not taking sides though often pressured to do so; not personally implicated in the dispute, but worried about the situation and hoping to improve it.

What mediators do is to try to establish, or re-establish, sufficiently good communications between conflicting parties so that they can talk sensibly to each other without being blinded by such emotions as anger, fear and suspicion. This does not necessarily resolve the conflict; mediation has to be followed-up by skilled negotiation, usually directly between the protagonists, supported by a measure of mutual tolerance and by determination to reach agreement. But it is a good start.

This would apply whether the conflict were between individuals or nations, and irrespective of culture, political ideology or religion. Although the circumstances of an international dispute, economic, political and strategic, are very different from the emotional tangle of, for example, a marital one, both ultimately focus on human beings who have to make decisions and to act, and whose passions, fears, hopes, rage and guilt are much the same whoever and wherever they are. This, at least, has been my experience.

Non-official mediation

Within the context of violent conflict, the forms of mediation may differ considerably. Some involve short term missions having a very specific objective, such as those of Terry Waite to secure the release of captives in various parts of the world, or the shuttle diplomacy of a Henry Kissinger hurrying, often without great success, between one capital and another. There is also the longer-term work of United Nations officials such as Dag Hammarsjold, Brian Urquhart or Sean McBride, struggling year after year to resolve one bitter quarrel after another.

These and many other patterns may be useful and appropriate. What I shall discuss is mediation usually of long duration, carried out by non-official groups or organisations, churches or other religious organisations, charitable bodies, academic bodies or concerned individuals without institutional backing (although individuals without such support tend to experience difficulty in launching and maintaining their mission, suffer considerable strain and naturally incur considerable costs). I shall not speak of UN mediation, most valuable though it is; the aegis of a great international organisation creates conditions, occasionally less favourable where there is unilateral distrust of it, different from those pertaining to both governmental and to private or non-official mediation. What I have to say derives from direct experience of mediation initiated by the Quakers who, of the half dozen or so organisations I know of that have worked in the field, have the longest and most varied experience, as well as from efforts which were personal although carried out with much help from others.

It is perhaps hardly necessary to emphasize that those engaged in private mediation are never, so far as I know, paid, except for their expenses. Nor do they, being constrained by the need for confidentiality, make money or achieve any ego-enhancement by such means as writing articles or giving interviews. Their mediation is perhaps more appreciated because in no sense is it influenced by the profit motive; there is no reason why they should submit to considerable trouble and inconvenience except to contribute if possible to the reduction of human misery. In the same vein, I sometimes point out to people that I have been retired for several years and would sooner spend my old age at home than gallivanting around the world.

There are, of course, some disadvantages to non-official mediation. There is no automatic entree, such as an ambassador would have, to recognised authority; there is no established source of intelligence information; there is no help in making appointments and travel arrangements, and with secretarial chores, all of which may be a considerable burden in some conditions; above all, there is no *power* such as would be enjoyed by the representatives of an important country who could reinforce arguments by a combination of threats and promises. Oran Young (1967, 1972) concluded that private intermediaries without political power and resources, lacked the 'saliency' to achieve major diplomatic results.

There is, however, one very considerable advantage. Paradoxically, it derives directly from the major disadvantage. The protagonists with whom mediators work soon discover, if the mediators act correctly, that their sole motivation is concern for the suffering occasioned to both sides by the conflict, and determination to do everything in their power to reduce it. They are not concerned with who wins or loses, they do not take sides, considering the only enemy to be war and the waste and suffering it brings; they are consistent in their honesty, concern and goodwill. Unlike official diplomats, however humane they may be, their aim is not to promote the policy of their own country; by contrast it is recognised that a country's official representative must carry out the instructions of the country he serves, even if they go against the best interests of the one to which he is accredited. Thus in certain respects the nonofficial or private mediator may be confided in and trusted more than the official. A further advantage of the private position of mediators is that they may be disavowed if for some reason they cause embarrassment, or even expelled from the country without causing a diplomatic furore; they are both useful and expendable.

What then do these people do? First of all if, as may well happen, they are not already well known or have not been specifically invited in, they must get approval for a visit to the country or countries concerned and then gain acceptance from the people with whom they must work, preferably key members of the governments concerned — this process will be considered shortly. Their proper work, when it actually begins, is to open up better communications between the warring parties. This includes such tasks as taking messages from one side to the other, usually enlarging on the implications and the meanings behind the message; they do a considerable amount of explaining the motives and intentions of one side to the other; they interpret the statements or the cryptic 'smoke signals' sent up by either combatant; they correct wrong information and mistaken impressions obtained from statements and speeches by leaders of the other side; they attempt to identify the common interests of the protagonists; they make suggestions about how to improve communications between the protagonists and how to avoid obstacles to reaching a settlement; they try to establish friendly relations with as many people as possible, especially decision makers, on both sides; and they try to keep as well informed as possible about the situation so that they can speak about it constructively without making fools of themselves and so discrediting their ability to act in an informed and helpful fashion. In order to carry out these tasks they may often have to make difficult and even dangerous journeys, seek people out in remote camps, and suffer some of the discomforts and privations of wartime conditions. Although they hope for friendly relations with all concerned, they will probably also make enemies, for there are always some who do not want peace, the hawks who think that it would be possible to get a better deal by continuing to fight. A mediator who favours peace, especially if listened to sympathetically, may be a threat they would wish to dispose of.

We should also consider what mediators do not do and what they are not. They are not negotiators. Negotiators are concerned with the nature and details of any settlement being considered and with the bargaining by which it is achieved. They are usually representatives of the conflicting parties and so by no means impartial. Mediators, on the other hand, have no partisan view on the character of a resolution. By the same token they would consider it improper interference to promote their own solution; their job is to facilitate an acceptable one by helping to clear away obstacles of prejudice and misunderstanding that impede the protagonists in reaching an agreement together. This is not to say, of course, that mediators may not move between the negotiating parties trying to help maintain good communications.

Mediators should also be very cautious of involvement in conflicts in which one side obviously possesses far more power than the other and is genuinely confident of victory. The reason is not that the weaker, and often oppressed, side should not be forsaken, but that mediation simply will not work. The strong are not going to heed any appeal for clemency or compromise. Why should they? They are confident that they can get what they want without giving an inch. If they do not reject the idea of mediation outright, they use the mediators to do their own dirty work by proposing terms to the weak which are tantamount to surrender; terms which, if accepted, would in many cases simply restore the conditions that led to war in the first place. Mediators can only make it clear that they will have no part in such trickery; their purpose is to work for a just and harmonious peace, not the passivity of subjugation. Submission at this stage without any resolution would in any case most probably be followed by a renewal of the conflict, for no situations are permanent.

What else can mediators do in such circumstances? Firstly, before they withdraw, they must ensure that their evaluation of affairs is really correct, that the strong are implacably obdurate, or that the weak have no chance of matching their power and so engaging in fair negotiations. Even if they decide they were in fact right, it could still be wise to try to build up relationships, perhaps with opposition leaders or significant non-official people, which could help initiate mediation when/if the situation eventually changed. For example, friendships made by some mediators with Zimbabwean African leaders several years beforehand greatly facilitated mediation when that became possible.

Mediators may possibly decide that they must temporarily abdicate that role and its impartiality to throw in their lot with the weak; this is purely a matter of personal conscience and judgement. However, if they do decide to serve the victims of violence directly, their best and most appropriate role may be to help empower them through understanding their situation more clearly, and organizing and practising non-violent resistance. I might add that in different circumstances, rightly or wrongly, I have responded in all these ways.

Long-term mediation

A major feature of this sort of mediation is its long duration, running often into several years. Admittedly there have often been brief mediations, persuasive arguments brought to bear upon the parties in a quarrel that has suddenly flared up and which, when tempers have died down, is as speedily put right. More often, however, what seems superficially like a short mediation is only an incident, even if a crucial one, in a process that started before and will continue after it; such was the mediation that led to the Camp David agreement; there a process lasting days was preceded by a long preliminary period and is still in some senses going on.

The truth is that peacemaking of any sort *is* likely to be a very long process. The greatest virtues for mediators are hope and patience, for during the period they must stick with the intransigent problems of peacemaking endless obstacles arise, often when the prospects seemed brightest. Sudden changes on the battlefield, the replacement of a 'dove' by a 'hawk', some external intervention, a rumour, a tactical error, may all demolish months of painstaking preparation for a peace initiative.

But the work of mediation, by its very nature, can seldom be carried out speedily and for the very same reason that conflicts cannot be terminated speedily: they depend more upon human perceptions than on external circumstances, the former being more stubborn and hard to influence than the latter. In the slow move towards negotiation, settlement and the eventual restoration of fully peaceful relations, the significant stages are the changes of vision rather than the signing of agreements that result from them, the gradual erosion of fear, antipathy and suspicion, and the slow shift of public opinion. By contrast, the cessation of actual violence as a result of military victory may lead to a speedy settlement which usually is by no means peace in the sense of harmony and mutual regard. The victors dictate terms which cannot be refused, it is as simple as that.

It is therefore appropriate for mediation to be carried out by non-officials who do not run the risk of being transferred but who can remain with the job, consolidating the relationships on which all peace making depends and following the ramifications of the unfolding situation, the rise and fall of the various actors.

To become associated with such a mediation is to make a commitment to becoming an element in a scene of conflict for a significant period of time. Those I have been involved with have lasted up to four years and never less than two. My colleagues (when I had any) and I were not of course on the spot the whole time; I, for example, would return to my base at home or university and resume my usual activities of teaching and writing and being a husband and father. But the war is never far from the surface of thought; there are letters and telephone calls about it, many meetings in various places; the suitcase remains metaphorically and often literally packed. We keep in touch as closely as possible, debating the meanings of new developments, planning the strategy and timing of the next visit. As soon as we accept this role, we accept responsibility for playing a part in a terrible drama; and the part must go on, unless an understudy can be found, until the tragedy is over.

Beginning a mediation

It may be of interest to consider the ways in which mediation begins. Sometimes an organisation, or perhaps more likely an individual, is directly approached because of her/his reputation, and asked to mediate, perhaps on a very specific issue. S/he will then no doubt agree and go ahead with whatever support from her/his organisation is available. Where there is not a direct approach the entree is obviously more difficult. In my necessarily limited experience it may happen in a way that is either haphazard or on the contrary well planned. In one case I visited a scene of violent conflict because I was interested in what was happening. It was only after repeated visits that I found I had worked myself into a job, was known to and accepted by a number of people, and that my toing and froing between different groups appeared to be welcomed. So I continued for several years until circumstances made continued work less productive than it had been and I was asked to take part in a more urgent and at the same time more hopeful enterprise. But this kind of more or less solo effort is not often possible, if only for financial reasons.

A more organized effort also tends to begin with the concern of an individual for a particular situation which s/he then brings to, for example, the Quakers. Then (speaking only for the Quakers with whom I have been through the process several times) the sequence is likely to be something as follows.

The individual discusses the issue with the appropriate group within the Quaker organisation and a preliminary decision is reached. This might be to explore further; to say 'no' because it is impracticable (there might be no qualified person to undertake it) or it might have lower priority than other projects under consideration; it might be referred to another branch of the Society of Friends, possibly the Australian Quakers if it is a conflict in the Pacific area; or it might seem that the main need is for relief rather than diplomacy.

If, however, it is decided to examine the matter in greater detail, more people will be consulted. Visits will be paid to the local representatives of the parties concerned, to the Foreign and Commonwealth Office in London, the State Department in Washington, to the appropriate branches of the UN in New York and Geneva. The purpose of these visits will be to get further information on the situation; nothing will be said about mediation, because it would be premature to do so.

If these early enquiries appear to favour the possibility of eventual mediation, the next step might well be a reconnaissance. A small group of people will visit the ambassador(s) of the nation(s) involved to express their distress at the suffering caused by the conflict. They will ask if there would be any objection to visiting the country concerned to learn more about the situation, as their organisation feels that media reportage is inadequate. The usual response would be to welcome such a visit since it would 'enable you to see through the lies of our enemies'. It is the first demonstration of the mirror image that the representatives of each protagonist tends to make a similar observation, each implying that *they* are honest, peace-loving and truthful, while their foes are the opposite.

If all goes well, the reconnaissance team sets off. There will probably be two or three individuals: one is too few as the combined judgement of two or three is desirable; four is too many – they constitute a delegation to whom senior officials speechify rather than converse.

In general the team will find that people are only too willing to talk. It will have to listen, time after time, to almost identical recitals of the wrongs inflicted on them, and of the unrivalled barbarity and ruthlessness of their enemies.

But the transition from fact finding to mediating has yet to be made. The simplest crossing of the gap occurs when the team tell some senior person that they are going to visit the other side and ask, 'Is there anything we can do for you there?' The answer might be, 'I would be very interested in your impressions', or 'If you see so and so, you might say...' and perhaps a message of some slight significance may be given.

I have guessed that such responses are made as much to test the objectivity, impartiality and honesty of the team, as in the hope of learning anything useful, A friend and I met with a good example of this during the Nigerian civil war. At an early stage of our work, before we had met General Gowon, the head of the Nigerian military government, the Quakers had a tentative plan for a secret meeting of senior people on both sides. This, it was thought, could be more effective than previous efforts which had been spoiled by publicity. Such a proposal could be agreed to only by Gowon, but we had great difficulty in making an appointment. Various fairly senior officials tried to arrange one, but we were told that they were always vetoed by someone called Mr. King, whom we imagined to be a white adviser, a sort of *eminence blanche* (in fact he turned out to be a Nigerian and became a close and valued friend). However, at length the permanent secretary of the Ministry of Foreign Affairs thought our idea was good, and overrode King. We had a meeting with the general, who was slightly interested in the proposal but doubtful over our proposed visit to Colonel Ojukwu, his enemy, the Biafran leader.

'He will simply use your visit for propaganda purposes', he said, 'claiming that the Quakers support his cause.' We assured him that we would give Ojukwu no cause to say that, and asked if he was actually asking us not to go. 'No,' he answered, 'but please don't say anything that could be taken to mean that you are going at my suggestion. It would be a dangerous mistake for him to think I was taking that sort of initiative. Moreover,' he continued, 'you will have to fly on one of the rebel pirate arms-carrying planes which my fighter aircraft have orders to shoot down. I am afraid I could not make any arrangements for the safety of your particular flight.' We assured him that we would be tactful in our dealings with Ojukwu and that we were prepared to risk the possible dangers of the flight. He then said: 'When you see him you might tell him that in the event of a ceasefire agreement I shall order my troops to halt their advance and arrange for a neutral buffer force to safe-guard the ceasefire'. This in fact was an advance on previous conditions. Gowon finally wished us well and said he would be very interested to hear of our experiences and impressions if we returned safely, which he hoped we would. We did, and were given an immediate appointment with the general, who greeted us very warmly. This was the beginning of a very good working relationship which lasted throughout the remaining years of the war.

This is how one mediation began. There had been a round of meetings and discussions at the UN in New York and at Washington, and there had been a reconnaissance lasting several weeks. But the real mediation did not start until we were given a specific message to deliver by General Gowon, returned with a response (not in fact an acceptance, but the idea remained alive) and, as was shown by monitorings of the Biafran radio, our visit had not been used to promote our own publicity or the Biafran cause. The fact that we had been prepared to face a certain amount of danger for no personal gain also counted considerably in our favour on both sides. After this the scope of our activities increased greatly in all the four categories of mediatory work which will be considered in the next section. I should add that in cases where extreme ideological differences are involved coupled with rigid stereotypes derived from them, the process of gaining acceptance may last much longer and be infinitely more complex.

Difficulties of mediators

We have discussed some of the intrinsic difficulties of peacemaking. To these must be added those peculiar to mediation.

The essence of these is that mediators are trying to bridge with friendship the hate-filled gulf between people who may well be killing each other and so generating the paranoid anger and suspicion that justify ghastly excesses. How can the protagonists trust these people who claim also to be on good terms with their sworn enemies? In fact it seems to be a tribute to the genuine desire for peace and essential good sense of most of the leaders I have met, that they were able to tolerate and even develop warm relations with such ambiguous characters.

It is certainly true, however, that mediators have to be constantly alert lest an unguarded word give any suggestion of favouritism of the other side. For example, to refer to Northern Ireland as Ulster to a Republican or as the Six Counties to a Loyalist would immediately put impartiality in question. Even the most tentative suggestion that one accepts the enemy's case, or their explanation of a particular happening, re-arouses suspicions that had been lulled by months of tactful and consistent good will. On two occasions in my experience during the Nigerian civil war (the Biafran war) other branches of the Quaker organisation concerned, not knowing of the mediation, issued statements implying sympathy with the starving Biafrans. Although the mediators had known nothing about this, a shadow was cast temporarily over their relations with the Nigerian leadership; if these relations had not already been very good, they would no doubt have been broken off. (On the subject of Biafra, to have referred to it as such would have been disastrous; we used instead the euphemism 'the other side'.)

Of course there is no question of concealing from one side one's relations with the other. This is central to mediation. If mediators did not inform X that they were going to visit Y who he hates, they might be spared some embarrassment, but they would be suspected of doing something even worse. If, moreover, they were caught in deception they could be thought of as spies or informers. In any case their usefulness as mediators would be over. No, it is best at all times to be honest and open. It is only by unswerving truthfulness, friendliness and concerned impartiality that mediators earn the conditional right to be on good terms with both sides.

But here let me interpolate another difficulty. Mediators must indeed be truthful if only because even the whitest of lies would, in this highly charged atmosphere, be a proof of mendacity. On the other hand, they must also be true to their principles; they are thought to be motivated by moral values rather than profit and hopes of advancement, but any lapse would throw doubt on their probity. They must, however, not only be truthful but tactful. These three demands upon them may sometimes come into conflict.

Suppose some atrocity is committed, are they to make no protest, in which case the sincerity of their principles will be questioned; or are they to say they are shocked and horrified, thus possibly seeming to imply sympathy with the enemy, and so giving grave offence? Perhaps the best approach is to express sorrow, but in a way that suggests no blame except to the practice of war, which makes such tragedies, committed by either side, inevitable. Faced with this dilemma, I have usually found that taking this line did not violate my conscience. If, however, atrocities are denied or attributed to the enemy with suspicious regularity, mediators must decide whether to risk a blazing row, or to remain pointedly silent.

In the early stages of their work, attempts may be made to use mediators in various ways. In particular the protagonists try to win them over to their side. This appears to be a fairly natural impulse of those engaged in conflict, but if successful, it would obviously subvert any efforts at real mediation. However, if leaders really want the possible fruits of mediation, they soon get the message and exchange the potential propaganda value of 'converting' the mediators for collaboration with them. There are also, however, more subtle ways in which mediators may be used. They may be asked to give messages that are intentionally misleading, suggesting, for example, that one side is eager for negotiations when it really hopes to lull the foe into a false sense of security, facilitating the preparation of new positions or the launching of a surprise attack.

It is not always easy to guard against such dishonesty, though at the outset it may help to make a firm but diplomatic statement that any manipulation will mean immediate withdrawal. Fortunately, once their suspicions are aroused, mediators are usually in a position to consult with their own head-quarters and/or other concerned and knowledgeable persons on the spot. These might be officials of various embassies, representatives of international agencies, the Commonwealth Secretariat, the OAU and other bodies. In fact, such contacts and consultations are a regular feature of mediation. As a mission proceeds, a network of involved people is developed including such as I have just mentioned as well as members of local churches, human rights organisations, academic institutions and so on. Mediators are seldom completely on their own, though they must always guard scrupulously against revealing what has been told them in confidence — if they did not do so they would never again be trusted and their mission would be ruined. They must also beware of excessive intimacy with or dependence on friends, for example, in their own embassy; such intimacy might be taken to imply bias.

The practice of mediation

We have seen that would-be mediators have to pass through what might be termed a probationary period, unless of course they have been invited in by the protagonists. However, once they have gained a sufficient measure of acceptance, their work begins to take shape. Although it will obviously change and expand, following the contours of circumstances, it soon becomes possible to identify four aspects of mediation. These are interwoven and overlapping but distinguishable emphases of the unitary task of bringing together those who have been separated by violence.

Building, maintaining and improving communications

By this I mean the mediators' own communications with both groups of protagonists and indeed other involved groups, and — via the mediators — between the protagonists themselves, the second being dependent on the first and both being essential to mediation.

Discussion

There is obviously more to being a messenger than just carrying a message and delivering it like a postman. For one thing, it will often not be written down, but even if so, there is always much to say about the circumstances in which it was sent and the mood of the senders. In addition, it will probably need to be amplified and explained, ambiguities elucidated and so on. The first necessity, therefore, is that mediators should be accepted in this fairly active role (part of what I call active mediation, discussed below) and can in fact communicate with the leaders concerned; communicate in the sense of presenting material that they will listen to and understand and this in turn depends on both having reached a measure of mutual trust and liking. But this is somewhat more in the realm of befriending and will be discussed a little later — for the present I will only repeat that these dimensions of mediation are often inextricably interconnected.

The following incidents illustrate how mediators may attempt to serve as channels of communication between protagonists.

One of the major conferences intended to resolve the Biafran crisis was sponsored in 1968 by the Organisation of African Unity in Addis Ababa under the formidable and remote chairmanship of the late Emperor Haile Selassie. (I had met him once in Ghana, a nobly dignified figure as he stepped from his plane in built-up boots and ostrich-feathered hat; but in a lounge suit resembling a lizard with a squeaky voice — 'Bonjour, Monsieur' he fluted as we were introduced.) Three of us were waiting in the wings and, as usual, keeping in touch with both Nigerian and Biafran delegations. Soon it became obvious that things were not going at all well; both sides made angry statements of seemingly adamantine positions; there was no debate, no give on either side. Everyone was tense and preoccupied; it was difficult to have a reasonable discussion with anyone. The Biafrans were grimly obdurate, pinning their hopes on massive military assistance from France, although they had lost all but three of their larger centres of population. The Nigerians, under the implacable Chief Enahoro, were buoyed up by military successes and convinced that the Biafrans could not long continue organized resistance (in fact they did, for nearly 18 months). There appeared no hope of compromise and we could see nothing but an indefinite continuation of Biafra's anguish.

Then one evening we had a long talk with Eni Njoku, the chief Biafran delegate. We knew him well, having met him in different parts of Africa, in America and, in happier days, when he was vice-chancellor of the University of Nigeria at Nsukka. He was in a state of muted despair, saying that he had proposals that could break the deadlock, but which he could not make openly because they would appear, wrongly, to imply an abandonment of their position and a loss of nerve. Their only effect, therefore, would be to intensify Nigerian military pressure; the Federal Government would think they had got the Biafrans on the run, and hope they could achieve an all-out victory without any need to compromise.

Whether or not Njoku was right about the possible reception of his proposals, they seemed to us to be reasonable and constructive. They proposed that Biafra (which would even be prepared to relinquish the controversial and inflammatory name) should be accepted as a part of a Nigerian Union. All they asked for in addition were two measures designed to secure the safety of the people, the great fear then being a repetition of the horrible massacres that had preceded the war. These were, first, that they should be allowed some sort of military force; second, that they should have a measure of international standing to ensure that any aggression against them would attract international attention and could not be dismissed as a purely 'internal affair'. The military force, Njoku said, could be little more than an armed constabulary, and international standing could be achieved by a seat on the board of one of the UN special agencies or of one of the regional organisations. But since Njoku felt he could not present these proposals without eliciting precisely the opposite effects to what he wished, he asked us to do so instead.

There was no way in which we could present the proposals at the conference, at which we had no official standing, so we decided to return to Lagos. This involved flying up to Rome and then down to Nigeria. I remember the delight of a summer evening in Rome, where we strolled out for a good meal of pasta and a bottle of wine, sandwiched between the heavily steaming heat of Lagos and the wet thin air of the Ethiopian highland.

Gowon was as friendly as ever when we presented, indeed argued, Njoku's case. He promised that the Biafran's ideas would be given consideration, and we left to return to America, where I was then based.

A little later we were told that there had been much discussion of the proposals, but that the hawks had won. They said that nothing new was offered, it was all a trick, a device to gain time. So that, for the time being, was that. But shortly after one of us met the Nigerian ambassador at the UN, who had not heard what had been going on. When he did, he was horrified that the Biafran proposals had been abandoned, maintaining that they did in fact constitute an important new initiative. He hurried back to Lagos to revive the debate. But by this time the military fortunes of the Biafrans had to some extent revived; they no longer wanted the sort of settlement that would have satisfied them when things were going badly.

We had another comparable experience that illustrates the diversity of a mediator's life. Two of us agreed to transport $57,000 in cash (a formidable amount in 1968), which had been raised to help the centres which had been established for starving people driven by war from their homes in Biafra. It was a rather hectic journey — as we spiraled down at night to the Uli air strip, a mere widened roadway, incessant flashes from the battle down below lit up the jungle, and the tracer curled up towards us. Halfway through our journey to deliver the money we had a meeting with Sylvanus Cookey, a trusted lieutenant of Ojukwu. He said the situation was desperate, the federal army was constantly advancing along the main roads (as we discovered, since we had to drive through the jungle to avoid the armoured cars); it was essential that we arrange a meeting to discuss a ceasefire as soon as possible.

As quickly as we could, we flew out on a Red Cross plane to what was then the Spanish island of Fernando Po and thence to Cameroon. My friend went to Lagos to inform the Nigerian Government; I went to London to tell the Commonwealth Secretariat and the British Government, then on to America.

After a few days, however, our hopes were dashed once more. Ojukwu made a fire-eating speech saying that the Biafrans would never yield a square inch of their sacred territory. What did this mean, asked Gowon, who was quite ready to go ahead with the ceasefire; had they really changed their collective mind? The Quakers were asked to contact Biafran representatives in Europe to find out. But no one really knew. Soon, however, came an invitation to return to Biafra along with a number of Biafran representatives who had apparently questioned the wisdom of continuing the war.

I did not go, but my two friends did. On arrival, they were kept incommunicado for five days before being subjected to a tirade by Louis Mbanefo, the Chief Justice, and several others of the Biafran top brass. The main theme was that they would never surrender, and that we should let everyone know that they would accept no compromise. Finally they apologised for speaking so harshly, saying there was no one else to whom they could let off steam. And that, once more, was that. My friends returned puzzled.

The reason soon became clear, however. General de Gaulle had come through with his hoped-for assistance and there had been a massive airlift of arms from neighbouring Gabon, one of the four African states that had recognised Biafra. The Biafrans decided that, after all, they had a chance; they counter-attacked and recaptured Owerri. This made them bitterly regret the loss of nerve that had induced them to sue for peace.

Their behaviour towards us was designed to demonstrate that they had not weakened in their resolve to fight on.

Of course some message carrying has more satisfactory but perhaps less interesting results. For example, we once transmitted a plea for a ceasefire which was agreed to immediately without the need for any discussion or argument. But the ultimate success of efforts to act as a channel of communication comes when the protagonists themselves take over, no longer needing the intervention of mediators.

Providing information

This means attempting to be aware of facts needed to establish reasonable policies and so as not to be misled by rumour, misinformation or prejudice; peace and negotiation are jeopardised more by ignorance than by truth, however unpalatable. Providing information is, of course, also an aspect of communication, especially because the manner of transmission and the quality of the relationship determines whether it will be heard or understood.

Discussion

Mediators are often in a good position to supply important information for the initiation of moves towards peace — and for keeping them moving. Much of this information tends to be negative, refutations of statements made by each side about the other, such as the following: 'We want a negotiated settlement, but it's no good, because our enemies are set on a military solution'. Mediators moving between the sides may be able to provide evidence that each side's interpretation of the other's intentions is faulty.

But in fact, any remarks about the other side must be made with caution. Both, while not being so crass as to ask obviously military questions, will be eager to glean information of tactical or strategic relevance; mediators hoping to promote peace may unintentionally satisfy their curiosity. If, for example, they hope to prove the sincerity of peace feelers by mentioning the other side's low morale and fear of losing, the enemy might instead take it as an incentive to attack.

But, of course, the opposite would also be true; if morale was high when the peace feeler was floated, it might be a reason to consider negotiation. However, every case is likely to be different and would need consideration on its own merits, and generally mediators do well to steer away from all military matters which are often subject, especially to the uninitiated, to contradictory interpretations. If, for example, mediators become aware that conscription is being introduced or extended it could imply either a determination to wage war more fiercely, or that losses were great and the bottom of the man-power barrel was being scraped.

One other sort of dilemma over military matters is moral rather than pseudo-psychological. Mediators may, in their travels or conversations, learn of preparations for an offensive in a particular area where great loss of life will inevitably be sustained. Should they give any warning? I think probably not. Firstly, they may be wrong and so sacrifice their impartiality for nothing. Secondly, even if they are right, the people to whom they give the facts would never again trust them as mediators — they would have shown that they were informers. But again there are different scales of violence. Nuclear or some other catastrophic attack should no doubt be prevented by any means possible.

Mediators are on clearer grounds in speaking of individual opinions. Most leaders, in attempting to evaluate the seriousness of peace proposals made by their opposite numbers, will want to know what various people have said about them, and mediators should be able to feel free to tell them as much as they know. They can give the context, possibly including the tone of voice and expression, in which comments reported in the media were made, and give details of happenings from personal experience or the often unavailable international press, which were relevant to the search for peace. In general, they can supply a full, objective and balanced account of crucial events rather than the frequently fragmentary details on which policies are precariously based.

They can be useful in other respects. For example, during the Nigerian civil war, the Biafrans, until a colleague convinced them to the contrary, were dubious about accepting the Commonwealth Secretariat as a mediating body because, being based in London, they assumed it must share the pro-Federal Nigerian views of the British government. In this instance and that of the Zimbabwe war, in which one side lacked the advantages of a foreign ministry and full intelligence services, there was always the danger of fatally faulty judgements. Mediators, free to travel around the world, can often fill a gap in information needed to develop sound policies for settling a conflict.

Befriending

This refers to the character of the relationship between mediators and those with whom they are dealing. They come essentially as friends, drawn by concern for the suffering of all concerned in the struggle, including the mental anguish of those in power. They play a different part from that of civil servant, diplomat or consultant; they come in a spirit of goodwill to do whatever they can to help the victims of the conflict to escape from the trap of violence. To the extent that their unconditional goodwill is accepted, the relationship of the mediators with leaders and other responsible officials may somewhat diminish the psychological tensions and the possibility of compulsive and unconstructive action.

Discussion

The first and most necessary step towards befriending harassed leaders (or anyone else, for that matter) is to think of them with respect and liking. But how is this possible when some of them may have a most unattractive reputation for, for example, cruelty and violence?

I have struggled with myself before going to meet a leader whose forces have recently committed an act of great barbarity. I felt an impulse to assuage my own distress by accusing him, but knew that to do so would impair my usually good contact with him. But I also knew that simply suppressing my emotions was not enough; my feelings would affect him even if disguised. So I made an effort to calm myself, practising what I had been taught as a child – count to 10 (in this case much more!) before speaking in anger. This helped me to realize what I had really known all along, that a general at the base could have little direct control of his troops on the front line. Beyond this, however, I realized – and have realized in many other instances – how people may be driven by circumstances, and that I had no cause to reprobate in others what I would have done or felt in their place.

Speaking in general, I then move on to consider the positive things about the person concerned, warmth, courage, sincerity, and indeed about the basic strengths of human nature. Finally I know that s/he is someone just like myself, that we are both in our different ways, up against the same fundamental problems, needing each other's help, respect and compassion and only damaged by each other's contempt or anger.

Understanding this, I break the shell of preoccupation with my own feelings and the equally cramping shell of preconception 1 had built around this person, crediting (or more properly discrediting!) her/him with unpleasing qualities that might not really exist and neglecting inner richness that might.

It then becomes possible to do what is one of the bases of building a human relationship; to listen and give full attention to the person I have come to see. Once we consciously try to do this, we realize how little we usually hear and give. We may hear the words our friend speaks but we do not reflect on or remember them for more than a very short while. But when the mind is relatively clear and uncluttered by distracting preoccupations, we are free to devote a much higher proportion of our attention to another. This means to be really aware of her/him; it means to open ourselves, to make ourselves available, in a sense to embrace. This is always felt by the other as somehow reassuring and encouraging, but only to the extent that it is done with genuine sincerity.

The listening element of attention giving is crucial. Everyone knows that listening, not necessarily profoundly but just letting people talk, is helpful to anyone in trouble. But to listen with real attention often, and unexpectedly, helps them to gain real insight into themselves.

Although this type of listening requires effort, it is different from the effort needed to hear a very quiet speaker. The effort is to maintain attention, to cut the distractions from one's own mind, and to open the hearing wide to include not only the words but the tone in which they are spoken and all other sounds within earshot.

I would not claim that this approach to befriending will lead always to an intimate relationship, rather to one of confidence and goodwill in which there is also a measure of warm feeling.

Since mediators, though deeply involved in the total situation, are separate from the quarrels, rivalries, clan and tribal antipathies and jealousies that often surface in times of stress, they may be able to provide some respite and relaxation from tension. This relaxation of the pressure of strain, of the threatened ego's quest for self-justification, tends to release the inherent capacity for sound and compassionate judgement upon which depend wise and humane decisions.

In conclusion I should explain, and perhaps excuse, the somewhat personal manner in which befriending has been discussed. I have done so because befriending another human being is a particularly individual matter. I have not pretended to give a prescription for what ought to be done, only an example of what one individual has found helpful.

Active mediation

I have coined this term to describe (inadequately) what might be thought of as the more specifically diplomatic activity of mediators. It is not their job, of course, to attempt persuasion or to promote particular approaches to the resolution of a conflict. On the other hand, they do not just passively and impersonally impart information and pass messages; they are not civil servants whose job it is to ensure that their political masters are aware of all the facts necessary for them to decide on wise policies, but who have no part in those decisions. Mediators, of course, attempt to do these things, but they do so with a specific purpose: to remove obstacles on the path to peace, and they argue strongly against the misunderstandings and preconceptions that strengthen those obstacles.

In order to illustrate this aspect of mediation, and also to a considerable extent the three others that have already been discussed, I have transcribed and suitably edited and modified to make identification impossible even by those concerned, since I have changed sequences, combined situations and fictionalised some details, a number of discussions between a head of state, prime minister or other high official, or a guerilla leader (P) and a mediator or mediators (M)[63]

Evaluation

What does it all amount to? People who have tried to mediate must always ask themselves whether they have been wasting their time. By the nature of things, anonymous private mediators are not going to be able to bring off dramatic coups. Even if they have made a great contribution to the changed understanding on which a settlement depends, they will not be the ones actually to engineer it. That happens in the public domain such as the UN, the Commonwealth Secretariat, the OAU or a powerful third-party government any of which will have the necessary resources and the technical administrative skills such as were needed, for example, to mount and conduct the Lancaster House Conference that brought the Zimbabwe war to an end. In any case, it would not be appropriate, and might adversely affect their future usefulness, to bring into the open people whose work depends on their invisibility, and it doesn't often happen; in my 20 years' experience, our activities have only on very rare occasions received attention in the media and then it was but slight. I have even wondered if I should write these pages. However, I felt it was legitimate to follow Mike Yarrow's book which I, as a practitioner, found useful, by something which I trust will supplement it. And I have preserved the anonymity of those not mentioned by name in this book, in which the narrative ends in 1970, and have given no details whatsoever of some later mediations.

However, a more important question than the degree of visibility of mediators is whether, seen or unseen, they do any good. Do they contribute at all to peace or do they put themselves and everyone else concerned to considerable effort and expense for nothing? I wish I could give a clear-cut answer, but does one ever know the full effect of anything done with or for other people? Is my wife better for having known me, have I helped my children deal competently and happily with life, are my students wiser because of my teaching, did my efforts in any way improve the quality of existence of the Third World people for whose development I worked? I will never know, just as I will never know whether the money my friend and I took to Biafra ultimately did more good than harm.

But this uncertainty doesn't worry me. I try to do what I think right to do, and my Quaker colleagues might feel that this was sufficient justification, provided I set about the task seriously and carefully, having taken the best available advice. Moreover, if we have any understanding of how things happen, especially in the complex weave of international affairs, we realize that there is never one person, one group or one event to which the final result can be attributed. What, in fact, is a final result? The peace conference or the settlement or the resolution (if they occur), are merely commas in a journal that is still going on and will be written until the end of time.

Of one thing, however, we can be certain: mediators *do* have an effect on the total situation. Admittedly, their effect will be very small if they never progress beyond the preliminary stages. However, the closer they get to the main actors and the longer they remain on the stage, the greater their influence on events. They are therefore under an obligation to make that influence a good one. This is likely to be so if they keep their egos in order, and tackle the external issues with informed common sense and sensitivity. At the same time, they should realize that, with all the goodwill and good sense in the world, they may not be able to help having a negative impact on some person or happening. But this, I think, is an acceptable risk. There would perhaps be a greater risk than that if they were not involved, their absence would have entailed the loss of important opportunities. I can think of some cases where, had we not been Present, a chance of peacemaking would have been lost; but whether it was taken by those empowered to do so is another matter.

Mike Yarrow, referring to the difficulty of assessing Quaker private diplomacy, says: 'Evaluation of the effectiveness of any one element... in a complicated series of historical processes, is difficult if not impossible. It is like asking for the effectiveness of one thread in a mainsail halyard of many filaments.'

Nevertheless, although there may be no hard evidence, I believe there are a number of hints of usefulness. Again I quote Yarrow: 'In the case of India and Pakistan just after the [1965] war over Kashmir, the heads of each government used the Quakers to communicate with the other opinions and intentions that could not be publicly stated, particularly with a view to testing the strength of moderate forces working to continue the truce. (It was in fact continued.) In the Nigerian war, the Quaker aim for a negotiated peace was not achieved, but peace by military victory resulted in an amazing degree of magnanimity towards the defeated side. The Quakers may have had a small part in this result, because their efforts were welcomed by certain Nigerian leaders.

'The one objective index of effectiveness available was the fact that the persons involved retained continuing access to the top leadership over a considerable period of time rather than being sent away as importunate meddlers. It is perhaps safe to conclude from this that the Quakers were carrying on an operation which others found useful and not just fooling themselves.'[64] There is little I would like to add to this evaluation, except that well-informed sources in Lagos confirmed to us what Yarrow suggested as our possible contribution to the paradoxically 'peaceful' conclusion to the war. Once the ceasefire was proclaimed the fighting stopped completely. The defeated Biafrans, who had expected to be massacred, were taken by their conquerors to feeding centres, loaded onto military trucks and conveyed to hospital if wounded; the soldiers handed over their own rations to the starving people and gave them money. Immediately Biafrans who had been civil servants or diplomats in the Federal Government had their jobs restored; if there were no immediate vacancy for, for example, a former ambassador, he was placed on full pay until one became available. Such a change of heart seemed almost miraculous.

Our contribution, if indeed we were not deceiving ourselves, was that we had been continually trying to explain to the Nigerians why the Biafrans felt as they did; that they did not resist so desperately because they were intransigent and filled with destructive hatred, but because, with reason, they were frightened but wanted peace as much as anyone. In addition, as I have described, on two occasions we carried and interpreted messages that could easily have brought a settlement many months before the actual end of the war.

After the end of the Zimbabwe struggle, where we were involved after the period recorded by Yarrow, Walter Martin, who planned and led the execution of the mediation with the greatest possible sensitivity and skill, received appreciative letters from African leaders and others who knew what had been happening. I also met an American diplomat who told me that it was recognised at the UN, where he had been temporarily attached, that the achievement of peace had largely depended on Quaker efforts; as he had no idea that I had been involved, the comment must be considered as completely unbiased.

As for me, having had my family life disrupted countless times, and often suffering inconvenience, loneliness and occasional illness and danger, I still go on because I believe, and have indeed been told, that it may help. This seems to me sufficient reason to continue trying, and sufficient cause to hope that the effort will bring a small measure of good results.

I am not sure, however, that this form of evaluation can be very fruitful. On the wide screen of conflict, any one happening is the product of innumerable converging forces. It would be rash indeed to attribute greater significance to any one of them. It is wiser, perhaps, to consider what mediation is designed to contribute towards, and how far the process as I have tried to describe it, is suitable for the purpose.

Mediation is intended to break down the barriers of suspicion, unreasonable fear, exaggerated hostility, misunderstanding and ignorance that keep protagonists at a greater distance than is warranted by the practical or material grounds of their quarrel. Only when this has to some extent occurred will there be an adequate chance of satisfactory negotiations.

Long term private or non-official mediation focuses on building relationships through which mediation can dispel some of the misconceptions, fixed ideas and irrational dread and hatred that develop all too easily in times of violence. It does so through the quadruple approach of communication, providing information, befriending and active mediation that has been described. This approach, if properly used, should both promote a more genuinely realistic understanding of the situation and diminish the distortions of ego compulsion.

It would be absurd to claim that diplomats, UN officials and negotiators representing various governments and international agencies do not, to a considerable extent do most of the same things; if they did not, they would have scant respect.

Mediators, however, have no other role that could interfere with their fundamental psychological, or it would be more correct to say human, task. They are tied by no policy, they have no other allegiance, they are entirely devoted to working on the mental obstacles to peace, believing that if these can be diminished so will be the material ones.

Why then, we may ask, is this form of mediation so insufficiently developed and employed? It is surely because we do not really understand the roots of conflict, seeing it primarily as an objective state of affairs and not as the states of mind that led to, and subsequently sustained and exaggerated that state of affairs. Consequently our approach to conflict resolution is confused and inefficient. We really know very little about it and after hundreds of years of diplomacy which have admittedly produced many brilliant practitioners, have little scientific understanding of it.

Our chief fault is failure to recognise that conflict is often largely in the mind and to that extent must be dealt with on that level; and that even when it is less so, as in the case of political oppression or economic exploitation, emotional factors exacerbate what is already serious. Consequently we have not developed good methods for dealing with it.

I believe from my own experience that the type of mediation I have tried to define represents a short, wavering step in the right direction. This would seem to be borne out by the very tentative evaluation that has so far been possible. I think, therefore, that mediation needs to be paid more careful and serious attention and, in the following part, present some proposals about how that might be done. These are comparable, in fact, to those made by Yarrow.[65]

Proposal for an International Mediation Centre

This centre should be set up as a non-governmental organisation (NGO) having consultative status with the UN. The first step towards establishing it might be for one of the bodies directly involved or else interested in mediation to convene a working party of concerned individuals and group representatives. If it seemed reasonable to proceed with the project, this group would (probably) suggest broad guidelines for the further development of the centre. It would obviously be premature to attempt to define the size, administrative structure or agenda of this centre; this could only evolve in a precise form after its establishment. Nevertheless, it seems safe to predict that the following functions would form part of its essential activities:

1. To develop criteria for the desirability and feasibility of the type of mediation discussed in this essay.
2. To maintain an overview of the global scene in order to identify situations where mediation was or might become desirable.
3. To compile a register of persons with experience in mediation and having qualifications, such as a language skill, appropriate for mediation in particular regions or circumstances.
4. To recruit and launch mediation teams when the directors considered it appropriate, and to give them backstopping assistance when they were in the field.
5. To raise financial resources for its operations, including funds for 'sabbaticals' to free persons in employment to carry out mediation.
6. To provide any necessary training or preparation relevant to mediation, especially with a view to ensuring a flow of younger people into the work. At present there is virtually no systematic training for mediation. Most mediators, who come from very varied academic and work backgrounds, have picked up their abilities 'on the job'. It is most important to find and impart better means of preparing women and men for this demanding task.
7. To carry out research on the field of conflict in general and on mediation and training for mediation in particular.

CHAPTER 8

Another way

POSITIVE RESPONSE TO CONTEMPORARY VIOLENCE[66]

We are stuck in the rut of conventional concepts of nationhood, state's rights, and diplomatic niceties. In particular we cannot get away from stereotyped ideas of intervention, and of the relationship of the strong to the weak, whether in helping them or controlling them.

In this third Part we shall try to suggest a different approach, one based on the actions and perceptions of a group of people in the Croatian town of Osijek.

EDITORS NOTE: *In a further piece Adam reflected more generally on what he learned from the Osijek experience, as follows:*

A role for citizen peacemakers

So what part can be played by the would-be citizen peacemaker from the United States or Western Europe or indeed anywhere else? The first step that they (we?) should take is to reject the central role of 'foreign expert'; the experts in this case are the local peacemakers, the members of the peace groups. The outsiders should come as sharers, supporters and helpers rather than initiators...

These workshops and trainings might cover such fields as: group dynamics; social change; theories of peace and conflict; psychological factors in violence; helping the traumas of victims of violence; mediation; negotiation; conflict resolution; the practice of non-violence; responding to violence; human rights and their protection; organization and administration; computer use and electronic communication; building a database; peace education; community development; small-scale economic development; adult literacy; appropriate technology; problems of refugees; and mine clearance.

There is, however, one issue of transcending importance upon which the effective use of all other skills and abilities depends; the development of the local peacemakers' inner resources of wisdom, courage and compassionate non-violence...[67]

Osijek

I should explain how it was that I came to visit Osijek. My wife Anne and I had been asked to attend in March the annual meeting of the Helsinki Citizens Assembly, the non-official arm of the Commission on Security and Cooperation in Europe, to join groups discussing mediation and conflict resolution. In one of these groups was a delightful and articulate Croatian woman, Vesna Terselic, from Zagreb. She was very active in the cause of peace and had set up Anti Rama Kampgne (ARK), the anti-war campaign. This was a brave thing do to in a country inflamed and angry from attacks upon it, and one in which the civil rights of protesters were not too well defined.

She told us that some people in Osijek were planning to establish a branch of ARK and intended to launch it with a series of public meetings, seminars and discussions in April. We were all invited to attend. In fact two friends of mine did so, one who had also been at the conference, and one from the Bradford University department of peace studies. We were joined in Zagreb by Erich Bachmann, an American peace worker living in Germany, and three from Zagreb ARK, Vesna, Aida Bagic, and a Dutch volunteer. We supped together and next morning went by train to Osijek, a trip of about four-and-a-half hours. This was longer than it could have been but the direct line had run through a chunk of now occupied country.

As one approaches Osijek the rail and the road traffic pass through a corridor between the surrounding UNPAs. The smashed new post office building faced arrivals at the station. It had been unwisely – as it turned out, but who could have foretold the coming rain of bombs? – constructed mainly of glass. It seemed to me a symbol of the town's agony. Now it has been rebuilt. A symbol of hope? Or of vain optimism?

The people

We were welcomed in the most friendly fashion by some of the people who were planning to set up the peace group. They took us to lunch at the hospital where one of them worked, Katarina Kruhonja, whom I referred to before. Later we had a formal meeting with the director, and were then shown around the underground ward.

Katarina, with a man, Krunoslav Sukic, were the leading spirits of the embryonic peace movement...

Katarina had been deeply distressed not only by the death and devastation of the attack on Osijek, but by the effect that this had had on the psychological climate. Fear and anger were to be expected, but these were now coupled with demonisation of the enemy and acceptance of the logic of war as the sole means of survival. At the same time there were urgent tasks in caring for those maimed in mind or body by the bombardment, and the 30,000 people displaced from their homes in the by then Serb-occupied areas, who had flooded into the town. But when she and Kruno, who shared her feelings, discussed their views, they met with almost universal hostility. How could they even for a moment consider any course of action except to win back the land they had lost; and how could this be done without fighting?

Serbs with whom they shared the whole area of Eastern Slavonia became devils overnight. Those who actually lived in Osijek in their thousands, who were Croatian citizens, and were by no means Serb nationalists, were ostracised, dismissed from their jobs and later evicted from their homes.

A further element of social pathology was growing with sinister speed: criminality. As I mentioned before, in times of disturbance – especially where guns abound – this virus seeps in through the widening cracks in the social order.

Katarina, I think, was even more upset by the poisoned minds than by the wounded bodies. How could the semblance of peace ever be restored when people were dominated by such venomous feelings?

The people of Osijek, even those so intelligent and generally sophisticated as Katarina, were far behind those of West Europe and America in their understanding of the issues of peace and violence. In London, Bradford and Cambridge, Massachusetts where I had lived for the past few decades, we had wrestled with them constantly. We had debated and demonstrated over the questions of nuclear danger and disarmament, the Cold War, and the Vietnam War. We had studied and sometimes worked with the prophets of the age, Mahatma Gandhi, J.P. Narayan, Martin Luther King, Cezar Chavez, Danilo Dolci.

But Katarina and her friends and opponents, living in a communist society, although a somewhat dissident one, knew virtually nothing of all this. Moreover, as someone put it to me, Osijek is a provincial city, literally very much at the end of the line from any centre of cosmopolitan culture.

When I first met Katarina and Kruno they had, I think, only recently come across the word 'nonviolence'. However, it had immediately resonated excitingly in her mind. Although she questioned me at length about it, tentatively, and saying how little she knew, I could see at once that in the depths of her heart she knew all about it. She has a deep religious faith from which quite naturally flows a creatively compassionate nature which recognises the divine in everyone.

With a handful of collaborators, she and Kruno had planned the launch to which the other visitors and I had been invited. Vesna too had been very helpful. The launch consisted of two or three rather formal discussions with perhaps 30 people: teachers in the university (where we met), members of various civic and educational bodies, and social workers. As far as I can remember (and I didn't hear everything either) these were not particularly controversial – more civil exchanges of view than anything else, but the underlying tensions occasionally surfaced.

There were also seminars led by us, the visitors. One was on medical and another on educational issues. I facilitated one on mediation. There were about 15 people, including Aida as interpreter. I had already discovered at the HCA conference in Bratislava that no one really knew what mediation was but felt it was some sort of mysterious technique for solving all problems of conflict.

Mediation, of course, requires two protagonists whom the mediator can try to bring together. Naturally in Osijek, there were a number of people and groups who disliked each other; for example, Glavas whom I have already mentioned, the authoritarian Zupan, and Zlatko Kramaric, the mayor who was a liberal and had a PhD in Macedonian poetry. Moreover, the cliques and enmities in the town were complex and interwoven, but did not affect feelings about the common monolithic foe, the Serbs.

And there was no obvious way of mediating from a provincial base about an international matter. Anyway it was impossible practically; there was no contact between the people of Osijek and those of the surrounding UNPAs. The frontier was guarded by the UN and even if it had been possible to cross, it would have been extremely dangerous (though as we shall see later an alternative procedure was developed). But, in any case, the potential outcomes even from successful mediation were not really attractive to most people: either to resume hostilities, or to return to their old homes (provided they had not been taken over by Serbs) under continued UN protection in a country still Serb dominated. In fact hardly anyone, Croat or, I think, Serb, was willing to consider compromise, which is, of course, the prerequisite of mediation.

This, my first visit to Osijek lasted less than a week. I left with a feeling of dissatisfaction. I had been there long enough to develop a great regard and liking for Katarina, Kruno and some of the others. But I felt I was leaving unfinished work behind. I told Katarina I would be happy to return fairly soon at a time when things were less hectic with seminars (which hadn't worked out very well!) and public occasions, so that we could talk more and explore the possibility that I could make some useful contribution.

Katarina felt this would be a good idea, and I returned in about a month to give an informal seminar/ workshop to a group of people she knew. We thought the best approach would be to talk and feel our way into and around the types of situations which can arise, and had indeed arisen, in embattled places like Osijek.

The early days of the centre

I returned to Osijek in June. I had given a good deal of thought to what we might do in the workshop that Katarina had organized. I had given a number of workshops on mediation, but this was different. What might be helpful to people who might be faced with the multifarious problems of crisis and chaos, problems I could only envisage in a most general way? The main feature of the context in which we would be operating was violence, so the focus of the workshop should be nonviolence. But nonviolence training is a very idiosyncratic business. I tried to understand what would be most useful to help a group of young people (to those in their late seventies anyone under 55 is young), who were facing almost any imaginable exigency, to function best both as individuals and as members of a team.

A facile answer would be to list the qualities to develop. But how to develop them when listed? I would prefer to think that what is needed, and is always needed by all of us, is the fullest possible development of our humanity, our potential as human beings. This means becoming able to escape from the mindless automatism that governs so much of our lives, from senseless worries and fears, from prejudice, from ego cherishing and irritability, from vanity, from illusions of guilt and badness, from belief in separate existence. These and all other negative emotions are like a fist tightly closed around the heart. They imprison our consciousness within the narrow confines of the self. But to be fully human our consciousness must expand, gradually embracing all others, including all nonhuman others with whom we share the planet. It means losing the lonely sense of separation. It means to be rather than to do.

But pondering these ideas, I thought, how could I profess to 'teach' others to be more human? I would have to be as much as I was expecting others to be. The answer, it seemed to me, was to use the workshop for sharing and mutual help; the learning would come to all of us from this, rather than from any formal instruction. In fact, the first lesson would be that we all have something to give and something to learn.

I felt, however, that there would be need for some loose and probably overlapping sequence of emphases in our exploration. This is how it worked out:

> Using the metaphor of the fist around the heart we considered the things that made it tighter or looser; for example, what threw us off balance and what made us more confident. We tried various awareness and listening exercises. Also I emphasized that I believed in the essential soundness of our nature, saying that in my experience if we approached people with respect and expecting them to behave decently, it would evoke their better nature. But if one expected the worst, one would find it.
>
> Moving on from this, but on the same track, we tried to become aware of some of our blind spots, prejudices, irrational reactions including anxieties, dislikes and guilt; things that could impair our judgement and our relations with colleagues and others.
>
> We considered our interconnectedness with all human beings, with all life, with the planet. In so doing we examined and tried to rid ourselves of conventional views of completely dichotomised self and other, friend and enemy.
>
> We traced the connections between what we had been discovering and different facets of violent situations; we explored

these from human, economic and political points of view, considering refugees, homelessness, psychological and physical traumas of war, separation of families, social dislocation, deprivation, and poverty. All of these were, of course, examined in the context of Osijek as well as generally.

We learned something of the basic principles and practices of nonviolent protest and conflict resolution and thought about their application in particular situations.

Throughout we devised what seemed to be appropriate role plays and other exercises.

The workshop lasted five days and about 20 people came. Since some were working, they could not all come all the time, but attendance was generally very good. We met for the first four days in a room loaned to us by a charity but they needed it on the last day, so we migrated to a garish disco, incongruously located in a picturesque building in the old town.

Most of the members of the workshop had either not met before, or knew each other only slightly. They came as individuals, rather than as members of an existing group. But it was noticeable that a warm and cooperative atmosphere developed very soon.

About half way through the meetings, a very significant thing, happened. Individuals who had mainly talked about 'I' and 'me' began to talk about what 'we' should do, how 'we' should arrange the next meeting, who should take notes, send out invitations, and so on. It seemed that, without anyone making a specific proposal, everyone had reached an unspoken agreement that we formed the nucleus of a group which would do the things we had been discussing.

Assessment

The genesis of the idea for a centre came late in 1991, when Katarina and Kruno, horrified by the violent and militaristic atmosphere, began to speculate on alternative responses to the situation. They were revolting against the growing alienation that violence creates and that in turns creates more violence. It is an automatic, completely unaware response, in the sense I give to unawareness. It is the response of people who are blind with anger or fear or grief or hatred, or all four, and who in consequence become estranged, alienated from parts of their background, their society, themselves.

When I mentioned alienation recently to a friend, he asked me, 'Alienation from what?' I paused, wondering if I had used the word too glibly, then realized that I meant it in a most profound sense: estrangement from life, from the world of the living, a descent into the realm of death, disaster and despair.

Consider the alienated killers, whether sadistic murderers in Bosnia and Liberia, or the five young teenagers I read of this morning in England who knifed to death by a blind old man, and later listened impassively as the charges were read. These are people who have nothing but their terrible compulsions; no ambitions, no hopes, no faith in anything, no sense of their own reality, no guidelines of morality. They are alienated from society, of course, but from themselves as living creatures, from everything alive.

It would clearly be a gross exaggeration to suggest that there are many people like this, but plainly the number is growing. When the milieu is openly and horribly violent, the growth is more speedy. I have spent long periods in areas of great violence. Usually I have found that humane and decent people would start by avoiding being judgemental or angry about insurgents or others the government was fighting. However, they gradually tended to became hard and callous. (I must say that I have not found this in Ireland nor, as I have described, in Nigeria.)

The centre's work as an antidote to alienation

I do not think that Katarina and her companions actually thought of their work in these terms. However, they greatly disliked the atmosphere in Osijek and wanted to show that the continued expression of vengeful hatred was doing no good to anyone; that what was needed instead of the militaristic bombast was getting down to the job of helping the victims of the war, completely irrespective of their ethnic origin. And this they proceeded to do.

At the same time as they were building up the centre, they were thinking constantly about the meaning of nonviolence. What does nonviolent help mean? Surely more than just providing what is needed to alleviate some hardship or disadvantage. They came to understand that in all human relationships there is a chance to give help at a variety of levels. The crudest level is purely material: providing the bread or the bed. But at another level we can provide solace and affection, and advice if needed on how to tackle difficult problems. At a yet higher level it is possible that the act of giving can include provision of stimulation and/or the opportunity for the recipient to do something which will contribute positively to the situation in which they suffered need. Maybe they will join one of the centre's projects, or in some other way help to maintain or rebuild the civil society. All this helps to restore meaning to life, a sense of hope and purpose which is nourished both by the formal activities of the centre and by the personal contacts and the friendships which have flowered between those engaged in the common enterprise.

Apart from those few who may still see the centre as a threat to their war mentality, the Osijek community values and trusts it as an organisation that is doing good and has no power or party political axes to grind. It is recognised as having no doctrinal bias beyond a compassionate concern for human well-being.

The centre members have close and friendly relationships with a number of other bodies, such as those set up among the communities of displaced persons, but are also themselves setting up new institutions. These, without any particular effort being made, embody the nonviolent ethos of the centre. Such a group is that of the Laslovo community, and those associated with the Peace Education Centre and with the various social/economic enterprises which have been established for the refugees and displaced persons. These developments have not been exactly planned, but have coalesced out of the association of people with common interests and common purposes.

If one has to define the nature of the centre, I suppose one would have to say that it is a non-governmental organisation, an NGO. But this would give a false impression. Most of the myriad of NGOs exist primarily for a particular purpose: to care for some aspect of health, the environment, education, welfare of the old, animals, children, victims of famine or oppression, etc. But this centre, which came into existence to demonstrate a different way of reacting to a violent situation, is expanding into the entire realm of human life to find ways of solving every human problem and healing every human pain of which they become aware.

The extent of this expansion cannot wholly be explained, it seems to me, from the effect of what the centre members are heard to say or seen to do in relation to particular difficulties and problems. It is more the effect of what they are, of the qualities that are evoked and nourished by their awareness. This has spread like leaven through the community, changing it; to use another metaphor, it is the antidote to the death-dealing virus of alienation.

The centre and peace

The prime purpose of the centre is peace, the establishment of peaceful relations at all levels; peace is the first descriptive word in its title. There is little it can do in relation to the existing state of war between Croatia and Serbia. The only thing possible is, to some extent, to mitigate the fever of violence in one small area. There is a continual quiet effort to probe through the barriers of suspicion into Serbia and to build relations with individuals and groups there. However, even if this is allowed to continue unabated, it could be years before the general climate of opinion is sufficiently changed to affect the governments concerned.

What seems to me extremely important, however, is that the work of the centre is to both stimulate and preserve the values on which harmony can eventually be restored. Respect for human life, concern for the other, the de-demonisation of the enemy, concern for justice, sensitivity to the great variety of pains are essential if a state of non-war is to be transformed into a truly peaceful relationship in which the other person is cherished to the point where they become the same.

This is the constant and all-pervading thrust of the centre's work. It serves as a repository for all those attitudes, so damaged in the fury of militarism, upon which peace depends. When the fighting stops and the peace accords are signed, bitter feelings may well continue to ruin the future with poisons of the past. However, to the extent that bodies like the centre and its equivalents which are springing up in many areas of former Yugoslavia have retained the values of peace, real harmony may come with the political decision to end the war.

This is a hope on which to pin our faith; a reason for giving all the support we can to these brave groups which have resisted the dangerous hostility of the violent without the degradation of hating them.

It is hardly necessary to say that Osijek should not be taken as a universal model. Different cultures, different conflicts and different levels of material development will demand different varieties of antidote to violence. Given the essential foundation of loving respect for human life, for peace and for justice, a great variety of approaches to meeting human needs and establishing civil society will be relevant and effective.

It is also clear that what I have related is only the first chapter, the opening of consciousness, the awakening of a new awareness. Ahead lies the vital question of how these largely inward developments can be ratified within the framework of appropriate policies and structures: legal, social, economic and political. Many authors have tried to write these chapters in their own idioms; the marxists, Margaret Thatcher and her sort, and the fascists are just a contemporary sample. But their first chapters, beguiling as they may once have seemed, were faulty and things went terribly wrong. The societies which they had hoped to create became monstrous, cruel, corrupt — and inefficient.

My friends in Osijek have, I believe, written an impeccable first chapter. I have no detailed idea of how the book will continue, but I believe that some of the arrangements they have made to implement their ideas promisingly adumbrate subsequent chapters. I hope to live to read some of the future instalments.

CHAPTER 9

Social healing of the wounds of war[68]

Half a century ago, when the Second World War came to an end, the survivors, soldiers and civilians returned to their homes. But for some, all that remained were the ruins of a home; for yet others, exile or the cold rule of a tyrant. Most had suffered in mind or body, most had lost something – peace of mind, a beloved person, a community, a country, a way of life, happiness.

The prisoners of war

The challenge of a new life in a new world lay ahead, but some could not meet the opportunities or excitement of that challenge. They had suffered too much. One group facing this challenge were the tens of thousands of British prisoners of war returning to Britain after five years of captivity in Europe. (These were initially referred to as PsOW, but at some subsequent stage – and in this writing – as POWs.) Later we will consider whether what we can learn from them could be applied to the difficulties experienced by others elsewhere whose lives have been disrupted by war and other catastrophes in the 21st century.

As it became clear in 1945 that the war was coming to an end, a group of very senior officers approached the government with an urgent plea that some provision should be made for the 120,000 British POWs who had mostly been captured in 1940. These officers had themselves been captured during World War I and argued that their lives had been ruined because no one had recognised the damaging effect of long-term captivity. Some provision must be made, they said, for the young men who would soon be returning to Britain from German prison camps. With an amazing lack of bureaucratic delay and with the assistance of two remarkable psychiatrists, A.T. Macbeth (Tommy) Wilson and Eric

Trist, the army set up therapeutic bodies called Civil Resettlement Units (CRUs). The task of the CRUs was to help the returned POWs bridge what turned out to be a very wide social gap between captivity and freedom. There were 20 such units, each servicing the needs of some 240 men, usually for a month at a time. (The awful physical plight of captives from Southeast Asia required special conditions and treatment not provided by the CRUs.) The first job for Wilson, Trist and their colleagues was to meet the fairly large number of men who by one means or another had managed to return to Britain early.

Most of them had enjoyed a blissful first few weeks, but then after a month or six weeks, their mood had changed. They were depressed, felt they were losing touch with their families, and wanted to return to such minimal military security as was offered by the CRU. They suffered from insomnia, and from loss of appetite and sexual drive. Some had aimlessly left home; a certain number had committed petty crimes. Many felt vaguely guilty for having allowed themselves to be captured, seeing this as failing both the army and their families. There was no single symptom apart from a strong sense of malaise and dissatisfaction, of being no longer part of society. There was therefore no obvious treatment. The psychiatric staff of the CRU organisation did not feel, however, that these POWs, with the exception of a few individuals, were suffering from any sort of psychological sickness. Wilson and Trist rejected any idea that they were 'ill'; or 'abnormal'. They were, however, unhappy and felt alienated from the society to which they had returned – and in tragic cases this included their wives and other members of their families. They were, in the rather horrible but expressive parlance that evolved, desocialised or unsettled.

CRUs as transitional communities

The CRU structure provided ample medical and dental facilities for the POWs, but the emphasis of the effort was social: the POWs were to be helped to 'feel at ease', in fact to be eased into the social and familial roles in which they had previously felt comfortable but from which they now felt estranged. Their alienation from normal civilian life had occurred during the whole process of militarisation. This is a process which transforms the civilian into the fledgling soldier through an increasing identification with the army unit, a process cemented by the experience of battle in which small-group solidarity and mutual trust is essential to survival. If it happens that the action ends in capture, reliance on the group intensifies. Without their weapons and their military leaders (who, if captured, are sent to other camps), the captives have to depend entirely on each other. It might have been assumed that the outcome would have been a chaotic anarchy. But from the available accounts, it was a tender democracy in which its members followed the mandate of reciprocal respect and care.

It seems that this democracy persisted as an ideal socio-psychological form, one looked back on with nostalgia during periods of painful re-patriation. However, although the culture of the camps was democratic, this was not entirely conducive to resettlement. The POWs were return-ing to roles – as father, citizen, neighbour, employee, especially perhaps husband – from which they had been progressively and often ruthlessly estranged. How could a sojourn in the CRU help these men recover the sense of being truly part of a society? At present they were still soldiers and must be eased back into more gentle, and – in a different sense – more 'democratic' roles. Wilson and Trist saw that they must also learn to combine the civilian skills of family and occupational life with those of citizenship. The role of the CRU was to serve as a stepping stone between military and civilian worlds, to be a transitional community.

The CRU curriculum

The permanent staff of the CRUs wore uniforms and were subject to normal (but relaxed and non-doctrinaire) military discipline. The POWs, though nominally soldiers in that they had not been discharged from the army, were all volunteers. Nothing was compulsory. They could come and go as they wished. In fact, perhaps encouraged by the complete lack of restrictions, the great majority took full advantage of available facilities and opportunities. These included:

- Psychiatric treatment if the volunteer felt he needed this. The psy-chiatric unit was located in an inconspicuous part of the camp to avoid the chance that 'old so and so' might be considered 'a bit potty';
- Help in mastering the complexities of post-war society: the ra-tioning of food, clothing, furniture and so forth; taxation and oth-er financial issues; problems of accommodation;
- Studying employment possibilities – the term used was 'job re-hearsal'. A number of businesses, trades, crafts and so on, gener-

ously provided time and skilled practitioners to give volunteers a chance to find out about building, farming, clerical work, the law, teaching, nursing or various forms of further education;

- Seminars or workshops. These were held fairly regularly with a participating (rather than a chairing or 'facilitating') officer on the staff. The exchanges that took place during these sessions gave volunteers the chance to break down feelings of shyness, or to deal with experiences in a way that could help them to become closer to their families and others in the civilian community;

- Finally, regular weekend home visits – the most important stepping stone. Until towards the end of the (usually) four or five-week stay at the CRU, the volunteers were not ready to open themselves to family life. However, the security of the CRU experience gradually lowered the barriers. The gap between the stepping stones grew narrower.

Evaluating the CRUs

We now come to the crucial problem of assessing the effectiveness of the CRU system. To what extent did these transitional communities succeed in resettling volunteers who had entrusted themselves to their care? We had carefully considered possible symptoms of deterioration or improvement, but none was very plausible. I should interpolate that my CRU role was as a research officer. It was particularly important that I should avoid any bias towards the CRU system and my thought constantly returned to many discussions with Wilson and Trist, and also with Ben Morris, Henry Dicks, Isobel Menzies and Harold Bridger. I mention these then eminent names because they may jog the memory of readers who know their work and will better understand the work of the CRUs. I had by this time resumed post-graduate work at Oxford where there were a considerable number of ex-POWs within easy cycling distance of my home. It had been decided that the best way to assess the performance of the CRUs would be to study the products of the system, and to compare these with a larger number – larger because there were more to choose from – who had not volunteered for the units. A total of 150 men were selected according to criteria chosen by others of our colleagues. I do not have a list of the criteria, but they were chiefly aimed at ensuring a certain rough balance, for example, with regard to age, marital status and level of education. Among these men, 100 had been to CRUs; the rest, not. A further 40 took part in the study who had not been in the services at all because they were in reserved occupations, though they otherwise conformed to the CRU/non-CRU sample. These comparisons, we thought, should be revealing. For weeks I spent much of my time with all the members of the samples. We met in their homes, at their places of work and in pubs (though there was an unfortunate shortage of beer!). At first I didn't know what I was looking for. After a while, however, we began to recognise various patterns of role behaviour and identified 15 illustrative types of relations which we termed Criteria of Social Participation. These included relations with partners, children and other close family members, with neighbours, employers and work mates, and with the wider society. However, the 'local culture' within which people played these parts varied greatly, from warmly close and cooperative to indifferent or hostile. It seemed to me that the men performed their roles at four different levels of skill and competence which we defined as the statistical norm, the ideal or supranorm, and two narrow and limited infranorms. Looking back at this material with which I was so deeply involved half a century ago, I am struck by how many aspects of human relations, or failures of relations, have remained basically unchanged. An able statistician, Hugh Murray, who was associated with the development of the CRUs, undertook detailed analyses of the scoring of the Fifteen Criteria of Social Participation (four for supernorm, three for norm, two for infranorm -one, and one for infranorm-two) in relation to the ex-POWs and the 40 men who had not been in the army at all. This analysis showed that a significantly larger proportion of those who had been to CRUs were better settled than those who had not. To put it simply, this vindicated the CRU experiment; statistically there is a very low probability that some other factor could have been responsible for the result. I think it was Eric Trist who spoke of the significance of 'creative casualties'. These were people who had coped with pain, confusion and separation from their loved ones without losing hope or the ability to help and encourage their companions in captivity. These were the men who, after repatriation, scored supranormally in the survey. A further way of expressing the idea would be that these 'creative casualties' had, by surviving threat and hurt, gained an exceptional new awareness and power. Obviously this development does not depend on having been a

POW, although this may sometimes have helped. There are other exceptional people whose inner growth does not depend on comparably demanding conditions.

Contemporary relevance of CRUs

Since the early days of my own career, which was really kick-started by my work with the CRU organisation, I have had the chance to meet creative casualties in many parts of the world. Several of them have in fact been former prisoners, though sadly a far greater proportion of former prisoners become victims. We cannot, alas, say that the world has become a more peaceful place. Those subjected to violence and those practising it are very numerous. Although the last 50 years have seen a wonderful growth of agencies working for human peace and well-being, there can be no certainty that they are winning the race against violence. Among the losers are millions whose lives have been ruined by wars, economic disruption, injustices or a damaged environment. These millions need to receive and to give help to their fellow women and men, and to the material world we live in. I believe that the experience of the CRUs provides grounds for hope and that units of this kind, adapted to suit present day circumstances, might help those who have experienced the trauma of war and violence in recent years. When this idea first came to me, I turned it nostalgically aside: ludicrous, I thought, too difficult, too big. But I then realized that the basic idea was simple. Throw out the frills and what is left is a frame-work of fundamental principles which remain relevant.

The first practical step in applying these principles would be to provide a restorative refuge where people could free themselves from shocking experiences. Here they could be helped by the priests and elders, the creative casualties, the inner shamans. They would be guided away from shame by discovering that many others were also plagued by illusory guilt. They would talk to each other about what, as a result of this process, would no longer be secret degradations. Respected relatives and friends would guide them back into the community of life. The character of each group would depend on the local culture, the types of pain its members had suffered, and the types of inner skills members brought to the group and developed within it. The healing power of the refuge would come from the trust, confidence and affection that it generated.[69]

CHAPTER 10

Peacemaking – public and private[70]

I only began to study peace after having been involved in the practical
work of peacemaking. It came about by chance. I had lived and worked,
mainly on development problems, in Asia and Africa for several years,
but having been trained as a psychologist and anthropologist, I had no
experience of politics or diplomacy. However, since I knew the places and
some of the main actors, I became sucked in as a mediator in wars in both
continents. For several years I was absorbed in the processes of negotiation, bargaining, seeking compromises, face-saving devices, attempts to
explain enemies to each other, trade-offs and all the other methods by
which a third party attempts to promote a settlement or to reduce the
level of hostility. This was how I understood peacemaking – the effort by
an outsider to end hostilities between warring parties. This, of course,
was public peacemaking, not that most of what we did was not highly
confidential, but because the general situation was well known, as were
the procedures of diplomacy and mediation.

Before long, however, I began to see that preoccupation with war
could merely distract attention from other situations that were almost as
damaging. These were situations in which violence was done to people by
injustice, oppression, manipulation, exploitation, by the infliction of terror, by degrading or inhuman practices and all the other countless ways
in which we demean and harm each other, physically or psychically. Indeed these forms of violence are just as important as wars, for they are the
seedbed out of which wars grow. If we were to analyse the approximately
110 wars of the last 30 years we would find that a very large proportion
originated in such circumstances – in colonialism, the victimisation of a
minority (or on occasion a majority) group, or exploitation for economic
or strategic purposes. Once the wars begin they develop a terrible momentum and are hard to settle except by military victory, but if the right
action is taken early enough the worst violence may be forestalled.

These pre- or non-war situations cannot be tackled by the same methods as wars, at least not those with which I have been involved. When the violence stems essentially from inequality, there is point in negotiation and bargaining: the strong are not going to give in to the weak, to surrender the advantages they derive from their position because of anyone's persuasive tongue. They may, of course, feel that it would be sensible for them to make some concessions, but that is a completely different matter. Essentially the only course open to the weak is to become strong enough to change the structure of inequality. This is what was achieved by Gandhi's struggle for the independence of India and subsequently, peacefully or violently, by many colonial countries. (I should note sadly in passing that independence obtained in this way was not always absolute! Often the colonial powers relinquished their control only to impose an equally harmful, because hidden, economic stranglehold.) Here one role for the peacemaker is to help empower the weak. This may be thought of as a subversive or revolutionary role, for if it is successful there would almost inevitably be a period of turbulence, but this can be justified on the grounds that it is a necessary stage in the establishment of a peaceful society in which justice and harmony eventually prevail. Another important task for the peacemaker is to find ways of making the change as non-violent as possible.

I would not wish to imply that all these peacemaking activities are on a large scale, involving nations or big groups. I have come to feel more and more that anyone who is seriously concerned with peace, by which I mean positive, warm, cooperative and constructive relationships between people, must be attentive to relationships between all human beings, friends, members of a family, teachers and students, doctors and patients, neighbours and so on. Obviously the scale of a relationship to some extent determines its character – there are some elements in an international relationship which do not exist in a relationship between a woman and her husband – on the other hand, there are also some which do. The common factor is, of course, the human one. Although the structure of a relationship may have been built up over centuries, eight of them in the case of Northern Ireland, it is the men and women of today who maintain that structure. They may be born into circumstances which impose certain pressures, but however they may have been moulded it is they who make the decisions, give the orders throw the bombs, pull the triggers. But it is also they who can talk to each other, help each other, influence each other, break the age-old pattern.

It is the structure of the relationship that is public objective, capable of analysis in terms of social-scientific concepts. But there is something else, an underside to these more objective peacemaking activities which I call private. It is not very easy to define. I can even say that it is the personal as opposed to the structural or institutional. It is personal, certainly, but then it has always been acknowledged that individual peculiarities do affect larger issues. Prime ministers and presidents are carried along by the momentum of history and have less influence on events than they might like to think, but there is a significant modicum of difference between the reactions of, for example, American presidents Eisenhower, Truman, Kennedy, Johnson, Nixon, Ford and Carter that no statesman can afford to ignore. No, I am referring to something that is more subtle. It has nothing to do with the specific situation, although this must obviously be well understood. It is not even concerned with what we call the personality of individual leaders, meaning their quirks, idiosyncrasies and peculiarities. It is concerned with the extent to which those involved in the situation are liberated from the forces that would make them see both it and themselves inaccurately.

Fairly early in my experience as a mediator I began to be aware that the leaders who have to make momentous political and strategic decisions are not simply icy thinking machines, moved only by a logical evaluation of all factors in the situation, and coming like a chess Grand Master to the best possible conclusion On the contrary, however able they may be, their judgement is also affected by their fears, anger, resentment, ambition, vanity and by the largely unconscious memory of long-past pains, anxieties and feelings of powerlessness. Often the tenser the situation the more dominant are these feelings, and the more dominant they become the faster the flight from reason. I have sometimes had the impression that if the greatest diplomatic and military minds of history, say Alexander, Napoleon, Machiavelli, Talleyrand, Metternich, with Aristotle thrown in for good measure, were to offer their solutions to the problems of Northern Ireland and the Middle East, they would be rejected. The actors in a conflict view the situation unclearly through a haze of violent emotion and only when this is dispersed can they properly assess the situation. To blow away the haze is a very important part of private peacemaking. But of course the peacemaker is in very much the same situation. He carries around with him the legacy of the past and the pressures of the present, both of which interact to impair his judgement, and he cannot help others to be free of this legacy until his own liberation has begun. It is not enough, moreover, to consider only the leaders. They are very important in taking the first steps towards re-establishing peace, but the consolidation of peace as a peaceful society needs many peaceful people, and peacefulness is a quality of people not driven by violent or desperate feelings. This, it seems to me, is a very important argument for seeking non-violent methods of changing cruel, or corrupt, unjust or unequal social structures. Some dedicated and intelligent people believe that we cannot affect human nature until we have altered the society that flawed it, and that we are unlikely to be able to do this without violence. But the habit of violence and the accompanying insensitivity to suffering tend to persist. Thus all too often in history, and we can think of several contemporary examples, a tyranny is overthrown and those ardent lovers of justice who overthrew it become equally tyrannical. If this were not so, there would be many utopias in our unhappy world. There are, of course, numerous complex reasons for the difficulty of establishing ideal or even relatively decent societies, but the acceptance of violence as a means of achieving ends is certainly one of them. The ends may at first seem good, but with practice we become less discriminating.

This implies particular responsibilities for peacemakers engaged in working towards the establishment of a peaceful society. I have phrased this positively instead of talking about changing or eliminating an unpeaceful one. Peacemakers may indeed devise strategies of social, economic and political change: this is in the public domain of peacemaking, but it is even more important for them to help their collaborators to work on their problems of personal unpeacefulness. This is the private approach, and it is as indispensable as public negotiation in reaching the final goal, not just the cessation of hostilities or the overthrow of a particular regime, but the establishment of a lasting peace, based on justice and non-violence.

Our tendency to inner unpeacefulness is very pervasive. At the centre of all human conflicts, whatever their cause and whatever the rights and wrongs of any particular case, are our apprehensions, anger, resentment, vanity, hurt pride, insecurity, prejudice, the sense of hopelessness, and above all the blurred understanding and the obscure but potent impact of old pains and fears. Even when we struggle for the most splendid cause, these things render our struggle harder and less effective.

In making this generalisation, I am not suggesting that human nature is in any fundamental sense pathological. Below the confusions that characterise so much of our lives are enormous potentials. Every so often we perceive these, unexpectedly revealed, in each other – great funds of creative ability, powers of concentration, profundity, intellectual clarity and grasp, determination, persistence, courage, love. We have all been taught to believe that to be 'normal' (a synonym for healthy) is a desirable state, but the norm is the average and our average is low – minds fettered by poor concentration, inability to exercise self-control (how many people can keep their minds empty of stray thoughts for more than 30 seconds?), and the compulsions of unconscious motives. If by normal we really mean healthy, or whole, we should not accept the standard of the average; we should aim at the best of which we are capable (perhaps Maslow's peak experiences). The question of intelligence is illustrative. A number of studies have shown that intellectual performance (and test scores) can be vastly improved simply by treating people as though they could do better. But we find it convenient to classify people according to a dubious concept of intelligence, and the more we act upon it the more true does it seem to be; just as people behave 'intelligently' when they are treated as competent human beings so they behave stupidly, and eventually cannot do otherwise, if treated as stupid, thus proving the myth. I have, however, so often found that people are capable of infinitely more than is generally believed that in my view the real normal, what we should be like, is a thing of wonder. We are capable of being, as our experience shows, incredibly strong, diverse understanding, sensitive, while the average is a pathetic travesty, from which comes most of our miseries, of what we might be.

How is it, then, that most of us, most of the time fall so far below our potential? From a very early age society impinges upon us. First we learn from our parents and then increasingly from relatives, friends, school, which things are acceptable and bring rewards, and which are in some sense punished. We become 'socialised', learning how to respond to social stimuli according to the prevalent social code. We also receive through various media an enormous amount of information about the world and ourselves. Much of this is, of course, factual and accurate, but much is also distorted or untrue giving rise to those habits of mind (a significant phrase) we call racism, sexism, ageism and a limited view of the nature and potential of humankind. We also add to our mental baggage the innumerable fears and hurts which we inevitably sustain in the process of growing up. All these feelings and attitudes are fed into that great computer, the brain, the organ through which we experience the mind. There they remain, some frequently and some infrequently activated, but all ready to be triggered by the right associative stimulus.

The brain is amazingly swift, and highly efficient, except in so far as false information has been fed into the data bank. It responds almost instantaneously to any stimulus by assembling and presenting the appropriate – or what we have been conditioned to consider as appropriate – information. Just consider how much we leave to our computers. Not only do we dress, feed or wash ourselves without consciously thinking out each move, but we greet acquaintances in the street, exchange conventional enquiries and comments in a completely automatic fashion and then pass on almost without memory of the incident. I can even do something as 'intellectually' complex as giving a lecture by computer. It takes over when I am speaking on a familiar theme and in a sense I can then go to sleep, just as if switching on the automatic pilot, but after a while I may awake and not know what point I have reached in my talk. At such times we are what is known as absent-minded. I use the analogy of the computer advisedly because a computer is a machine and there is much that is machine-like and automatic about our behaviour when the 'mind is absent' and there is no real awareness of what we are doing. This is inevitable: we are not fully conscious. While the computer works it dreams, wandering away along a train of associations that we call day-dreams. There is, of course, much about us that is necessarily automatic, not only the autonomic nervous system, but the learned muscular responses enabling us to walk, talk, swim, play games and so on. It is only when what should be conscious becomes automatic that malfunctioning begins.

Some of the elements in the computer which contribute to the diminution of consciousness are also those which tend to make automatic behaviour damaging or violent. I am speaking of these complexes of fixed ideas about people and society that I would collectively call 'isms', and of memory traces of fear, rejection, loneliness and other painful feelings. Often the isms and the feelings of pain interact: we seek refuge from pain in the false security of an 'ism' that boosts our self-esteem, and so act in a way that pains others – and may thus indirectly contribute to our own hurt. In countless ways our response to pain, especially the pain whose origin and nature are hidden from us, is destructive. We protect ourselves from future hurts, or shield our fragile identity (itself a protective device) by manipulating or dominating others, by pestering them for attention, by assuming artificial or unnatural roles, by trying to demonstrate our superiority, by hurting or humiliating. Like most of what are called neurotic mechanisms these things do nothing to give more than temporary relief from the conditions that evoked them. In general they make things worse.

For most of us the moods come and go, unbidden and often unrecognised, in response to the stimulus. They may not be very important, but also they may determine a whole complex pattern of life. Whenever we find ourselves suddenly and unreasonably (as we realize later, but not at the time) irritated, resentful, alarmed, depressed, it is because something has stirred the dregs of an old hurt which has then taken over and dimmed our consciousness. The anger that we express at that time against a particular person, may well have nothing to do with that person, who in all innocence merely did or said something to stir an association. The pain inflicted upon us is transmuted into anger that we direct against others, who in turn receive it as pain and pass on as pain-giving anger to yet others and so on in an endless spiral of violence – all semi-conscious.

I should mention in passing that it seems unnecessary to debate whether human beings are innately violent, killer apes as we have been termed. I do not believe that we are, and if there are any individuals or societies which are or have been completely nonviolent – as I think can easily be demonstrated – we have to find another explanation for the all too prevalent violence. A wise psychiatrist, John Rickman, said that violence was the fruit of unlived life. By this graphic phrase I think he meant that violence stems from the frustration, pain, fear, anguish, desperation, sense of loss and confusion that we have all suffered, though some no doubt more than others. But life *can* be lived and we must learn to do so more fully.

If it is the common predicament of humanity to be less than half awake, to behave – often violently – like machines, to mask our high potential with misinformation, preconceptions and negative emotions, then the would-be peacemakers must work on themselves as much as or more than on those whose violence they would wish to curb, for they are also violent and violent people cannot create lastingly unviolent situations. Only by learning to control their own malfunctioning can they help others to control theirs, and only thus have a fully human relationship with them rather than a largely mechanical interaction.

First it is necessary to recognise how little real autonomy we have; how much we are dominated by the flow of thoughts, memories, ideas, feelings that flicker across the screen of consciousness; how little we are capable of attention (this is an activity of the whole self as compared with an absorption that can be as automatic as anything else); how, for all our vaunted free will, we cannot choose our feelings or control our thoughts. At the same time we have to recognise that this is the general human condition and that we must not castigate ourselves or forget that below the surface confusion is a deep source of strength. For all our normal lack of complete consciousness, we are not impotent.

Next, we must seek some means of becoming more and more constantly awake. This is an individual matter for each person. Let me, however, mention a few things which I believe to be of general validity. Our normal state is one of inner noise distracting us from reaching the inner parts of the mind. First, therefore, it is necessary to practice quietness. This is not difficult, if we can only remember to do it. It is only necessary to compose ourselves, sitting comfortably but not slouching, for two or three minutes two or three times a day, but preferably between different types of activity. The mind then comes to rest and intruding thoughts ignored or nudged gently aside. During these periods, whatever we are engaged with, we should awake. I mean that we should become conscious of who we are, where we are, what we are doing, what is around us, and particularly what our bodies feel like.

These things are very simple; the only difficulty is in breaking the bad habit of being asleep by the good habit of being awake. If we could be conscious of ourselves the whole time, life would be transformed including, of course, our relationships with others.

It is particularly important to remind ourselves constantly that our essence is flawless, that we are all in that sense perfect. But at the same time we are machines. If we are to prevent the machine taking over what should be the function of mind, of consciousness, we have to understand the machine and so should observe it. Paradoxically we can sometimes get the best insight into its nature from the way in which it impedes consciousness – for example, by the difficulties we have in remembering to be quiet.

It is also very important to trace to their sources those invaders that all too often dominate our minds. These are the paralysing fears, the feelings of impotence, the destructive impulses, the desperate need for reassurance, the miseries, the oft-repeated patterns of behaviour that always lead to the same sort of undesired consequences, the sense of worthlessness that arise unreasonably and unbidden. They not only make us unhappy and distort our relationships with others whom we try to manipulate to assuage our pain, but make us much less effective than we might have been. How can we deal wisely and comprehensively with a complex situation when we are, as we significantly say, 'out of our minds' with worry – or resentment, or hopelessness, or whatever it may be? The best we can do on our own is to try to maintain perspective, understanding that these invaders are unreal, that they have nothing to do with our genuine natures, or the present situation, and to try not to treat them seriously. As we become more self-conscious their origins may become clear to us, and their hold over us weaken. There are, however, certain sorts of help which may be sought. Among more accessible techniques, I am struck by the efficacy of co-counselling which identifies the sources of the dominating pains and fears and enables us to dissolve them by discharging the emotion we originally felt, but for various reasons could not properly express.

The practice of meditation is of great help in our efforts to escape what is inappropriately automatic in our natures. Meditation is, in one sense, a journey inwards. It may be contrasted with consciousness-raising exercises which lead outward and which make us more aware of the body and surroundings. These help to stem the draining of energy in daydreams and destructive emotions but meditation leads us to the source of that energy. Again I would emphasize that this is a very personal matter, private indeed, and we must seek the help that seems most suitable and most available.

Lastly, I would suggest something very practical. It is not enough simply to recognise as a general principle that we have great untapped potential, but to demonstrate to ourselves that this is true. We are dominated by ideas, usually because people have told us, that we are stupid, no good, inartistic, impractical, lazy, hesitant and the like. Here are a few hints. Never waste time worrying about not having time to do something – get on and do it and you will find you have all the time in the world. If there is something you would like to do but feel you are unable to – painting, playing an instrument, driving a car, doing household repairs – just do it, and you will find you can as long as you don't think you can't. If you find yourself being overcome by the fear of failure don't dignify this erroneous belief by paying it attention, or it will overcome you. Have you ever stayed awake all night because you were afraid you were not going to be able to get to sleep? Just push the idea away without focussing on it. But beware, also, of another pitfall. When you find you can draw or play the piano or whatever, don't get pleased with yourself. To know calmly and objectively that you have capacities is very different from claiming personal credit for them. To say 'look at me, how clever I am', is as destructive as saying 'how stupid I am'. Our success has merely demonstrated one individual realisation of a universal potential. A wrong concept of 'me' and 'my' is the source of much pain and confusion.

The efforts that we make to liberate ourselves from the invaders that become a part of the dominant data in our computers must obviously be connected to our relationships with others. If they are not, if what we gain is kept hugged to our bosoms as personal profit, nothing will come of it – even for ourselves. In what I have suggested as some of the approaches to self-liberation much is implied for our dealing with others. In this context, I am referring to our contact with people in the peacemaking relationship, but it would be almost equally valid for virtually all other human interactions.

First, and most important, we must learn to give people complete attention. We must make ourselves absolutely available to them, not interposing our own fears, needs or preconceptions. This means that we must as far as possible switch off our computers, with their automatic and built-in needs, and respond to human beings as human beings rather than as objects who can either hurt or help us. This type of attention creates an aura of safety in which people can abandon their prickly defences and, as we say, be themselves. But even this fully human interaction is always precarious, because we are not usually very good at it. I recall one counsellor who told me that if her attention to her client wavered for a minute he or she was aware and resentful – the contact was lost, and the expectation left unfulfilled. In order to give attention we must be constantly conscious of the value and importance of the other person. This means also that we must ignore the possibly bad things we have heard of her or him. I remember visiting a well-known and very dangerous guerrilla leader and attempting to give him attention. After a while he said with some surprise 'no one else has ever come to see me smiling and relaxed'. We became fast friends and were able to explore ways of finding humane rather than violent solutions to the situations he was involved in.

A part of giving attention is listening, not only hearing the words and noting their meaning, but listening to their sound which may convey something different — if you ask me how I am and I answer 'fine' in a depressed tone of voice the sound conveys more than the actual words. And listening involves also sensitivity to unspoken feelings that are conveyed by other means. The native Americans, as I have myself experienced, are very adept at this sort of listening. Attentive listening to another person reaches far below the surface and has a profound influence on the relationship of those involved.

A contact based on attention and listening is far from being a machine-like one. In a machine-like relationship we base our interaction on what is machine-like or automatic in each other. If, at this level, I am asked what I think of a particular man I shall describe him in terms of what we call personality traits. And these traits are simply the quirks, patterns of behaviour, habits of thought, automatic responses derived from his fears and pains that dominate his computer: they are nothing to do with the essential him and I must ignore them. It may not be easy to do this: most of our human evaluations are based on this sort of superficial judgement. I must therefore avoid giving 'character sketches'. I must reach below to what is living and vital. It will help if every time I meet people I consciously avoid the temptation to stereotype them and remain absolutely open to an understanding of their real selves. Moreover, when I meet people I already know well, I must always be as open to them as if I were meeting them for the first time. To say, oh, its poor old Joe again; we all know that he is this that and the other will surely make Joe this that and the other, thus frustrating his capacity to do something quite different. Especially, we must be ready to see great beauty and goodness in the person we thought of as poor old Joe.

Not only must we avoid making judgements about people, we must avoid criticizing them – we are all in the same boat, creatures who respond in a way that appears foolish or selfish but which we cannot help until we have learned differently; and if I see something ridiculous in you, you can no doubt see something similar in me. But if we once give in to the impulse to criticize and label people as silly, opinionated, self-centred, or whatever, they tend to live up to our assessment. Tell a child often enough that it is stupid, or can't do mathematics, or draw and he or she won't be able to. I have suffered this myself and to my shame have inflicted it on others.

Instead of criticism, therefore, we must give support, encouragement, validation. Most of us have a poor opinion of ourselves because we have been told we are no good, or feel we have failed. And most of us, I am sad to say, have told someone else, a child, student or mate, in a fit of irritation or to get rid of some hurt or anger, that they are in some way deficient – and so contributed to their diminishment. On the contrary, we should do all we can to counteract the miserable sense of incompetence, inadequacy, impotence or folly from which most of us suffer. It is very easy. We simply have to tell people that we see them as wise, brave, good and strong. But we cannot deceive them, we must really feel it because we really perceive it.

This does not mean that we must never tell our friends that they are wrong or behaving badly. There is an Indian legend about a snake that was converted by a guru and swore never to bite another person. But the local villagers took advantage of this and stoned it. The snake, angry and disillusioned complained to the guru who answered: 'but I never told you not to hiss'. We, too, must hiss if we see people doing wrong to themselves and others, but to hiss does not mean to harm. This is part of the obligation to explain and to help others to understand what they are doing. At one level we are able to do this by helping them to identify the fears and pains that dominate their computers, at another by explaining the ways in which they unconsciously manipulate and victimise others.

There are other duties we have towards our fellow human beings. We must refrain from subjecting them to our own fits of depression or anger or other negative emotions; these can only make life harder for them and to make them share our self-centred miseries cannot help us. In general, and at all times, we must be aware of them, conscious of the common ground of our being. I began to try to apply these principles several years ago when it became clear that the skills of public peacemaking, diplomacy, bargaining and so on, were insufficient. At first I acted more or less intuitively. Later, when I tried to understand the apparent effectiveness of those methods, I had the opportunity to learn more of the principles behind the practice. I am now certain that what is essential to peacemaking is also of the greatest value in all human interaction.

In conclusion, I would like to reintroduce the public dimension of peacemaking. The public and the private, the inner and the outer, the large and the small are merely different facets of the same whole, the same truth. If we consider them as being opposite or irreconcilable principles we won't see that truth. If we concentrate on one to the exclusion of the other the right things will not happen. If I simply work on myself and on my relationship with individuals to whom I am opposed or with whom I am acting as negotiator, I will not take into account the very different principles that govern large-scale events: the large is not just the small magnified; in some ways they differ in kind. Likewise, if I give all my attention to the large, the public, the outer, the right things will not happen because the large, although different from the small, private and inner, is composed of these hidden dimensions. One might say the same of the relationship of a body to the cells of which it is composed. If I simply work on myself and ignore the other how shall I know myself since the other is part of myself, from whom my separation is illusory? If I simply work on the other, ignoring myself, I shall not know him either since I can only see him clearly through eyes lightened by self-knowledge. Peacemaking is the science of perceiving that things which appear to be apart are one. It is the art of restoring love to a relationship from which it has been driven by fear and hatred. And one last definition: public peacemaking is what we do; private peacemaking is what we are, the two being interpenetrating.

PART 3

THE FRAGILE VOICE OF LOVE

We concluded Part 2 with an early essay by Adam, published in 1978, on peacemaking as a public and private activity. We have given Part 3 the title 'The fragile voice of love' which is the title of his last book. The title expresses not only the preoccupation of his later work but much of how throughout his life he saw higher levels of awareness as the driving force for peacemaking. In Chapter 14, John Paul shows that Adam's life pedagogy suggested the need 'to live in the liminal space that navigates between the inner and outer world'. The idea of the liminal space is used in anthropology and in-depth psychology to mean transitional spaces where normal limits to thought and behaviour are relaxed, where the barriers and boundaries determined by excessively rigid norms of what Adam called belonging identity are softened or dissolved. In these spaces new perspectives and understandings can be generated. Barbara Mitchels, in her study of Adam's work on the relationship between trauma therapy and conflict, especially in Croatia, where he worked with his wife Anne, his daughter Deborah, as well as with Barbara, suggests that their peacemaking work in Osijek 'shows that liminality achieved within a community can be a very powerful agent for change". She goes on to say: 'With increasing awareness, the definition and boundaries of self and other may disintegrate and merge into a collective "we", as the Centar za mir (Centre for Peace) found in its very first workshop with Adam Curle. A safe, therapeutic space created by professionals, friends or a community can provide the environment in which we can experience liminality within which lies the opportunity for the psychological change from unpeacefulness to peace.'[71]

Part 3 contains four chapters, three of which deal with Adam's continued reflections on the inner and outer dimensions of peace, a preoccupation which deepened in his later years. Extracts from his last two books feature here: the material in Chapter 11 is from *To tame the Hydra*, published in 1999, when he was 84. The *Hydra* is the term he used to define the systemic presence of a malign force which generates discord and violence. It equates to the term more familiar in mainstream peace research – the 'culture of violence' – the sets of exploitative institutions, ideas and behaviours that harm people and communities. 'The Hydra, like other creatures, has now evolved the attitudes and attributes needed to survive in its hostile, marshy environment: these, shared among its nine heads, are rage, ferocity, greed, cruelty, hatred, lust for power, pitilessness, distrust and illusion.' His thinking on the Hydra is developed further in his last book, *The fragile voice of love*, published in his 90th year, in 2006, where he explores the idea of the conflict between what he called the Black Cloud and the Mind of the Universe, or the universal mind. This is the subject of Chapter 13.

It is important to recognise that Adam did not use these terms as simple metaphors or as beliefs derived from religions or theology. It is true that during the time he was writing these books he became, as we noted in the introduction, deeply influenced by the Dalai Lama and by Buddhism and in the process described himself as a 'semi-lapsed' Quaker. But he saw Buddhism, or the way it has meaning for him, as a non-credal, non-dogmatic and agnostic value system which was not theological but based on psycho-philosophy – another way of understanding the *philosophia perennia*. He explained the reasons for writing the *The Hydra* (the global interconnection of destructive forces based on military, economic and political power) as the need to create a shift in our ideas about peace. While the tools and techniques remain important – mediation, negotiation, problem-solving and so on – '...we need to understand and learn to *withstand* and to *transform* within ourselves and our own societies the attitudes and activities out of which the culture of violence develops'.[72] In order to better understand the culture of violence (the Hydra and the way it permeates collective thinking – the Black Cloud) and the transformations needed to move cultures of peace, he explored the forces underpinning them and the lessons to be learned from systems theory, psychology and neuroscience. Chapter 6 of *The Hydra* is called 'Mind, system and society', where he draws on a wide literature which explored the nature of mind and consciousness. Jung held that there was a 'collective unconscious' shared by all humans, and which was the 'foundation of what the ancients called 'the sympathy of all things'. He also cites Gregory Bateson's *Steps to an ecology of mind* (1972) which argued that mind is 'the essence of being alive' and is a basic requirement for all living organisms to adapt and change. The work of Ken Wilber extended the concept of mind/consciousness to levels beyond the individual. Reading Fritjof Capra's *The web of life* (1996), helped Adam to understand and make connections between neurobiology, psychology and philosophy. From all this reading and his own meditations and reflections, he concluded that 'there is probably some kind of collective awareness, extended mind, or whatever we may like to call it, that has an enormously powerful – but often unacknowledged – impact on human feeling and action'.[73] Taking all this closer to the goals of peacemaking, Adam went on to suggest that 'those of our values that epitomise the harmonious and creative civil society – peace, justice, human rights and respect for life – are a collective possession, possibly a facet of a shared mind, rather than merely individual ideals. It may be plausible to regard them as constituting the heart of a fully human system. If so, like our human potentials, they are always available'.[74] We could say also that the attempts to develop cosmopolitanism as a political and cultural theory for peacebuilding shares a similar objective, as does the rich and creative work of Wolfgang Dietrich on transrational peace and cosmopolitan perspectives on global cultural traditions of peace and peacemaking.[75]

With this idea of values as a collective possession, Adam comes close to an implicit revision of needs theory in conflict resolution – that the satisfaction of basic human needs (for security, identity, recognition) are non-zero sum – that is that they are capable of universal satisfaction. In Adam's work on the mind-system-society connection to the nature of peace, he suggests that there may be underlying values in the collective or extended mind capable of finding satisfiers or at least a motivating energy to enhance the satisfaction of needs. One of these values is the pursuit of happiness, the subject of Chapter 1, which is an extract from the *Hydra* on happiness, in which he suggests that 'the pursuit of happiness (following Jefferson) is a dominant and universal human drive'. (p. 37)

Chapter 13 presents an extract from *The fragile voice of love*, published in his 90th year, in 2006, where he explores the idea of the conflict between what he called the Black Cloud[76] and the Mind of the Universe. The concept of *awareness* is central here as the key to self-knowledge and the connection to the universal or extended mind as defined above. *Medita-*

tion and the connection between *meditation* and *mediation* is a theme in this chapter, meditation being a technique for the inner aspect of peacemaking, mediation the outer. Chapter 13 also contains some of his poems (*Lama, Mind, and Mediation/Meditation*) which are also used by him as reflective meditations, a way of enriching awareness of the inner and outer, the public and private dimensions of peacemaking.

In Chapter 1, we included the poem *The policeman calls*, a reflection on his interrogation in South Africa in the early years of the anti-apartheid struggle. The introduction to *Recognition of reality* in which the poems were published was written by Joanna Macy. She asks how can we deal with the pain and suffering of war and conflict, with atrocities and the general misery and alienation of modern living (Adam's Black Cloud). We can respond, she says, either by turning our backs on it, ignoring it, or by responding 'with such desperation to do good that, run ragged between organisations and meetings and faced with frequent defeat... we burn out'. The third way is to 'embrace the world that we move into as our own heart, compassionately recognising its afflictions as extensions or mirror images of the conflicts and delusions we nurture in ourselves. When that movement – or stillness – of the mind occurs, something is released in us. Our firm grip on our separate selfhood dissolves and in its place springs a sense of identity with all life so real, so profound, that it can, buoying us like a river, be our strength and our hope'.[77] She goes on to say that Adam's work enables us to understand this liberating sense of awareness. One of the distinctive qualities of Adam's work as a mediator is that he connected mediation with meditation. He tried to meditate alone first before meeting parties to a mediation, in order to reach this stillness, to befriend and to open up spaces in which he might be able to connect adversaries through an understanding of common humanity.

As happiness is the leitmotiv of *The Hydra*, so love is of *The fragile voice*:

> So, above all, love, let's love and do it generously and with a full heart; and be deeply sorry for those who find loving hard; and if you do, be courageous to face the difficulties on the way. And spare an affectionate thought for the Black Cloud; its displeasing ways are the products of its pains.[78]

Much of *Fragile voice of love* contains Adam's reflections on this inner journey, on becoming peaceful as well as on making peace. The point is made poignantly in the concluding advice at the end of a short (unpublished) memoir, written for the benefit of his daughters and grandchildren:

> The fate of the world doesn't depend on you. It would be wrong and arrogant to think it did, and to do so might make you ill: I know this from my own experience. On the other hand it would be equally wrong to think that you can contribute nothing to the peace and happiness of the world. The great relationships – between nations, communities, cultures, religions – are built on a foundation of millions of small relations between people, between you and me, for example. Anything we can do to bring harmony, to comfort, to give hope, to encourage another person contributes to the world's reservoir of love. No one can or need to do anything else. But one day you may see, and then take the opportunity to do, something more. But whatever you do, nothing could be better than to be, to nourish your good heart and open it to others.

The arts, unsurprisingly in view of the family environment in which he was nurtured, provided another pathway for him to share understandings of universal values and to illuminate the nature of being as positive peace.[79] The art of Goya and Picasso, he claimed, can tell us more about war and peace than the tables of statistics which academics compile. Chapter 12 presents his essay on *Peace and love: the violin and the oboe*, which refers to Bach's Concerto for Violin and Oboe in D Minor as a musical expression of the polyphonic and harmonious relationship between peace and its essential relationship with love. This was an early example of linking music with peace. The theme was developed some years later by John Paul and Angie Lederach in their book *Soundscapes* (2011), exploring the deepening of feeling and understanding in peacebuilding through music, sound, stories and 'the poetry of presence'. In the final chapter of this book, Chapter 14 – Remembering forward; the visionary practical scholarship of Adam Curle, John Paul highlights the continued importance of Adam's work in responding with compassion, conviction and creativity to the peacemaking challenges of our time.

Here, we reproduce a short prose poem which he placed at the front of *The Hydra* as a tribute to women peacemakers:

Mars asked the planet Earth:
'Who is winning the race?'
'What race?' asked the Earth.
'The human race,' said Mars.
'But you can't win the human race,' said Earth.
'No,' said Mars, 'but you could lose it.'
Venus said, 'If you don't interfere,
Perhaps I could help humanity find itself.'

CHAPTER 11

To tame the Hydra – happiness[80]

Happiness

The title of this chapter speaks for itself, but the concept of happiness as applied to issues of conflict, peace and social change is perhaps new. For me, however, it symbolises the central issues we shall be discussing and so is introduced at some length here.

For a number of years, I have been preoccupied with the relationship between what we are and what we do, our inner and our outer lives. The concept of happiness has been for me the key for unlocking the sad mysteries of inner hatred and outer violence. The reason for this is that true happiness implies freedom from many of those illusions that cloud the essence of our nature, of which happiness is surely a part. Enlightened by it, we can see that anger, fear, hatred and ambition which lead to violence reside in our own minds; any quarrel is a clash of misconceptions. For this reason, happiness is an essential element in the struggle to erode violence; although the work may be hard and the conditions in which it is carried out grimly sombre, it is impassioned by a longing for the happiness of others. If these ideas may sound strange, I should explain that as a half psychologist (the other half is anthropologist) I believe that the pursuit of happiness, as Jefferson put it, is a dominant and universal human drive.

But why happiness rather than some other strong human drive, such as sex, or survival or protective aggression against predators or sexual rivals? My reason is that the quest is the basis of everything we do. Even if what we do is unpleasant, boring, dangerous or painful, *not doing it would be even worse*. Shame or guilt at our laziness or cowardice would, we feel, bring even more unhappiness than doing the displeasing job. What is at stake, then, is preserving as much happiness as is possible in the circumstances.

Our feelings about what we should do or not do – that is, basically, about what will make us more, or less, happy – are greatly affected by our culture. Paradoxically, in a virtually atheist society our moral code is one that was largely implanted in the social culture by the churches; some of their underlying principles, such as original sin, play a part in the confusion of life today.

Unfortunately, just because happiness is so powerful, it may easily swerve off course to bring about its antithesis. If things go wrong, we blame the circumstances or other people, not realizing that the degree of happiness is also a reflection of our own inner state – and so may often be more important than the actual situation. But not understanding this, our efforts to make up for disappointment or frustration can read inexorably to a fresh cycle of pain, anger or despair.

But what, we may ask, has this to do with happiness? In one sense, of course, nothing. In another, everything; it is the quest for happiness turned upside down.

Happiness, I say again, is a drive. Or, to put it another way, it expresses an urge to restore the primal happiness with which, as William Blake knew, we are born:

> I have no name
> I am but two days old.
> What shall I call thee?
> I happy am,
> Joy is my name ...

And such happiness is shared by other species, as all know who have watched lambs or puppies playing. But it tends not to last because we do not properly understand it and so misuse it. Sex is a similarly powerful drive; it can bring wonderful joy and harmony, or the most bitter unhappiness and distortion.

But what are we really discussing? Happiness is far less easy to define than those conditions which have an apparently largely physical basis, like hunger or perhaps even fear. But however we try to describe it, whatever we think of as happiness is hugely significant, judging by the frequent references to it.

Here are a selection of these:

JEREMY BENTHAM: The greatest happiness for the greatest number is the foundation of morals and legislation.

Aristotle: Happiness is an expression of the soul in considered action.

Dostoyevsky: Happiness does not lie in happiness, but in the achievement of it.

John Keats: Wherein lies happiness? In that which becks/ Our ready minds to fellowship divine/ A fellowship with essence till we shine/ Full alchemised and full of space. Behold,/ The clear religion in the heaven.

The XIVth Dalai Lama: I believe that the very purpose of our life is to seek happiness... the very motion of our life is towards happiness.

Berthold Brecht: The right to happiness is fundamental. Men live so little time and die alone.

George Santayana: Happiness is the only sanction of life.

Immanuel Kant: Virtue and happiness constitute the *summum bonum* of life.

Emile Zola: I have one passion only for light in the name of humanity which has borne so much and has a right to happiness.

Alexander Pope: Oh happiness, our beings aim and end.

Thomas Jefferson: I consider these truths to be self-evident, that all men are equal, that they are endowed by their Creator with certain unalienable rights, and that among these are life, liberty and the pursuit of happiness.

These quotations, and many others, support my belief that the pursuit of happiness, to use Jefferson's term, is truly a drive, a main-spring of human energy as powerful as sex (which is in part one of its manifestations, the two being indeed very closely associated). The pursuit of happiness, like the quest for sexual gratification, can lead us to bliss or to realms of illusion and fantasy. When powerful energies are involved, both miracles and disasters often occur. But wherever the drive for happiness, and/or our illusions about the nature of happiness, may lead us, it must be reckoned an enormous force.

And one which is universal. It can be recognised in its least adulterated form in the play of young animals. Also in human babies – the fact that they also often cry may be attributed, at least in part, to the frustrations of their helplessness as compared with the mobility of youngest creatures. In terms of psychoanalysis the pleasure principle (the Freudian term for the drive for happiness) is deeply rooted in the unconscious, the id, impelling us to action, however disastrous.

Legitimacy of the happiness concept

Happiness may, of course, be eclipsed or at least weakened by many things: by childhood neglect or abuse, by violence or indigence, or by perverse example, by sickness – or simply and perhaps almost universally, by ignorance.

However, instead of now considering what drives it off course, let us consider its source. Here I must depart from the analytic assumption of a blind and essentially selfish happiness drive and posit a more positive human nature, one having a great potential for wisdom, generosity and compassion. This potential can perhaps best be cultivated by social or personal example, by wise education, and by the awakened consciousness of the individual.

Why should you agree with this approach? I can offer no proof, except to say that I have found it to be true. I have met a number of men and women whose acts, and our traditions, would encourage us to think of them as 'bad' but invariably, if they were dealt with generously and justly, their latent humanity and 'goodness' was evoked.

Also, of course, many of the world's great philosophies and religions have stressed our wonderful latent capacities. Buddhism, which is both agnostic and noncredal (the Buddha stressed that we must work things out for ourselves) and less a religion than a psycho/philosophical system, is pre-eminent in this respect. It holds that all beings have the Buddha nature. Neither is any action called 'sinful'. Instead, it is branded 'unskilful', that is to say an unskilful means of attaining the goal of understanding, of being aware of the nature of reality (this is often referred to as enlightenment, but this gives it a falsely mystical nuance). Our endowment is claimed to be inherently perfect in the sense that our *machinery*, our physical and mental *equipment* is essentially perfect. But we forget, misuse and become deluded about it.

Christianity is superficially very different. There is considerable stress on 'sin' as being 'original', though Paul and Augustine, rather than Jesus, must take most of the blame for the concept. The idea of innate wickedness has caused many millions to feel badly about themselves, and abjectly to pray forgiveness for the apparently unavoidable fact that 'there is no health in us'. But many Christians also think of the 'Christ nature' and the 'Christ within'which is not so different from the Buddhist belief.

So far as I am aware, no major religious system, certainly not Islam, Hinduism or Judaism, has any belief similar to original sin. Equally, however, not all would teach the basic goodness of human nature, except perhaps some versions of Hinduism and Sufi Islam. (I should mention, however, that religion is not the only source of guilt feelings. They are often based on ill-treatment or neglect in infancy, which makes a young child feel unlovable and therefore wicked, because it would otherwise be loved by its parents.)

In the realm of depth psychology, psychoanalysis particularly emphasizes the inexorable inner conflict of good and evil (though the eminent John Bowlby asserts that 'humans are pre-programmed to develop in a socially cooperative way'). Less so, however, those such as Jung in his analytic psychology, and Assagioli in his psychosynthesis, who go perhaps even further than the Buddhists in what some call (I personally question the term), *spiritual* psychology. So do various other forms of depth psychology including the transpersonal and humanistic, also Eastern psycho-philosophies such as various forms of yoga.

Once we accept that we are born with a basically pristine nature, we can without prejudice consider the psychology of happiness.

Primal happiness

First, we are born happy (apart from the potentially damaging character of birth). We experience primal happiness. This is a condition we rarely experience in adult life. It is pure joy, inseparable from any outside circumstances. It may come quite unexpectedly, on awaking perhaps from sleep. It can only be described as unalloyed delight in being alive.

But our initially pristine nature does not normally remain so for long. We are born into a web of relationship with parents, siblings and other close family members; this is our earliest educational experience. We learn from it what is good and what is bad, and since the behavioural idiom of all families differs, we all learn slightly different things and in a slightly – or indeed sometimes, greatly – different manner.

In particular, we learn how to strive towards happiness in adverse circumstances which, moreover, we do not understand. We make mistakes.

What we thought would bring an euphoric response has the opposite effect. What we hoped would arouse pity merely irritates.

In the face of adult or sibling disfavour, we build up defences which may only make things worse – and us more unhappy – so that a miserable cycle of mutual aggravation becomes habitual, and primal happiness obscured.

Of course the story is not all so grim. Care, sensitivity – and it must be admitted good luck – may create a very happy milieu in which the child may develop without conflict or manipulation.

In this case s/he will grow up with the original endowment of wisdom, generosity and compassion much less damaged than that of those who have had to struggle and in a sense distort their nature to obtain – or indeed to fail to obtain – a quota of happiness. But we have to admit that this is very much a matter of degree. Some have had to strive for happiness (and generally speaking, the more we struggle the more we fail) harder than others; but none escape without any effort. Everyone's capacity for enjoyment of pure primal happiness is impaired.

Existential happiness

A type of happiness which is somewhat less intense and less unusual I would refer to as existential happiness. This is felt, in my limited experience, after some difficult or dangerous ordeal. It does not, however, relate to the ordeal, which fades into the mental background. I assume that some combination of relief and relaxed tension breaks through the veil of misconception and externalisation that obscures the primal source. It is important to recognise that both primal and existential happiness differ from what we shall discuss in the following paragraphs in that they do not make demands, they are self-sufficient.

Conditional happiness

This is not the case with two related forms of the drive [for happiness]. Both are conditional in the sense of the *if* qualification; if I had... could... knew... etc. I would be happy. These are divided into the *rational* and the *ignorant*.

The rational conditional (apologies for the cumbersome terms) drive for happiness is felt by those who need what is necessary to fulfil themselves and care for the essential needs of their families for such things as food, shelter, healthcare, education and justice. When these are satisfied, a far greater quota of primal happiness is restored.

By contrast the drive I term 'ignorant' is towards goals that, in the material though not the psychological sense, are non-essential. They are for recognition, popularity, admiration, envy and similar ego-boosters. The means of achieving these would, for example, be through owning a new car, going on holiday to fashionable resorts, keeping a good cellar, the tasteful decor of one's home and, in general, possessions. position and power.

The drive adapts to different levels and types of culture and sophistication. I knew one unfortunate man who had served many years in gaol for trivial offences. His proud boast was that it had been a maximum security prison, not any ordinary clink, where his friends had been the Great Train Robbers.

The main purpose of this distorted aspect of the drive for happiness is to enable us to look in the mental mirror and to like what we see; to free us of the feelings of worthlessness and guilt arising, perhaps, from experiences that have made us feel unloved, and so in great need of the reassurance of popularity and approval.

An additional and perhaps more universal source is the sense of having lost or failed to cultivate our wonderful inner potential. This is often felt as a poignant but unidentified bereavement.

I must emphasize that the differentiation between the two conditional drives is not in any sense judgemental. Virtually everyone experiences both according to the shifting circumstances of their lives. If the conditions that emphasize the rational should improve, we may enjoy the luxury of the irrational drive with its ego-serving aspirations and desires. The more we do so, however, the more our peace of mind is jeopardised and the true primal source of happiness obscured.

The gratification obtained from both conditional drives, particularly the ignorant drive, is likely, because of ever-changing conditions both material and emotional, to be short-lived. We are commonly deluded into feeling, although we intellectually know this to be untrue, that conditions in which we are happy will last forever.

Our gratification is based on a second illusion: that happiness depends on external circumstances. I was disillusioned about this at the age of five. I longed for a particular toy – a gun, in fact! This my mother at first refused to give me, yielding at last, however, to my importuning. Now, I said to myself, I shall be happy forever, I shall never want anything again. But a few days later I found myself in tears over some trivial mishap. I realized I had been wrong; I saw that happiness did not come from outside but from within.

Wanting and yearning

The main difference between primal and existential happiness on the one hand, and on the other the conditional happiness drives, is that the latter are inseparable from wanting and yearning; where these are present, there is potential conflict and violence. Issues of identity are often involved with desiring and thus easily side-step into rivalry and hostility. This almost invariably generates a potentially vicious cycle in which the chances of true happiness are enormously diminished through the very drives which emanate from primal happiness.

Visualise a circle. One point on it is labelled 'ignorance and illusion', another is marked 'longing, desiring, lust' or other comparable words, a third is designated 'hatred, anger, dislike' etc. Start anywhere, but ignorance is perhaps easiest. It means ignorance of our true nature, our basic identity which is our great potential for happiness, wisdom and compassion. This, however, is to some extent clouded over, as we shall see as we progress round the circle. Next comes longing. This is the attempt to compensate for the loss of happiness, and forgetfulness of the true nature, by getting things or arranging situations which will serve as substitutes. But these all fail later, or probably sooner.

The failure of longing to assuage our pain disturbs and distresses us. We feel anger or resentment towards the people or situations on which we pin responsibility for our failures.

These negative emotions further obscure the source of happiness and our other great potential qualities; the yearning desire for something to make up for our loss grows stronger, but our increasingly frantic efforts fail yet more bitterly; our furious hatred grows; our illusions become more obsessive... round and round it goes.

Threats to happiness: externality and identity

As we mature we tend to become infected with what might be termed externality (the second great illusion referred to above): the happiness drive turns hopefully towards the enjoyment and manipulation of what is outside us. These things are not only not the source of happiness, however good they may be, but what they are is inherently impermanent. Thus they become the occasion for disappointment, frustration, desperation, the sense of loss and, perhaps in the end, rage and violence.

This illusion, however, not only affects our happiness, but the character of our whole civilisation. Over long periods of time, these externalities may become crystallized in military, economic or social institutions, or in traditions which to a considerable extent freeze our expectations, and consequently patterns of behaviour, in a relatively lasting fashion. We expect to have more and more wars, so we create and maintain armies, staff colleges, intelligence agencies. We expect to carry out our affairs with money, so we create and maintain banks, stock exchanges, corporations (but what if, instead, we used barter and exchange of services? What if the taking of interest, as still in some Islamic banks and in early Christianity were illegal?). The symbiosis of our need for happiness and the external means we devise for its satisfaction contribute to destruction and rivalry throughout the world.

But the essence of joy, the great happiness potential, is an integral part of our nature. Though obscured by preoccupation with externalities as memory may be by alcohol, its primal source still pervades our being with its warmth. It may, however, feel like central heating set very low; and the greater the obscuration, the deeper the chill.

Paradoxically, however, although the peaceful joy of primary happiness is dimmed, the great driving force, the 'pursuit of happiness', persists. In fact, its degree of power is the very function of its failure. The urge to achieve, to have, to be, to overcome what is wrong with our lives, becomes stronger with our lack of success. We want these things, however paltry. Without them we feel we are to a greater or lesser extent empty, incomplete, uneasy – in a word *unhappy*. No matter that what we want is trivial, to the degree that we desire it, we feel it is the one condition of happiness. But being based on externals it is fragile and evanescent and, at best, simply a state of less pain. But it may, of course, lead to something of terrible import – the crazed ambition of a Hitler!

A major aspect of the ignorant drive, which like the others, affects almost all of us to some degree, is the quest for identity. We long to feel we are someone, to be identified as distinguished by particular set of qualities. We all have an idea of who we are. It is cobbled together of things which belong to us or to which we belong. What seems to us to be distinctive may be our appearance, our education, our particular skills or profession, our family and so on and so on. These locate us in society and, if we are important enough, in the world – but of course for some unfortunates a sad self-image locates them in a rather miserable spot.

Our identity is partly a conscious and partly an unconscious construct. We take an open pride in being the woman or man who has achieved this or that. When we prepare our c.v. for a job application we marshal all the facts we think will make a good impression – carefully tempered not to sound too boastful. This much is of course conscious. I recall, however, how my award of a certain academic honour unconsciously affected my self-view. I was working with a group of exceptionally brilliant people and from time to time suffered a displeasing sense of inferiority. When this happened, however, a ray of comfort from an unknown source would lighten my depression. It was months before I realized that my largely forgotten award (not shared by most of the others) suggested I was not as stupid as I feared I must be.

Most importantly, our identity gives us a sense of our own reality. This is ME, and I am separate from and different from you. But this is another illusion to obscure our perception of reality and to cover primal happiness with the fog of ignorance.

We are not simply the product of our parents, genes, but of our whole human environment, its culture, teachers, our experiences, the artistic and philosophical influences that have played on us. All of these are incorporated in our being, just as our being is incorporated into that of countless others. Every change in our circumstances also changes us. Today I am different from what I was yesterday – how much more so last year, a decade ago, a half century ago. How differently I feel and act with people I love from how I do on formal occasions; when being professional and when being social; when jolly and when miserable; thoughtful or frivolous.

Who, in fact, am I? What is my true identity – indeed, do I have one?

We shield ourselves from these awkward questions because we base much of our social philosophy and psychological belief upon the traditional concept of 'I'. The prospect of recognising it as a fiction is very alarming.

It is, however, necessary, if we are to understand how to deal with the problems of violence, hatred and despair which are largely the subject of these pages. It is necessary to do so if we are to enjoy fully our birth right of happiness.

First of all, I should say that the deconstruction of the self as a completely self-existent, separate entity does not mean that you and I do not exist as recognisable individuals. The nature of our being can be perhaps best reconstructed by analogy with the Tibetan parable of Indra's Net described in the following short poem.

> At each intersection of the endless net
> of Indra's heaven, according to the myth,
> there is a bead that represents a life.
> Each bead reflects every other
> and every reflection of every other.
> In the sub-atomic field every hadron
> Affects and is affected by all the rest,
> resulting in a flux of energy and movement
> in which little can be foretold
> save unpredictability and endless change.

We do in fact possess unique individuality but it is an individuality forged from the flow of energy and wisdom from countless multidirectional sources, playing upon our original inherited endowment; a wonderful paradox of unity in diversity as an endless source of happiness.

Money and wealth

These words exemplify another of the great illusions. Advertisements for lotteries and other money-making schemes show the successful investors grinning, prancing or expressing other physical symptoms of supposed great happiness. In fact, what many people believe they want most of all is money, equating money with joy. However, except when cash enables us to save a sick child or avoid some dreadful adversary money of itself does not stave off misery. This is something known to us all, but we do not act on that knowledge.

We should, however, learn better. Unless some means is found for controlling the speculation that is devastating the world's markets, we may all face poverty and must learn to live with it without loss of happiness.

But loss of money does not mean loss of wealth. The wealth that enables us to live richly is the cultivation of our great inner resources of wisdom, loving appreciation and the deep primal happiness. These are far more than compensatory substitutes for crass cash; they are the true stuff of life, the real stuff of all these pages.

Discussion

To end this chapter, I should explain further the relevance of happiness to an examination of the Hydra and the culture of violence.

The degree of clarity of primal happiness is like a thermometer measuring our ability to deal constructively with these things. This source of happiness does not, of course, depend on circumstances, it is not conditional. It is happiness unrelated to the satisfaction of cravings – which are often very evanescent and always impermanent, usually leading to unhappiness, more craving, more disappointment, more unhappiness... The more free we are of the illusions of the ignorant conditional drive and of the false identity associated with it, the more we are liberated to transform the Hydra and to erode its related culture.

The extent, frequently mentioned, of our own implication with the Hydra depends on the extent to which we are entrapped by these illusions. This in turn depends to some extent on the shifting flow of circumstances, but – as with seasonal temperature – we tend to have an average degree of hallucination. The higher it is, the less our capacity for sustained positive action; and the lower, the greater.

It is often said that our age is particularly materialistic. In the clumsy terms used here, this would suggest domination by the ignorant conditional drive; a great need for and strong expectation of happiness gained from acquisition.

Although it is not hard to assess addiction to consumerism in individuals, it is very difficult to judge whole societies in this respect. Nevertheless, I have known communities in which people who had very little seemed to want very little, but appeared, contrary to what might be expected in the West, happy and high-spirited.

By contrast it appears, superficially at least, that the members of our high consumption society are less relaxed and light-hearted than, for example, my beloved Chakmas[81] before their communal destruction. This suggests that we are more overwhelmed by, and by the same token, less able to resist the allure of the glamorous opportunities of the Hydra and the culture of violence.

I should emphasize my belief that it is possible for us to lower the average threshold of craving, of the ignorant conditional drive. Or, if the circumstances provoking self-pity, fear, vanity or longing are aggravated, to raise it. I have pondered the usefulness of suggesting measures for lowering the threshold. However, there is such a variety of measures suited to an equal variety of individuals that this could simply prove confusing. I will only say that the essence of virtually all approaches is *awareness*.

I hope I have shown clearly the significant interconnectedness of Hydra and happiness. Because of our failures of understanding, our happiness drive easily degenerates to the ignorant conditional – we shall be happy IF... we have, or can do this, that or the other particular thing. If we can only achieve this at the expense of another, *tant pis*. Slaves, for example, have seemed particularly desirable acquisitions to increase our prosperity in some places at certain stages, beginning perhaps in Babylon and continuing in various ways until today, and until recently in South Africa.

(It could be argued that, rather than happiness, the love that 'makes the world go round' should be considered as the greatest clue to understanding violent, as well as tender and cooperative human behaviour. It certainly is one of the great clues; without doubt, moreover, love and happiness are inextricably interwoven at the summit of human bliss. It is, however, also a complex and contradictory clue, in large part because of the sex factor, also because it had been romanticised in so many and such diverse ways. Happiness, as I understand and have tried to explain it, can be more clearly analysed and directly related to experience.)

Postscript

It may seem surprising that the word peace has hardly appeared in these chapters. It is a complex and confusing concept, very often used simply to indicate the end of fighting. However, this would leave us with a very limited and shallow view of the condition. Some decades ago I coined the terms peaceful and unpeaceful relations as applying to any relationship from the transpersonal to the transnational in which, if peaceful, the parties did each other more good than harm; and if unpeaceful, the other way around.

It may be that in thinking of happiness, I am referring to one component of peace or peaceful relations. Certainly the two are very compatible, perhaps sometimes identical.

Nevertheless, my vision of happiness is of an all-embracing cheerfulness and confidence, a joyous acceptance of life; the French phrase *joie de vivre* is highly significant. This is a quality I find rare even among those whose relationships with everyone are delightfully warm and friendly. But apart from this, what I think of as happiness adds a zip, a zest. It has a force most urgently needed to impact the world, and it seems to me to be in very short supply.

Many possible reasons for this lack are embedded in the personal history of women and men, but it is heightened by their belief that there is nothing they can do, that they are helpless against the implacable forces of militarism or the market.

But these essentially peaceful people must be transformed into *powerful* people eager to struggle valiantly against the rule of the Hydra, not in order themselves to dominate or control, but to turn the focus of its undoubted energies to peacefully creative action. With this in mind, they must first recognise and then cultivate the tremendous strength and wisdom of their own nature.

CHAPTER 12

Peace and love

THE VIOLIN AND THE OBOE[82]

NOTE: *Part of the Bach Concerto in D Minor for violin and oboe was played before the delivery of the lecture. You might like to play it and listen attentively before reading the text!*

I often receive letters, particularly from my younger friends, which end by wishing me peace and love. Their generation, I believe, is wiser than mine, for if we can learn the true meaning of peace and love, and the significance of their relationships, many things will be revealed to us.

The ensuing lecture explores some aspects of these themes. In the hopes of making what is perhaps a compressed and clumsy argument easier to follow, I will begin by outlining the sequence of ideas.

To start with, I give a brief description of the objective qualities of peace. I move on to the more difficult question of subjective peace, describing three of its manifestations, of which only the last is entirely positive. I identify the main obstacle to attaining this form of inner peace as what I term the computer – the process by which we think and act mechanically, often unpeacefully and violently and at variance with our true natures. I then devote some attention to how we might behave if we were more closely in touch with ourselves, and conclude that the more we are so, the more deeply we experience love. But there is a powerful need to seek unity with what is beyond ourselves, a cosmic drive of which human love is a manifestation. It is through love that we find peace, and in love and peace we find the capacity for right action. But in order to achieve this to the fullest extent it is necessary to be reborn, to evolve inwardly.

It might have been expected that a lecture by someone holding a chair in peace studies would sagely analyse the global situation, suggest policies for the United Nations and our own government, denounce violence, propose panaceas for Northern Ireland and Southern Africa, and so on. Now, although I have not withdrawn from outward action I realize that the human being I am determines the value and effect of what I do; and that what I am is a function of my capacity to give and receive love, and to experience peace.

I have consciously been concerned with the quest for peace for about 15 years. I say consciously, because now I realize that much that I had always done was a part of the same quest. There was, however, a definite period of my life when I began to concentrate my attention on war and violence and, shortly after, I became involved directly in mediation efforts in various parts of the world. But although I do not avoid this work, I now see peace as being very much more than the absence of war. An unpeaceful situation, to my mind, is one in which human beings are damaging each other's potential for fulfilment and development in any of a number of ways; not merely by killing and maiming, but by oppressing, exploiting, manipulating, cheating, making excessive demands on others, corrupting, enslaving, humiliating, deriding, frightening or deceiving. These are all forms of violence (the etymology of the word implies the 'unlawful use of force') of violating a person, of doing wanton damage. The fact that the damage need not be physical in no way affects the degree of potential harm for the victim and, albeit in a different way, the perpetrator.

To widen the definition of peace so greatly may sccm to make its achievement impossible. How can human affairs possibly be ordered so as to eliminate all harm? Obviously they cannot. But to the would-be peacemaker this should be taken as encouragement rather than the reverse, for whereas the great conflicts may seem grimly intractable there are many on a lesser scale which are soluble. Moreover, sometimes the vast and lethal issues are built on a foundation of many smaller and less intractable ones which, if dealt with, render them less daunting.

These unpeaceful conditions are based upon relationships dominated by injustice or violence or, very often, both. Peaceful conditions, to reverse the definition, would be those characterised by both justice and the absence of violence. But such a negative description is hardly adequate. We must add to it the positive qualities of mutual respect, toleration, cooperation and, above all, love. Indeed, a peaceful society could hardly exist without these, but mention them to emphasize that peace must be positive, not merely a condition from which certain ills are absent.

So much for the outer conditions of peace. The question of defining inner or subjective peace is far more difficult. We may talk about feeling peaceful, enjoying peace of mind, finding certain places peaceful; and of course we also speak of feeling unpeaceful, and so on. These inner states are clearly very important for both our happiness and our actions, but they are nebulous, fluid and highly personal: when I say that, for example, I feel peaceful, do I mean what you mean when you say the same thing? In attempting to describe three types of experience which might all be considered as forms of inner peace, I shall try to be as precise and factual as possible, because although we are bound to touch upon matters which are virtually ineffable or transcendental, it is good to go as far as we can on the relatively solid ground of common experience.

When we say we are feeling peaceful, or use some equivalent phrase, I believe that we may be referring, without much discrimination, to one of three levels or dimensions of feeling. These levels are separate, although it seems to me that they may overlap in certain circumstances, and that at times the second may lead naturally to the third. I would refer to these three, for brevity and clarity, as lethargy, the release of tension, and bliss.

Lethargy, which could equally be described as indolence, sloth, inactivity, passivity, a condition of being neither agitated nor excited, may be either appropriate and desirable: or the product or some excess or of physical or psychological imbalance. For example, it is good to feel 'peaceful' and quiescent before going to bed, but the heavy drowsiness which follows a large Christmas dinner is much less functional – it is not a part of the process which maintains our strength by ensuring a good sleep. Still more non-functional are those heavy moods by which we are all at times overcome for no easily identifiable reason: there is no desire for activity, one is sleepy. One's incentives are blunted. In a certain limited sense one is peaceful, but this state is hardly the psychological equivalent to the positive peace of cooperation and mutual support we look for between groups.

The peace following release from tension could also be related to satisfied desire, or the removal of worry. We may experience this in many different contexts: relaxing with friends, walking in calm and beautiful surroundings, after danger, after love-making, after reaching a difficult decision, when freed from a nagging anxiety, returning home after a journey, and so on.

This facet of inner peace consists of a quietening of those thoughts, feelings and emotions which normally to some extent keep us active and busy and, on occasion, tense and distracted. Perhaps most of us associate this quietening with things that are good, positive and constructive – love, companionship, beauty or the overcoming of difficulties. But they need not be. What if we are driven, as some are, to seek release from tormenting inner stress by sexual assault; or if the worry from which we are freed came from fear of discovery in some crime: or if our desires are satisfied by great profit from a shady business deal? These are, of course, extreme cases. But most of us must recognise that we too have experienced states in which we were less inwardly restless precisely because we had done something unworthy. We have experienced a sort of peacefulness because we have got our own back on someone who annoyed us, or we have assuaged our sense of inadequacy or guilt at the expense of someone else whom we have manipulated, embarrassed or made to feel foolish or unhappy.

This dimension of inner peace may, then, be selfish and arise from violence, but not necessarily so. The elements of love, awe, reverence, selflessness, can transform it, or at least add a transcendental element. Loving God and loving our neighbours are, after all, our two greatest obligations and they may lead towards each other.

It is mainly love which, I believe, forms the bridge to the third dimension of inner peace. This form of peace is not negative, as is the lethargy characterising the first dimension; nor is it the quiet – which may be good or bad – following the release of tension of the second dimension. It is a condition of untroubled joy, strength and bliss out of which will come very effective and purposeful activity when it is required. One could say that the second form of peace is the *sequel* to activity, and the greater the inner stress leading to that activity the more hectic, exhausting, energy consuming and inefficient it was. The third type of inner peace is the *precursor*, even the source of energy and efficiency. It appears to be one which is natural to humankind and one we have all known on rare occasions. Nevertheless, we have somehow lost much of our understanding of it.

I may be correct in believing that these three levels of peace correspond to the three kinds of happiness described by the Lord Krishna to Arjuna in the Bhagavad Gita, Sattwa, Rajas and Tamas. Please note that they are described in the reverse order to that in which I have described lethargy (Tamas), release of tension or the fruit of action (Rajas) and bliss (Sattwa).

> Who knows the Atman
> Knows that happiness
> Born of pure knowledge:

The joy of Sattwa.
Deep his delight
After strict self-schooling:

Sour toll at first
But at last what sweetness,
The end of sorrow.
Senses also

Have joy in their marriage

With things of the senses,

Sweet at first

But at last how bitter:

Steeped in Rajas,
That pleasure is poison.
Bred of Tamas

Is brutish contentment

In stupor and sloth

And obstinate error:
Its end, its beginning
Alike are delusion.

How is it that we have become ensnared by negative forms of inner peace? From a very early age, society impinges upon us, first through our parents and the pattern they impose upon our behaviour coupled with their expectations of us and increasingly through our contacts with the wider world of people and things. As a result, we become what the sociologists call socialised – that is to say, we learn to respond, and to want to respond, to social stimuli in an acceptable fashion. In the process we all acquire our individual experiences and so build up sets of ideas and beliefs which are peculiar to ourselves. But we also all have some things in common.

The first is that we bear the imprint of our society, whatever it may be: this enables us to make recognisable generalisations, though often inadequate so far as any individual is concerned, about various groups.

The second thing we have in common is that ideas, information, prejudices, desires, needs, etc. that we receive through various media are fed into the great computer we call our brain, the mechanism through which we experience mind. There they are stored, some lying dormant virtually forever perhaps, some constantly activated. Every circumstance of our lives, however trivial and minute, calls for a response from the computer which will, literally with the speed of light, assemble through its infinity of associative channels the information needed to make the appropriate response. In addition to the acquired information, there is no doubt some which could be termed hereditary or instinctual which help to shape our reactions. Thus we behave, to a large extent, automatically. Consider how we can fly, as the saying goes, into rage and do unkind or violent things, for reasons which we afterwards recognise as petty or absurd. Consider how little careful or conscious thought goes into a casual conversation with an acquaintance at a party. The situation calls for certain things we have already learned – a tone of voice, manner, topic of conversation; we can speak with animation, joke, mention matters of current interest without reflection or much subsequent remembrance – the computer had taken over. I could use another analogy, less accurate but perhaps more illustrative – we become like an airman who has switched on the automatic pilot while he rests. But I would not wish to give the impression that the work of the computer is confined to insignificant or what we sometimes call mindless occasions, such as parties or quarrels, in which our main interests may not be engaged. It is just as much in operation when two academics are debating some academic point in their own field. The machine responds equally to an intellectual stimulus by retrieving the appropriate information, arranging and presenting it; the stimulus will probably not, however, be wholly intellectual – there may also be the impetus of hurt pride, the desire to show off, to prove the other person illogical or ill-informed, to prop up flagging self-esteem. The computer is in operation the whole time and its operation covers every aspect of our lives – intellectual, emotional and physical. Even when we are in a condition of passivity and subjected to minimal external stimulus, the computer is, so to speak, idling. If we can stand back from ourselves at such times, we will be aware of a constant flickering flow of thoughts, feelings, memories, ideas – some pleasant, some unpleasant – as one association triggers off another.

The computer is, of course, very useful. It turns us into fairly competent machines, although some computers are less well stocked with information and the channels of association may have broken down – this, I believe, is what has happened in many cases of what we call mental illness – so that the response does not relate properly to the stimulus. But we pay a heavy price. The continuous activity of the computer uses up psychic energy, just as a normal computer uses up energy in the form of electricity, and we waste precious resources in spurts of depression, anger, self-pity, anxiety and so on. Its constant noise drowns out our ability to listen to more subtle sounds. The everlasting flow of associations drives us to unnecessary – indeed, at times frantic and obsessional – mental and physical activity. Most importantly, in the context of a discussion of peace, the fact that our computer – controlled activity is mechanical – implies that violent and destructive behaviour is also automatic. Thus unpeaceful behaviour is an inescapable product of the human condition, which can be avoided only by changing that condition. I have often wondered whether this is not the psychological essence of the theological concept of original sin.

I will approach this from a slightly different direction. The chatter of our computer makes it hard for us to hear other people. Who has not gone to a meeting where everyone spoke past everyone else, and where people were so busy making their own speeches that they never listened to the person actually talking? Sometimes, in my experience, a proposal made early in a meeting is rejected because no one really heard it, but is accepted when repeated later because for some reason the group have become more able to listen. Many of the Native Americans, whom we used to call American Indians, make it a regular part of their children's education to teach them to listen. When my Native American friends came to visit me, they would sit very quietly for a few minutes. They were stilling the noise of their own thoughts and feelings so that they could better listen, not only to my words, but to my feelings, to sense my mood, and to understand what they could best do to help, encourage or strengthen me; and this they were always able to do.

However, if one really listens to others, one also listens to oneself. By the very fact of quieting oneself, switching off the computer, which usually requires a conscious effort, a purposeful giving of attention to a task or – in this case – another person, one is in touch with the non-automatic part of the self, the part below or beyond the computer. What one then says in response to the other person constitutes a very profound contact. It is not one machine reacting to another machine, but one inner self, or whatever term one uses, communicating with another inner self. This communication may seem like a meeting on common ground, as though below the computer there were a shared base of universal knowledge. We might use fingers and a hand as an analogy. We are like fingers joined to a hand in which we have a common existence, but we have forgotten about the hand and behave as though we had been severed; thus we communicate with each other very ineffectively.

It could be argued that what I am talking about is only another more sophisticated computer. I can only say that, in so far as my experience goes, it feels quite different. Not only is it lighter, happier, more effective and constructive, and completely non-violent, but it appears to reach beyond what I thought I knew. Let me give a couple of examples. A friend was discussing a strange personal problem with me. My computer dredged up every possible scrap of relevant knowledge and experience in an attempt to say something helpful, but I could see he was increasingly disappointed by my failure to be at all constructive. I then decided I must switch off the computer and made the effort to compose myself in quietness. Very soon and without any premeditation, words simply came out of me, and I could see by my friend's expression that I had said something which had real meaning for him. A second example concerns a recent trip to America. I visited several universities and in one of them gave as many as five lectures a day, to different groups and on different topics. Since it was out of the question to do detailed preparation for them, I decided to go to the opposite extreme and give them no advanced thought whatsoever. Before each lecture I made myself as inwardly quiet as possible, trying both to reach into my own depths and to listen to the group I was to address. Then I spoke spontaneously, and really believe that have seldom given better talks. Moreover, at the end of what might have been gruelling days, I was perfectly fresh. I was perhaps helped in this because, being a Quaker, I am accustomed to waiting quietly for what we call a 'moving of the Spirit', and I have also learned something of forms of meditation emphasising inner stillness.

I am sure it will be obvious where this discussion is leading. We are to a large extent dominated by potentially destructive automatic responses which derive from a combination of heredity and conditioning, and the first two dimensions of what we might refer to as inner peace are, apart from the saving grace of love in some, as much a part of this conditioning as is unpeacefulness. To this extent they are neither positive nor purposeful, being either a product of lethargy, or of the release of tension. If, however, it is possible to go below or beyond what I have been calling the computer, we touch an entirely different level of our being. It can tap great springs of energy and has access to extraordinary knowledge. There is no need to debate whether this knowledge is 'esoteric' or 'supernatural': it is enough to recognise that there are within us and all creatures incredible mechanisms which regulate our growth and the functioning of our organs, enable us to adjust to changed conditions, mobilise our defences against disease and respond, as in the case of menstruation, to extra-terrestrial forces. The wisdom inherent in the human organism is so amazing that we need not bother with mystifying or controversial epithets. This universal human knowledge is quite apart from the specialised knowledge stored by the computer, much of which, such as knowledge of a particular language or set of circumstances, is special to a particular person. The deeper knowledge could be thought of as an ocean in which our individualities are dissolved, so that we are in touch with – indeed, perhaps form a part of – all other human beings. Or it could be considered as something which all human beings have in common, such as two arms and legs and a head: and that when we enter our own deeper territory we can understand that same territory in others. But again, such a debate is academic. The fact is indisputable to all – which means most of us – who have experienced it and recognise that they have done so: there are within us endless sources of strength and wisdom. In addition, there are capacities for communication which go infinitely far beyond the normal exchange of verbal symbols. Once again I would not wish to discuss whether or not this constitutes telepathy: I would simply suggest that the level beyond the computer retains the capacity to communicate in ways the computer cannot.

To the extent that we can switch off the computer and reach this more universal and far greater level of awareness, we may experience the third, and true, dimension of inner peace. By disconnecting the associative and retrieval mechanism however temporarily we achieve stillness, and in stillness we can experience that calm and radiant bliss, which is not only in itself delightful, but transforms our whole self and replenishes our depleted stores of energy. This peace, although infinitely restorative, is far from passive. The energy it enables us to draw on or create is given a teleological direction, because inner peace and knowledge which makes clear demands on us, coming from the same level, are one. We are enjoined to 'Be still and know that I am God.' Am I then asserting that the third level of inner peace is the peace of God? I do not know, and can only be sure that there are many spheres of which I have no awareness. I must indeed apologise for discussing things of which I have such limited experience, but my experience, such as it is, points me in this direction and I am following the shadowy sign-posts as far as I dare without irreverent and presumptuous claims.

It seems to me that if we can approach, however briefly, this ground of our being where inner peace truly dwells, we find love. I suggested earlier that the element of love in the second dimension of peace could transform it, leading it deeper and farther. It may essentially lead us to the source of all love, the element in which we and all creation exist and without which we should be nothing. The love which we individual human persons feel for each other draws us, unless we use it selfishly in the hopes of enhancing our identities, to a universal love which is the energising dimension of universal knowledge, powering the whole creation. At some moments of inner peace, we may be privileged to glimpse the stupendous reality of objective love.

I would now like to return, from a slightly different direction, to the definitions of peace and its relationship to love. I can add to my original definition of outer peace as a situation or relationship in which damage is done by suggesting that it is also one from which love is absent. As a consequence of the absence of love, people are separated from each other, sundered by hatred, fear, suspicion, prejudice, pride, ignorance or traditional enmities, or by barriers of colour, politics, religion, caste, class, language or sex. Peace, by contrast, is a condition in which people are united, in which those who were separated are reconciled, in which they are joined in love.

Love and peace, however imperfectly we understand them, are forces which have enormous power over us. We yearn for what we conceive as peace; we constantly seek, both to give and to receive, what we call love. The reason, I believe, is that we all have a deep longing for a union which transcends the painful limitations of our constricting individualities. Even though we pass through life half-awake to reality, we have a faint and unformulated memory of a state in which our loneliness is dissolved by merging with a greater whole, uniting with what is beyond us.

This striving for oneness might be thought of as an expression of the sexual drive. I would think rather that the opposite is true. Apart from its specifically reproductive function, sex could be thought of less as the motive force for union than as an instrument to be employed in the quest to achieve it. Indeed, sex may have nothing to do with union, or only at the crudest physical and loveless level as in rape or the coupling of two people without mutual affection. Equally sex may be completely irrelevant to love, to the love of children, of old people, of friends, of many for whom we may feel deep but not sensual affection. Sex may well be quite unnecessary to the true closeness of those who, such as long-married couples, have experienced and enjoyed the fullness of pleasure and fusion. Even more important and utterly separate from sex is the burning yet in a sense impersonal love for the poor, the oppressed, the suffering, the deprived, which has impelled so many fine human beings to lead sacrificial lives of service: this is perhaps the most noble dimension of human love. Yet we all, in whatever circumstances, yearn to be closer to each other, just as a lover yearns to be closer to the beloved; there is a slight, wistful melancholy that we must be forever apart.

In some settings sex may, of course, have an important role in bringing about greater closeness between individuals and indeed leading them towards an even wider union. It may provide for many people their nearest approximation to the spiritual states significantly described by many mystical writers in allegories of physical love. Here sex is the tool of love, helping men and women to move beyond their painful and artificial isolation to a state of peace in which they are freed from the burden of conflict, doubt and illusion. It can serve as a mechanism for both actualising human oneness, and vouchsafing a glimpse of the transcendent, a foretaste of the mystical union. The sexual union of people who are in tune with each other is not only physically fulfilling: it also helps them to escape from the normal limitations of time, space and personality and enter a world of wider and more vivid reality, an experience from which their lives may derive greater purpose.

All who love deeply, not only lovers in a physical sense, make love, or – to avoid ambiguity – create love. This is to say they together weave a beautiful filament of warmth, comfort and caring, which of course is of incalculable value to them as individuals and has I believe an even deeper significance. Loving, the creation of love by whatever means is, I am sure, our most important task. In carrying it out we replenish the world's supply of this most precious fabric – perhaps fuel would be a more appropriate word – and approach our own rebirth. Through loving, that is through right action conforming to the eternal principles, we draw nearer the centre of things, the still, everlasting, vibrant source of creation both within and outside ourselves. Then we begin to understand the reality behind such overworked but perhaps little understood sayings as 'God is love', and learn that through love of each other we have been led towards the great objective love that rules the universe: that quite literally, in the words of another cliché, makes the world go around. All the world loves a lover goes yet another saying, and it is true. People who love each other deeply create around themselves an atmosphere of calmness and joy which is enormously attractive. This is because they have reached the constant and universal in each other's being and those who meet them cannot fail to be touched by what is revealed. At the same time, we learn the inner meaning of peace. It is only as we move towards the eternity of love that we free ourselves from anger, fear, pride and ignorance that are the source of disquiet in our minds, and sow disunity between ourselves and others.

I had sometimes wondered why peacemakers are referred to in the Beatitudes as the children of God, that highest of all designations. I now understand it is because they must not only be at peace within themselves, that is free of inner disharmonies, but also carry the crucial responsibility for establishing unity, of bringing together what had been separate. This it seems to me, emphasizes that our striving for oneness is far more than a dislike of loneliness. We have a potentiality for spiritual evolution, however dimly we perceive it, and the way of growth is the way of union. This we seek, often vainly and foolishly, driven by a half-remembered dream. But our underlying motive is not selfish satisfaction, because the evolution of individuals into wider consciousness serves the purposes of creation. Those who do evolve become the salt, that is to say the preservative, which protects the world from decay.

In those final words of counsel and comfort which Jesus gave his disciples, according to the Gospel of St. John, the themes of love and peace are brought together with compelling power. 'I give you a new commandment,' he admonished them, 'Love one another; as I have loved you, so you are to love one another.' Later he said, 'Peace is my parting gift to you, my own peace, such as the world cannot give,' and later again, 'Dwell in my love.' But the whole message is one of love, recurring time after time: the love of God, the love of Jesus for the disciples, of them for him and of their love for one another; and of peace, the complement of love. These great themes can be identified in another inspired but very different work, the Bhagavad Gita, which actually ends with the words 'Shanti. Shanti. Shanti.' ('Peace. Peace. Peace.')

I have just mentioned rebirth and evolution, related themes common to many of the great teachings. We must change; we must be reborn. As I have tried, over the past years, to grapple with the problems of violence and injustice, I have realized increasingly how little I can do as I am. Without an inner evolution I cannot act wisely, I cannot predict the results of my actions, I cannot understand the nature of the problems I am presumptuously attempting to solve because I view them through the same distorting lens as those who created them. Above all, I am the slave of my computer, with its stock of mind-cluttering ideas and information and consequently am just as prone to violence as those I might wish to curb. The world is awash with political, economic, psychological and technological panaceas, some of which I have tried with naive enthusiasm, but my experience has led me to the boring and old-fashioned conclusion that to act with effectiveness and knowledge, I must be a knowledgeable and effective human being. I do not mean, of course, that I should do nothing until I am perfect – in that case I would indeed do nothing. I must do what I can in the faith that if I try with inner stillness to act for the good my efforts will not be wasted; and in humility recognise their limitations.

Like many others, I know some of the answers theoretically, both at a practical and a philosophical level. For example, I believe I know how to bring to a conclusion one of the world's more violent situations, but I cannot act on my knowledge – which means that it is not in the real sense knowledge! I know that we should love our enemies, and if we did that we would have made peace, because when we loved them they would cease to be our enemies. But this we cannot do until we are reborn, until we become again as little children to whom belongs the Kingdom of Heaven. Jesus did not refer to them in this way because of a sentimental liking for young people, but because he knew them for what they are: beings whose computers have not developed, whose vision has not been swamped by the myriad trivia of ideas, prejudices, misconceptions and so-called facts.

Children in time become adults, but adults have the chance, if they have the courage and strength to take it, of burning off their conditioning and becoming once more as children, that is being reborn and developing anew so that their inherent knowledge and strength may be properly used, for peacemaking as for all other purposes.

Return to the purity and accuracy of childhood vision is associated, at least in my mind, with return to the Garden of Eden. In the infancy of the world, according to the legend, all creatures dwelt there in peace and harmony. There then occurred a crisis comparable to the invasion of the mind by the computer, replacing its knowledge with lies and illusions. But if we are reborn and return to childhood it is not merely a personal return, in some sense we return to a different world, or perhaps I should say we discover we had always lived in Eden. We suddenly see that the people whom we had disliked or feared or felt alien to are very like ourselves, and that below the surface of quirk and idiosyncrasy, they are wise and good, and we can be at peace with them.

I have gone as far as my limited knowledge and the equal limitation of words to express it enable me to go. Peace and love constitute a kind of celestial double helix, a glorious pattern of interwoven powers reaching from our inner selves to the depths of eternity. They are like the solo instruments in Bach's Concerto for Violin and Oboe, separate but absolutely interdependent in the creation of ordered beauty.

I cannot do better than conclude with the valediction of the young, thus repeating the title of this lecture: peace and love.

CHAPTER 13

The fragile voice of love
and prose poems[83]

Cloudy self

The Black Cloud and the concept of the self are intimately connected, but not identical. The Black Cloud, as I have tried to define it, is the collective tainting of the human mind by catastrophic and horrible happenings, such as war. Such are megadeaths, torturing, destruction of homes and communities, concentration camps, massacres, brutal oppression that have dominated the world scene for almost a century. The misery and despair caused by these dreadful events have driven peace from the heart of many millions, even those who have not suffered directly. It shows in distorted community life, especially among the young through violence and addictions and – naturally – hostility towards adults who, they feel, have so distorted the world. This is somewhat unfair because the Cloud affects them too, if differently. Take me, for example: I have not undergone the frightful pangs and anguish that so many have suffered, but simply knowing of these things and from time to time and place to place being directly touched by them, I have shared a fragment of the pain.

But the harm of the Black Cloud is not simply knowing about or suffering from these catastrophes: it invades the mind with illogical dread and unease and in some cases despair. In this way we share the misery of those who have directly suffered the imprisonment, the persecution, the loss. One of the ills of the Black Cloud is that it distorts. We who sit comfortably at home watching the television reports of war or famine, may well be relatively untouched, but the waves of terror and despair emanating from those happenings impart a deep uneasiness, the full force of which we may not recognise. The misery or grief may come from a past incident, but once a mind is touched by it, the reverberations will spread, perhaps very widely.

Belief in the self is an illusion, the ultimate illusion that 'I' is the Supreme Being – I love, I AM everything that is. The reality of 'emptiness' and 'mind' are utterly incompatible with that of the deluded self. They are also completely different, of course, from that of the ego. The ego is the self-concept which someone tries, not always with success, to present a favourable enough view of (and to) her/himself. Someone with what is called a strong ego is one who is self-confident, assured, holds strong opinions and expresses them emphatically. This is not the same as being egotistical, which usually means selfish but not necessarily strong-minded. These somewhat niggling little definitions are unfortunately needful if we are to identify the Black Cloud syndrome as something different from, if linked to, other emotional conditions, primarily perhaps anxiety, paranoia and depression.

I am not suggesting for a moment that the Black Cloud effect should supersede the existing psychiatric categories, but am simply saying that it intensifies and probably ramifies existing problems. It may also complicate them by multiplying the elements which compose them. For example, we do not know (as far as I am aware) whether different sources of suffering – a wound, torture, death of a baby from famine or from bombing – call for different treatments. There are probably many issues of this sort which have not been elucidated.

These uncertainties are probably ill-informed. So much the better if that is the case. Of one thing, however, I am quite certain. The physical ills to which so much of humanity has been subjected during the last 100 years have caused, or been amplified enormously, by misery. But at the same time we are also reminded that the self is the stumbling block, the shackle that holds us back from what we might do or be.

Let's try, however, to think (or imagine) about how we can overcome the stumbling block of the self. Or rather, having gone so far, ask what next.

To think back, we envisage that the hold of the self has weakened and that the power of the Universal Mind has strengthened proportionately. I can say no more. I can only feel sure that when (if?) I reach that point, the next tentative step will be a long stride. But whither?

But it is pointless to inveigh against the Black Cloud, since we have all taken a part, however small, in its development. The most important task is to understand it. The first point is that there is a dynamic interaction between the Cloud and human beings. In the relatively normal situation, such as existed towards the end of the 19th century, a few decades after the end of the Franco-Prussian war and before the start of World War I in 1914, it was relatively weak and inoffensive.

There had, of course, been minor disturbances, but in the fairly calm atmosphere, the psychic wounds of grief could be more or less dissipated by the joys and affections of ordinary existence. But the beginning of World War I marked the start of a saturnalia of death continuing at least to the day I write. This is also a period of enormous technical development, much of it concerned with military hardware, particularly more lethal weaponry. That, of course, was part of our sad age – but just imagine a bizarre epoch in which people travelled in planes and cars, but still fought with bows and arrows!

As it is, however, whether we are actively implicated in conflict or not, we are greatly concerned with war and armaments. Many of us remember the social and political agitation seething around the now quaintly old-fashioned atom bomb! And such turmoil is in fact seldom far from our consciousness. Our young men are being killed in Iraq. We are expecting to be attacked by frantic Muslims in some desperate 9/11 suicide/murder outrage. And more and more people are armed to protect us.

I hope I have made the point that even if we may, thankfully, be spared the loss of a daughter or son, we share the anxiety, anger and misery of living in a world of futile and deceitful war (even if Iraq were peaceful), contributing to the opacity of the Cloud and holding back the healing that the world so badly needs.

Most people who read this, and I who write it, will dislike the Black Cloud, but even our opposition will give it some nourishment: paradoxically, we hurt ourselves, confused in our minds with love for the sufferers who contribute most to the Cloud and who bitterly oppose more muddled minds. Desperate reactions oppose their desperate source.

We are not only affected by the Cloud, but our response to it is to think and behave in a manner that creates yet more misery, as each enormity generates more of itself, and so on and so on ad infinitum - thus more muddled minds and desperate reactions. Examples of such horrible cycles have become increasingly common in recent years. The most humanitarian enterprises go wrong: the US mission to help the Somalis, the war in Sierra Leone, the recent violation in the Western Congo – all are examples of the knock-on psychic principles culminating, for the time being, in mayhem in Iraq.

The great increase in violent conflict in almost the whole of Sub-Saharan Africa in the last two decades, the size of some of the armies involved, the general international tension, all these bode ill for humanity. We already have a disruption of the world's moral standards: the maltreatment of prisoners and all too often of children, the execution of hostages, mob violence and the general growth of pathological social behaviour.

The dynamic interaction between humans and the Black Cloud causes, in relatively normal times and conditions, no more stress than can be absorbed in a comparable situation today in, for example, most of Western Europe: the balance remains more or less usual. But in times of violence and uncertainty, the stress increases. That is to say, the Black Cloud also grows relatively more powerful, therefore individuals are more seriously affected. As a result, they are more likely to do things that swell the Black Cloud and continue the process of escalation (as indeed is happening in many parts of the world today).

However, we are really all in the same boat with those suffering from the Cloud's miasma, and with those who take advantage of people already confused, upset or even incapacitated by it. We should cherish each other, together with the poor planet Earth. In the last few decades we have done so much, physically and psychically, to harm each other. We must bear it in mind that we are Earth's tenants, operating in a scene we are only just beginning to see clearly, but which our forebears understood in many ways so much better, and some of our present leaders, so much worse.

But we must realize that most of all these troubles are what Meister Eckhart might have called a 'Self-culture', a creature both of the Black Cloud and globalization, a planet desecrated by the conceit, greed and folly of those who have lived in it through the past century and particularly, some of those who have ruled and are now ruining it.

In concluding this section, let me turn a different ideological page and consider the culture of Islam. I am not referring to the beliefs of Al Qa'Ida which are both highly spiritual and wildly nihilistic – a strange and dubious combination. It seems as alien to the Islam of my many Muslim friends as it is to the mystical Sufism, which I greatly revere and which, I suspect, is not favoured by Al Qa'Ida. But my spiritual friends begin any activity by saying with deep attention: 'In the name of God [I would say Good] the Compassionate and Merciful.' There is no gentler balm for the malaise of the Black Cloud.

Different floors

It is always very difficult to describe states of consciousness. Those that are what might be termed 'unpleasant' – such as angry, miserable, lecherous or excited – are in general more easy to describe than those termed 'pleasant,' such as blissful, rapturous or ecstatic – such, at least, is my experience, if that is normal. But those are the wrong adjectives because it is not normal for me to experience them.

Let me try to describe a typical (but rare) experience.

I woke up after a rather deep afternoon rest and found myself in a different level of awareness from that in which I had gone to sleep. I saw everything quite differently. What do I mean by this? The closest I can get is that everything – the room, the furniture – had life. The things didn't move, but they shone burnished with life. I knew that I was looking into a new world.

I felt that I was at the top floor and that below me was another floor furnished with an ample supply of feelings and emotions – of awe, delight, happiness and other cheerful feelings which, ordinarily, I would have thought to indicate an exceptional, even perhaps sublime state of awareness. Now I felt they were fine, but not in any way exceptional, compared with my own consciousness.

And below this was a ground floor occupied by the sad detritus of the Black Cloud, aware only of misery, jealousy, confusion, anger, a horrid stew of negative feelings.

Approach to therapy meditations

The programme set out below can probably act as a pattern for users needing further confidence or insight before taking another step in what might be a difficult or risky enterprise in such fields as politics, the economy or social development.

I would propose:
1. Begin with something neutral, harmless and desirable such as treatment for a 'bad back' or some other not serious condition.
2. Then look at the strains, tension, bad posture, etc. Observe with attentive detachment, which is actually a form of meditation. Do this until you feel comfortable with it, not fussed.

3. The meditation is woven through gradual stages around the de-cluttering of the mind; first, simply observing the mind as it is, strictly not making any judgement of good or bad. Forget the back pain (or whatever was the original minor trouble). It has served its purpose, and will diminish or depart.

4. Concentrate on the Mind of the Universe as incorporating every-thing. Don't try to map it mentally. Just observe it. Or let it observe you. Envelop the Black Cloud in the Mind and watch it diminish and, if you do the exercise regularly, disappear.

5. Notice the diminution, and hopefully complete disappearance, of the original pain.

6. Maintain the practice and take up a role in whatever field you feel you can best serve.

Recognition of reality: reflections and prose poems

The Lama

He teaches us by simply being.
His presence, Kundun,
Opens a third eye
To see the other world, the true one,
Not one we've fabricated
Of illusion.
Now in his light we know again
What we had forgotten,
Miracles, gifts of poetry
Or music, things that family,
School or convention, the so-called
'Real world', blotted from awareness.

He gives us no new knowledge,
The truth is already with us;
Trendy fresh ideas and notions
Are ephemeral – instead
He shows us how to exercise
Psychic muscles for unblocking
The mind's channels, to release

Arcane wisdom within the heart,
To join the woman and the man
In our own being.

The teachings do not aim to rouse
Peculiar abilities -
Levitation, clairvoyance,
The bag of tricks called siddhis,
But to naught the blustering ego
Whose demands destroy compassion;
Then only can we really
Fulfil our proper task, helping
Others reach enlightenment.

Mind

Long years ago I saw, the inner
eye still sees, a small round pond
in the midst of a far off forest,
the water limpid but so deep
the eye could reach no bottom.
Once while I gazed a monstrous fish,
first a dim shadow far below
but then increasingly magnificent,
rose to the surface, made itself known
then slowly sank from sight to where
I felt certain that this single pool
must join with countless others in an
immeasurable subterranean lake.

But fallen leaves would often cover
much of the pond's surface.
I might have described it then
by the intricate pattern,
always different and shifting,
that they made, as one might say,
conventionally trivial,

someone has this quality or that,
pleasant or not according to
capricious taste, oblivious of clear
profundities below and magical
beings that inhabit them,
gliding mysterious wise and calm
throughout the hidden lake of mind.

Mediation/Meditation

An easy mistake, I often
Type meditation for mediation
And vice versa,
Slightly amused at the difference
The letter T makes to the meaning.

But perhaps it's not so great;
In meditation we become
More aware of reality,
Escaping from automatism
Of habitual responses
And from enslavement to
Our negative emotions.
Thus freed we live and love with
Greater strength and greater understanding
And so, among other things,
Can mediate with more effect.

We hope through mediation
To purify the atmosphere
Of needless somes inevitable
Suspicion, angry fear and
Misconception that impede accord.
We try in fact to introduce
Reality into the furious
Fantasies swathing both
Protagonists who now see each

Other not as human but demonic.
In this uneasy kinship
That we have with two hostile groups
We strive, as in our meditation,
To bring awareness.

But it is hard.
We only gain the measure of success
Achieved within ourselves -
Not always even that.

CHAPTER 14

Remembering forward

THE VISIONARY PRACTICAL SCHOLARSHIP OF ADAM CURLE

Introduction

The launching of this book comes on the heels of the 40th anniversary of Bradford University's peace studies degree program and Adam Curle's 100th birthday. These celebrations provide a rich opportunity to reflect back and look forward. Given the extraordinary extension of our field that Adam facilitated in the course of his pioneering engagement, we now enjoy a much wider acceptance in the academe and in policy circles. Adam's life, writing and commitments speak to a number of challenges that emerge as the field has grown. Three come to mind, sparked in part by noting the range of ideas and proposals found throughout the chapters that comprise this volume and will remain the formative narratives we need to understand and engage.

Liberal Peace

Over the last decade the breadth of application, investment and policy that has attempted to support the transition from war to peace in so many parts of the world has increasingly demonstrated the deficiencies of external mandates that devalue, ignore and too often invisibilize the centrality of embedded and local capacity, narrative and agency. The notion that models developed and supported by wealthier, liberal democracies provide the recipe for sustainable peace independent from deep understanding of local context and the nuances of relational patterns and histories, patterns that have emerged from long and harmful legacies of colonialism and neo-colonialism, have simply proven inadequate.

Our language reflects this bias. In the main, we prefer approaches of transition over transformation where the emphasis on stability seems more driven by international community needs than a robust embrace of the deep and difficult processes of relational, social and economic change required to shift the systemic dynamics driving repeated violence. We remain challenged by the 'vertical gap' of disconnect between local agency and national elite structures of politics. This is only further exacerbated by the challenge of global/local integration where the principle of operation should focus toward the agency of context and local communities but instead seems driven by the infrastructure of external expertise. A recent *Guardian* newspaper investigation reported that in the wider development field less than 1% of international funding reaches local civil society actors. From 'tools for transformation' to his view of education and the depth of his commitment to context and local process, Adam's core work provided an early capacity for radical critique and what today we refer to as criticism of liberal peace.

Ineffective timeframes of response and commitment

The metaphoric but deeply significant framework of 'post-conflict transition' exemplifies the very nature of the 'international community's' form of agency. The approach illustrates the paradoxical technocratic imagination about time as *both too short and too slow*. The mainstream orientation toward 'timeframes' shows a systemic bias that is very *slow* to respond to emerging risk of large-scale violence though early warning and repeated patterns are available and clear. This joins up with the *short-term* investment that privileges quick transition of complex political and social change through forms of economic agency we rarely problematize known as 'projects' that ultimately 'projectivize' human relationships. Templates, techniques and transitions provide the guiding metaphors from within this time orientation and dominate over notions of transformation, relational engagement, sustained dialogue and social change.

Adam's primary orientation in his seminal book, *Making peace*, required two forms of critical analysis: deep awareness of power imbalances and a fundamental orientation toward understanding the big picture of change processes. The deepest quality of his orientation emerged with a radical appreciation that social change is relationship-centric, that it emerges from and returns to quality of relationships people must ultimately understand and build.

Political Realism

By whatever name we may choose to call it in the more accepted field of international relations, the realist schools of thought that dominate national and international politics consistently suggest that containment and temporary political accommodation remain the only realistic horizon of change. This orientation, claiming political and military power as 'real' has rarely had any imagination of whole body politic, systemic interdependence or processes that link justice and social healing.

Adam long ago advocated for a holistic view of change and spent a lifetime exploring through interdisciplinary lenses the 'recognition of reality' that exposed the superficiality that assumes constructive change happens and will be sustained when placed in the hands of the few. He believed the deepest expression of reality emerges with commitment to confront dehumanization through engagement with systemic evil, honesty in interpersonal relationships and the personal journey of self-awareness. This comprises what we could call a radical centre not defined by his notion of 'in the middle' or political neutrality, but by his commitment to holistic re-humanization, the search to assure and develop the wholeness and integrity of personhood and flourishing human dignity.

These three dynamics systemically result in repeated and oft-lamented patterns. In many locations across the globe we live with deeply disembodied politics, artless and heartless social change processes that seem to create conditions of no war, no peace.

And less we judge outwardly, we should not forget that we in the academe contribute significantly. We are ever more proficient in our scholarly rigour on ever less budget moving us toward filling the ever narrowing demands for the professional technocracy needed to carry forward the less than satisfactory practice of peace.

I apologize for such a dose of pessimism, though perhaps as I argued in *The moral imagination*, a gift dances on her stage – the gift of getting ourselves squared with the challenges we actually face.

Into these challenges I would like to cast a personal eye back and forward at the same time, *remembering forward*, as I titled this chapter, to the first Professor of Peace Studies at Bradford University.

Adam was a beacon of orientation in my early career both as a practitioner and a scholar. I read Adam before I read Johan Galtung. I read

Adam well before I read *Getting to yes*. I ended up seeking out Quakers in Boulder, Colorado for my PhD studies (Kenneth and Elise Boulding and Paul Wehr). Prior to coming into teaching at a university my work in peacebuilding and mediation found orientation in Adam's philosophy and practice of peace. Throughout those early and formative professional years I had numerous, and what I considered significant, spaces of conversation with Adam about the dilemmas I was facing especially in larger-scale national mediation processes. He served as a mentor and wise practitioner. He rarely answered any of my questions directly. That was not his approach to deep listening; he much preferred a quality of presence that sat alongside the dilemmas. Yet I always left our encounters with greater clarity and sense of encouragement.

Following his death in 2006 I began systematically to collect all his major writings, and with recent help of the archives in Bradford, I think I may be close. During my last sabbatical year I read back through this body of work, much of which appears here in this volume. I recognized in a new way how much Adam provided the shoulders of my own work and scholarship. I would propose that Adam remains one of the most important influences relevant to many of our contemporary debates in peace studies. However, I also find that some of his most visionary contributions, ones with potential corrective qualities for the three challenges mentioned above, remain at the periphery of how mainstream peace studies and peace practice has evolved and the literature held as central. In this short concluding essay I share five observations I noticed in my re-reading of Adam's work that may serve as a way to provoke our reflection about the nature of the challenges.

I start with two observations related to his practice as an intermediary, then two related to his scholarship, and a final one pertaining to the overall impression about his quality of character and the meaning of radical peacemaking.

Lost art of conciliation

I start with what I would call the lost art of conciliation. Adam had a particular notion about his work as an intermediary. At times in his writing he provided specific advice about technique and frameworks. But underpinning his view was the deep core belief that conciliation developed around the relational requirement and practice of *sustained listen-*

ing oriented toward preparing people to overcome the psychological and deeply human challenge of encountering the enemy. This preparation requires that prior to meeting an enemy a person must feel safe enough to encounter him or herself, that is, people need the safety to face more honestly their deepest fears, internal barriers and cherished biases.

Adam called this safe and preparatory space conciliation. In *Mystics and militants* he described it this way. In conciliation 'hostile individuals are brought to the point where they perceive each other with less unreasonable fear and hostility so that they can, with some hope of success, begin the process of bargaining (negotiation) which leads to a settlement of the dispute and resolution of the conflict'. Of note and without shortcuts, conciliation must work separately with both sides – slowly, quietly and with long-term commitment. This deep commitment to the accompaniment of people, to the quality of radical listening – listening that understands and touches the soul attempting to speak from pain – provides for safety and honesty that builds out the meaning of conciliation. This deep and sustained preparatory work has largely not been at the fore of contemporary international mediation.

Befriending

Conciliation goes in hand with a concept I have only rarely seen cited in mediation literature, yet in my own practice, captures the core of what drives and orients much of my mediation work in settings of deep-rooted and violent conflict. Adam proposed the radical notion of diplomacy as friendship. He phrased this as an active verb: to befriend.

Adam literally understood befriending as the quality of relationship characterized by elements of care, concern, honesty and commitment that never was taken up for purposes of instrumental engagement to achieve ulterior purposes, even if those are noble. We can imagine why the term did not stick as the field grew professionally aiming ever more toward the technical and efficient definitions of roles, where at worst the approach was dominated by narrow views of neutrality and at best impartiality defined as equi-distance from each side. But at the core of Adam's engagement was not technique but rather his vocational impulse of seeking mutual humanity leading to what I would today refer to as a compassionate presence. He consistently focused on the discipline of re-humanizing the person he accompanied.

Reflective practice

Among the most dominant observations I had about Adam's scholarship when reading one book after the other emerged this observation: *he embodied an approach of reflective practice.*

Adam committed himself to a life of learning by doing. He reflected systematically on what he had experienced in the real world, whether at the highest level of negotiations with generals and presidents, or at the level of local communities under siege in Croatia. He did this in the fields of education, psychology and political science.

Among the elements we have not evolved well in the world of the academe is how to hold the space for and value the practitioner-scholar. Our bifurcation of value pushes us in two directions, both with deficiencies. On the one hand, the peace practitioner leads into a life driven by daily urgency and an overly responsible sense of activism embedded in the world of professional engagement with little or no time for deep, sustained reflection and renewal. On the other hand, the scholar separates out from the true messiness of the world they seek to study, interacting with the demands and confines of objective scholarship with too little space or time for the grounded views and complexities of what practice entails or requires.

Adam chose to live in both worlds, an example that informed my own vocation. If we are to take more seriously the challenges mentioned above, we in the academe need the radical reconsideration proposed by Adam's life of how we value embodied learning, a gap ill addressed in the very place where our future generations are formed.

Inner and outer worlds

I think it fair to say that Adam was an intrepid traveller. With Quaker intermediary teams Adam participated in places like Nigeria-Biafra that today could make for interesting travelling shows – the forerunners of second track diplomacy living unprotected in the wilds of open and violent war zones, moving between enemies at considerable risk. Less explored in Adam's work academically we find his deep personal commitment of the equally intrepid travel into the *inner world* of peacebuilding, seeking to find his *radical centre* – the rootedness he required to stay balanced, whole with commitment to stillness, mindfulness and the spirituality of engaged nonviolence.

We don't find many courses in our academic curricula that attend to the development of compassion, courage, health and wholeness of personhood for peace practice. As such, to be very honest, we experience significant burnout and professional apathy on the side of practice, signs that our preparation provides for filled heads and lonely souls.

Adam had a theory about this for himself. In an intriguing essay titled *Peace and Love: the violin and oboe,* a public talk that began with the Bach's Concerto in D Minor for the two instruments thus perhaps representing one of the first times that peace studies bridged into the arts, he spoke these words: 'As I have tried, over the past years, to grapple with the problems of violence and injustice, I have realized increasingly, how little I can do as I am. Without an inner evolution I cannot act wisely.'

Adam's life pedagogy suggested the need to live in the liminal space that navigates between the inner and outer world, a space most politicians, activists, practitioners and scholars fear more than any of their respective professional challenges.

The humility of learning

A final observation emerging from the full reading of Adam's work: across a lifetime he remained open to learning. He embodied the humility of a true scientist, a quality that at the same time *cultivates* the deep listener. This embodiment holds lightly the need to defend truth, whether in the form of academic battles over theories or whether in the form of ultimate religious belief.

Looking across the body of work, much of it found in this volume, I found it insightful to note that while his early work focused on educational models and evolved into multiple volumes on peace and engaged practice, he titled his last book *The fragile voice of love.*

Returning to where I started this chapter, if we look carefully at the deeper attitudinal forces that form the structural patterns underpinning the identified challenges, we would find what might best be described as arrogance: the belief that one's knowledge, approach and theory is superior. This subtle attitude in turn blinds the capacity to be with and alongside others in a common endeavour for the wider good. The antidote emerges only in the form of *radical humility* – a way of rooting one's life alongside humanity, to live with, rather than over, others. The lack of radical humility may be why we have disembodied politics and an academe that too often succumbs to the winds of arrogance and the trials of funding.

Throughout this chapter I have returned to the meaning of 'radical' peacemaker we find in the title of this book. The etymology of radical is less the notion of extremist views or obstructionist action – qualities hinted at in contemporary use of the term - rather it traces to root or rootedness. These represent Adam's deepest convictions seen primarily with how he chose to embody his peace practice and scholarship. Throughout his long journey Adam exemplified a *radical centre, the way he chose to be in the world* epitomized through his purposeful critique of systems, his commitment to relationship-centric social change, his constant search for re-humanization and listening, and his embodied humility and learning. These represent the core correctives we need to understand more fully as durable qualities defining the very nature of peace studies and practice.

PART 4

COMPLETE WORKS OF ADAM CURLE

Unpublished work

Published work

Co-authored published work

Unpublished work

The children of God.

Leading out or shoving in?

The man in the moon.

Poem to Corkie.

While there is life...

Todo y nada.

Civilian based defence and nonviolence.

Inner sources of peace and war.

Towards transforming a global culture of violence.

Peacemaking in the 21st century.

The worthlessness of war.

Steps towards pcaccmaking.

Heretical firefighting.

1926. Love and blackmail (unpublished).

1938. A desert journey.

Memoir: one branch of your roots: Adam's story. Unpublished, no date.

Published work

1946 'The teacher face to face with himself in relation to the community'. *The New Era in Home and School.* 36:1-6.

1946 *A follow-up survey of resettlement among returned prisoners of war.* War Office, London. 15 pp.

1946 *Some methods of facilitating the resettlement of returned prisoners of war.* War Office, London. 12 pp.

1948 With E.L. Trist. 'Transitional communities and social reconnection' in *Human Relations.* 1:74.

1948 'A theory of psycho-social interaction ' in *Proceedings of the eleventh*

International Conference of Anthropology and Ethnology. 1948.

1948 'Human satisfactions in rural life' in *Proceedings of the Sixth Agricultural Conference of Agricultural Economists.* 1948:248-251.

1949 'Toilet training in early childhood' in *Proceedings of the Royal Society of Medicine.* 52:905-909.

1949 'A theoretical approach to action research' in *Human Relations.* 3:269-280.

1949 'The sociological background to incentives' in *Occupational Psychology.* 23:21-29.

1949 'Incentives to work: an anthropological appraisal' in *Human Relations.* 1:41-47.

1949 'Participant action research with special reference to rural communities' in *Bulletin of the British Psychological Society.*

1951 'A conference on the methodology of social surveys' in *International Social Science Bulletin.* 3:629-634.

1951 'Human affairs'. *Biology.* 17.

1951 *Uses of Psycho-social research methods.* UNESCO.

1952 With A.E. Wilson, and E.L. Trist. 'Transitional communities and social reconnection: a study of the civil resettlement of British prisoners of war', in *Readings in Social Psychology.* Swanson, Newcomb, and Hartley, editors. 561-580.

1952 'War crisis seen in terms of human relationships' in *The New Era in Home and School.* 33:122-123.

1952 'Impressions of modern German psychology' in *Bulletin of the British Psychological Society.*

1952 'Education for Freedom' in the *Times Educational Supplement.*

1952 'The function of educational psychology' in *Bulletin of Education.* 29:12-15.

1952 'What Happened to three Villages' in *The Listener.* XLVIII:1027-1028.

1953 'Children and their social relationships 1' in *Bulletin of the Institute of Education of the University College of the South West of England (University of Exeter).* 2:3-5.

1953 'Studies of behaviour and concepts of freedom' in an inaugural lecture. University College of the South West of England (University of Exeter), 20.

1953 'Kinship and conformity' in *The New Era in Home and School.* 5:8-10.

1954 'Some psychological factors in rural society' in *Tribus.* 4-5:250-255.

1955 'The psychological theory of groupwork' in *Social Group Work in Great Britain.* Ed. Kuenstler, 135-155.

1955 'The contribution of psycho-analysis to the understanding of human behaviour' (a symposium with J. Nuttin and C. de Loncheaux) in *The Advancement of Science.* XII:548-563.

1955 'Education in rural areas' in *Looking forward in education.* A.V. Judges, editor. 156-173.

1955 'From student to teacher status' in *The New Era in Home and School.* 36:21-23.

1955 'A matter of communication' in *The Listener.* III:566-567.

1955 'Huxley's 'Brave New World' in *The New Statesman and Nation.* XLIX:508-509.

1955 'The Year Book of Education 1954' in *British Journal of Educational Studies.* 1955.

1955. 'The teacher face to face with himself in relation to the community' in *The New Era in Home and School.* 36:1-6.

1955 'Education and the Future in Rural Areas' in *Looking Forward in Education.* A.V. Judges, editor. Faber and Faber, London

1956 'Community organisation and family welfare in European problem areas' in *Ministry of Social Work*, the Hague. 22.

1956 'Problems of social change' in *The Government of Pakistan Planning Board.*

1957 'Problems of resettlement in the Chittagong Hill tracts' in Mimeographed Government of Pakistan Planning Board. 14.

1957 'Nomadism in Kalat Division' in *Mimeographed Government* of Pakistan Planning Board. 12.

1957 'The child and the community' in *Proceedings of the first all-Pakistan child welfare conference* 1957. Vol. 6. Proceedings of the first all-Pakistan child welfare conference, Pakistan.

1957 'The special areas and other tribal territories' in *The First Five Year Plan,* Government of Pakistan Planning Board, 639-652.

1957 'The school curriculum and social and cultural tradition', UNESCO. 57.

1957 *The first five year plan*, Government of Pakistan Planning Board.

1958 'Development in the far north of Pakistan' (Mimeographed). Government of Pakistan Planning Board. 33.

1958 'The present labour policy', Government of Pakistan Planning Commission. (Mimeographed). 11.

1958 'Principles of regional development', (Mimeographed). Government of Pakistan Planning Board. 15.

1958 'The desert areas of Thar Parkar district', (Mimeographed) Government of Pakistan Planning Board. 22.

1960 'Social Service'; Part III 'Human Resources and Welfare'; Part IV 'Regional Development ' in *The second five year plan*'. Government of Pakistan Planning Commission: 311-391; 329-396; & 397-414.

1960 'Tradition, development and planning' in *The Sociological Review*. 8.

1961 *The role of education in developing societies*, University of Ghana, Oxford.

1961 Foreword in *Social survey of Tefle: child development* (monographs). D.K. Fiawoo (ed). No 2 Institute of Education. Legon. 2.

1961 'Undervisningsvalsenets funktion i de underudviklede lande' in *Unge Paedagoger* . 22 Argana:10.

1961 'Dangers in Ghana' in *Amnesty*. 4:2.

1961 'Fra elev-til laererstatus' in *Unge Paedagoger*. 22 Argana:9-14.

1961 'Further thoughts on teacher training' in *The New Era in Home and School*. 42:1-4.

1961 'The role of education in developing societies' in inaugural lecture, University College of Ghana.

1961 'Sir George Robertson: an early fieldworker'. *Man*. LXI:1-25 & 15-19.

1962 'African Nationalism and Higher Education in Ghana' in *Universities Quarterly*. 16:229-243.

1962 'Social and economic problems of increasing human resources in underdeveloped countries' in *The Year Book of Education* by Bereday and Lauwerys (eds.). 528-538.

1962 'Some aspects of educational planning in underdeveloped areas' in *Harvard Educational Review*. 32.

1962 'Letter from Jamaica' in *Universities Quarterly*. 16.

1963 'Economic and social development' in *Educational Investment in the Pacific Community*, American Association of Colleges for Teacher Education.

1963 'Education, administration and development' in Occasional papers. Comparative Administration Group, American Society for Public Administration.

1963 *Educational strategy for developing societies: a study of educational and sociological factors in relation to economic growth*, Tavistock, London.

1964 'World campaign for universal literacy: comment and proposal' in *Occasional Papers in Education and Development*, No 1 1964.

1964 'Education, politics, and development' in *Comparative Education Review*. 7.

1965 'The goals of education in underdeveloped countries' in *Challenge and change in American education 1965* by M. Yudelman and S. Harris (eds.).

1965 'Critical implications of the education explosion' in *The Year Book of Education 1965* by Bereday and Lauwerys (ed.).

1966 *Planning for education in Pakistan : a personal case study*. Tavistock Publications, London, Sydney, Wellington.

1967 MSS of book on Education and technological change.

1968 'Universities in a changing world: innovation and stagnation' in *The New University*. J. Lawlor (ed.). Routledge, London.

1968 'Problems of professional identity: an examination of training for human resource development and educational planning'. *Education and World Affairs Report*. No 6 1968, New York.

1968 *Educational Planning: the Advisers' Role*. UNESCO, Paris.

1968 'The new university' in *The new university*. J. Lawlor (ed.). Routledge and Kegan Paul Ltd, London.

1968 *Problems of professional identity: an examination of training for human resource development and educational planning*, Education and World Affairs, New York.

1968 *Educational planning: the adviser's role*, UNESCO International Institute for Educational Planning.

1969 'Education, politics and development' in *Scientific investigations into comparative education*. M. Eckstein and H.J. Noah (eds.). Macmillan. Toronto, Ontario.

1969 *Educational problems of developing societies with case studies of Ghana and Pakistan.* Praeger, New York.

1969 'The Devils advocate view'. In *Agents of change: professionals in developing countries* by G. Bereviste and Ilchman, W. (eds.). Praeger Publications, NY, Washington, London. Chapter 4 : 50-56.

1970 'The professional identity of the education planner' in *Fundamentals of education planning series,* International Institute for Education Planning, Paris.

1970 'Aid and its implications' in *Problems of economic development* by D. Prasi (ed.). WRI, London.

1970 *Educational strategies for developing societies,* Tavistock, London.

1970 *The professional identity of the education planner,* UNESCO International Institute for Educational Planning.

1970 *L'identité professionelle de l'education,* UNESCO Institut international de planification de l'education.

1970 *Freundschaften: in der Offentlichkeit und im Privaten,* FWWCC, Luxembourg.

1971 'Education cast in a broader development role', *Modern Government.*

1971 *Making Peace,* Tavistock, London.

1971 'Education, politics and development' in *Education in comparative and international perspectives.* K. Gezi (ed.). Holt, Rinehard & Winston Inc, Chicago, SF, Atlanta, Dallas, Montreal, Toronto, London, Sydney. 302.

1971 *Gelisen Cemiyetlerde Egitimin Roli.* Cahit Okurer Sosyal Lhimler, Kamisonu Yayinlari : 3.

1972 *Mystics and militants – a study of awareness, identity and social action,* Tavistock, London.

1972 *Mysticos y militantes,* Tavistock, Buenos Aires/ London.

1972 Seminar notes peace studies and the U235.

1973 *Education for liberation,* Tavistock, London.

1973 *Educational problems of developing societies: with case studies of Ghana, Pakistan, and Nigeria,* Praeger, New York: London.

1973 'The education of teachers' in *Education at home and abroad* by J. Lauwerys and G. Tayar (eds.), Routledge and Kegan Paul Ltd, London.

1973 *Educational psychology a contemporary view,* Communications research Machines Inc, Del Mar, California.

1973 'Professor of peace studies' in *The Friend*. 131:2-3.

1973 'Adam Curle appointed to the Chair of Peace Studies, Bradford' in *The Friend*. 131.

1973 'Teaching peace' in *World issues*. 27:6.

1974 'Contribution of education to freedom and justice in *Education for peace proceedings for the First World Conference of the World Council for Curriculum and Instruction*. by M. Haavelsrud (ed.), ISP Science and Technology Press, University of Keele. 64-97.

1974 'Peace and cooperation' in *1974 Ernest Bader Common Ownership Lecture* Vol. 5. Scott Bader Commonwealth Centre, Scott Bader Commonwealth Centre.

1974 'Education for peace: the international dimension' in *London Educational Review:* 33-38.

1974 *Education in developing societies* (Hindi edition). Oxford University Press, Bombay.

1975 *The scope and dilemmas of peace studies, an inaugural lecture,* University of Bradford, Bradford.

1975 *Reconciliation, violence and anger,* New Malden, Fellowship of Reconciliation, 9 Coombe Road, New Malden, Surrey KT3 4QA, New Malden.

1975 'Conspiracy case in context' in *The Friend*. 133:139.

1975 'A word for this time' in *Friends Journal:* 515-518.

1976 'Education for a technical explosion' in *Hidden factors in technological change*. E. Coggin, and E. Semper. (eds.). Perganon Press, Oxford, Toronto, NY, Sydney, Paris, Frankfurt.

1976 'Peace studies' in *The Year Book of World Affairs*. Vol. 30. G.W. Keeton, Schwartenberger (ed.), the London Institute of World Affairs. Stevens and Sons Ltd, London.

1976 'Violence or non-violence? A Christian dilemma' in *The Clergy Review*. LXI:44-49.

1977 'Reflections on working in a university' in *Studies in Higher Education*. 2.

1977 *Peace and love the violin and the oboe* in Lindsey Press, London.

1977 *Educacion liberadora problems de pedagogia,* Editorial Herder, Barcelona.

1977 *Estrategia educativa,* Editorial Herder, Barcelona.

1977 'That of God' in *Quaker Monthly.* 56:81-85.

1977 'Reflections on working in a university' in *Studies in Higher Education.* 2.

1978 *Peacemaking, public and private,* Wider Quaker Fellowship, a program of the friends World Committee for Consultation, 1506, Race Street, Philadelphia PA 19102, Philadelphia.

1978 'Towards a different society' in *Quaker Monthly.* 57-8:150.

1978 'Peace studies at Bradford – the first five years' in *The Friend.* 136:1213.

1978 *Vredestichten als Openbara en Prive Aktiviteit,* Queens University Publishing, Canada.

1978 'Seven Enemies' in *The Friend:*1121-1122.

1979 'Looking abroad: the material and the sacramental' in *The Friend.* 137:329.

1979 'Looking abroad: vigour and veritas' in *The Friend.* 137:1167.

1980 'Life styles: human and machine' in *Friends Quarterly.*

1980 *The basis of Quaker work for peace and service* in Friends House, London.

1980 'Action research as part of peacemaking' in *Social science – for what?* Festschrift for Johan Galtung. H.H. Holm and E Rudenberg, eds. Universitesforlaget, Oslo, Bergen, Tromso.

1980 'Life-styles – human and machine' in *The Friends Quarterly.* 22:213.

1980 'Bears and lions' in *The Friend.* 138:217.

1980 'Wars of liberation: a fact of international life' in *The Friend.* 138:1 August 1980.

1981 *True justice: Quaker peacemakers and peacemaking,* Swarthmore Press, London.

1981 *Preparation for peace* in Canadian Yearly Meeting, Canada.

1981 'Do our nuclear weapons protect us more than they imperil us?' in *Science and Public Policy.* 8:350-360.

1981 'Looking abroad: Tibetans outside Tibet' in *The Friend.* 141:1039.

1981 'Looking abroad: digging into Pendle Hill' in *The Friend.* 139:307.

1981 'Security through disarmament' in QUNO Seminar, Geneva.

1981 'South Africa in bondage: time for compassion and action' in *South African Working Party of the American Friends Service Committee.*

1981 *True Justice: Quaker peacemakers and peacemaking,* Swarthmore Press, London.

1982 'A letter to Sigrid Helliesen Lund' in *Quakerism, a Way of Life: in homage to Sigrid Helliesen Lund.* Kvekerforlaget, Norway.

1982 'What do Friends really mean?' in *The Friend.* 140:1165.

1982 'Universities in the third world' in *Pacific Perspective.* 12:4-7.

1982 'Sources of peace and violence' in *Churches Register.* 3:20-21.

1982 'Can we speak truth in love?' in *Quaker Monthly.* 61:193-196.

1982 With Dugan, M. 'Peacemaking: stages and sequences' in *Peace and Change.* July. Vol. 8, Issue 2-3 pp. 19-28.

1983 'The compassionate will' in *Quaker Monthly.* December 1983.

1983 *The fire in the peat,* Quaker Peace and Service Friends House, Euston Road London NW1 2BJ, London.

1983 'Do our nuclear weapons protect us more than they imperil us?'. Defence and Energy issues in *Science and Society.* Heinemann, London.

1983 'Looking abroad: the fire in the peat' in *The Friend.* 141:189.

1983 'Abnormality in the context of different cultural settings' in *The Friend.* 141:581.

1983 'Conflict resolution simplified' in *The Friend.* 141:911.

1983 'Tentative notes for the shambhala recruits' in *The Friend.* 141:975.

1983 'The compassionate will' in *Quaker Monthly.* 62:253.

1983 Das Feuer im Moor' ('The fire in the peat') in *Der Quaker.* 6:104-106.

1983 Europe and non-violent defence' in *European security: nuclear or conventional defence?* M. De Perrot, editor. Pergamon Press, Geneva.

1983 'Three stages in the process of peacemaking' in *The Internationalist.* 121:27.

1983 'Quakerhaltung im Konflict' in *Der Quaker.* 3:35-36.

1983 'Making peace' in *The Internationalist.* 121:27.

1983 'Conflict resolution simplified' in *The Friend.* 141:911-912.

1983 'Nuclear and/or conventional forces in European security' in *Groupe de Bellerive International Collloquium*, Geneva.

1984 'The nature of peace' in *Issues in peace education*. C. Reid (ed.). The United World College of the Atlantic, South Glamorgan. 8-12.

1984 'Looking abroad: visions of the future' in *The Friend*. 142:1331-1333.

1984 'Education for peace' in *Educare – Journal of Life Education*. 1:7-8.

1984 'Looking abroad: our common membership' in *The Friend*. 142:239-240.

1986 *In the middle: non-official mediation in violent situations*. Berg, Oxford.

1986 'Mediation: steps on the long road to negotiated settlement of conflicts' in *Transnational Perspectives*. 12:5-7.

1986 'Looking Abroad: a bureau of trained mediators in *The Friend*. 144.

1986 'Non-violent political struggle' in *Conference on non-violent political struggle*. Quaker Peace and Service, London.

1986 'Leading out or shoving in?' in *Educare – Journal of Life Education*. 2:44-46.

1987 *Recognition of reality*. Hawthorn Press, Stroud.

1988 'Labels' in *Quaker Monthly*.

1988 'The terminology of peacemaking' in *Conflict Resolution Notes*. 5:26-27.

1989 Document arising from the consultation on Quaker experience of political mediation.

1989 'A key to awareness' in *The Friend*: 1375-1376.

1990 'Peacemaking: 'inner' state and 'outer' act' in *The Friends Quarterly*, Friends Publications Ltd.

1990 *Tools for transformation-a personal study*. Hawthorn Press, Stroud.

1990 'Peace studies' in *Peace is the Way* by C. Wright and Augarde, T. (eds.). The Lutterworth Press, Cambridge. 121-124.

1990 'Letter from the Peace Brigade' in *Quaker Monthly*. 69:186-187.

1990 'Third party peacemaking' in *Interdisciplinary Peace Research*: 62-73.

1991 'A dialogue for universalists' in Quaker Universalist Group.

1992 'Small circles: work for peace in the former Yugoslavia' in *The Friend*. 150:1265-1268.

1992 'What prospects for peace in the former Yugoslavia?' in *The Friend.* 150:1229-1230.

1992 'Unclenching the fist around the heart' in *The Friend.* 150:1103-1105.

1992 'Peacemaking: the middle way' in International Division of the American Friends Service Committee.

1992 'A spirit of optimism' in *Waging Peace.* D.A.K. Krieger, (ed.). The Noble Press, Chicago, Illinois.

1992 *Peacemaking – the middle way.* Bridges. Quaker International Affairs International Division of the American Friends Service Committee, Philadelphia, Pennsylvania.

1992 *The transforming force. Aspects of non-violence.* Carlssons.

1993 'In a climate of moral anarchy' in *The Friend.* 151:1071-1072.

1993 'Peace and development' in *CHEC Journal.* 11:29-30

1993 'Small circles for peace' in *Horizons: Community Aid Abroad.* 1:14-15.

1993 'Steering the world away from violence' in *Voices on the Threshold of Tomorrow.* G. Fuerestein and T. Fuerestein (eds.). Quest Books, Madras, London.

1993 'Some notes on Quakerism and Buddhism' in *Quaker Monthly.* 73:212-213.

1994 'New challenges for citizen peacemaking' in *Medicine and war.* 10:96-105.

1994 'Forgiveness?' in *Fellowship.* 60:9.

1994 'Towards a global awareness of peace services' in *Towards a Global Awareness of Peace Services.* Christian Council of Sweden, Stockholm. Life and Peace Institute. Uppsala, Stensnas. Sweden.

1994 El campo y los dilemas de los estudios por la paz in 2nd Conference Europa de Construccion de la Paz y Resolucion de Conflictos. ECPCR, Prim 34, San Sebastian.

1994 'Reflections on forgiveness' in *Fellowship.* July/August:4.

1995 *Another way: a positive response to contemporary violence.* Jon Carpenter, Oxford.

1995 'Reconstituting the council' in *Fellowship.* 61:21.

1995 *Ways out of war.* Quaker Peace and Service, London.

1996 'Small circles for peace' in *Community Aid Abroad:* 14-15.

1997 'Public health III: hatred and reconciliation' in *Medicine, Conflict and Survival.* 13:37-47.

1997 'Public health II: the psychological dimension' in *Medicine, Conflict and Survival.* 13:23-26.

1998 'Happiness as a right' in *The International Journal of Human Rights*: 77-83.

1999 *To tame the Hydra.* Jon Carpenter, Charlbury Oxford.

2001 'Social healing of the wounds of war' in *Committee for Conflict Transformation Support* 14:3-6.2005: The fragile voice of love, Oxford: John Carpenter.

2006 'Happiness and Peacemaking' in *The Friend.* 7 July.

Co-authored published work

Curle, A. and E. L. Trist (1948). 'Transitional communities and social reconnection' in *Human Relations* 1(1 & 3.): 74.

Curle, A., A. E. Wilson, et al. (1952). 'Transitional communities and social reconnection: a study of the civil resettlement of British prisoners of war' in *Readings in Social Psychology.* Swanson, Newcomb and Hartley: 561-580.

Curle, A. and M. Yudelman (1965). 'The goals of education in underdeveloped countries in *Challenge and change in American education.* S. Harris, Deitch, K. and A. Levenshon (eds.). Berkely CA, McCutchan Publishing: 103-112.

Bibliography

Allport, G.W. *Becoming.* Yale University Press, New Haven, 1955.

Beckwith, Gerald. *Ouspensky's fourth way: the story of the further development and completion of P.D. Ouspensky's work by Dr Francis Roles.* Starnine Media & Publishing Ltd, 2015.

Berman, M. and Johnson, J. eds. *Unofficial Diplomats.* New York: Colombia University Press, 1977.

Bion, W. R. *Experiences in groups and other papers.* Tavistock, London; Basic Books, New York, 1961.

Borton, T. *Reach, touch and teach.* McGraw Hill, New York, 1970

Boulding, E. 'The child and nonviolent social change' in *Strategies against violence: design for nonviolent change* by Charny, I (ed.), 68-99, Westview Press, Boulder, CO, 1978.

Boulding, E. *One small plot of heaven: reflections on family life by a Quaker sociologist.* Pendle Hill Publications, Wallingford, PA, 1989.

Boulding, E. *Building a global civic culture: education for an independent world.* Syracuse University Press, Syracuse, NY, 1990.

Boulding, K. *Conflict and defence: a general theory.* Harper and Row, New York, 1962.

Chiang, H.-M. and Maslow, A. *The healthy personality.* Van Nostrand, Princeton, N.J, 1969.

Curle, A. *Another way: a positive response to contemporary violence.* Jon Carpenter, Oxford, 1995.

Curle, A. *Memoir: one branch of your roots: Adam's story.* Unpublished, no date.

Curle, A. *Planning for education in Pakistan.* Harvard University Press, Cambridge, Mass; Tavistock, London, 1966.

Curle, A. *Making Peace.* Tavistock, London. 1971.

Curle, A. 'Reflections on working in a university', *Studies in Higher Education,* Vol. 2, No. 1, 9-13. 1977.

Curle, A. *In the middle: non-official mediation in violent situations.* Berg, Oxford, 1987.

Curle, A. *Recognition of reality: reflections and prose poems.* Hawthorn, Stroud, 1987.

Curle, A. 'New challenges for citizen peacemaking' in *Medicine and war*, 10(2): 96-105. 1994

Curle, A. *To tame the Hydra: understanding the cultures of violence*. John Carpenter, Oxford, 1999.

Curle, A. *The fragile voice of love*. John Carpenter, Oxford, 2006.

Curle, R. *The last of Conrad*. The Joseph Conrad Society, London, (no date).

Curle, A. and O'Connell, J. *Peace with work to do: the academic study of peace*, Berg, Leamington Spa, 1985.

Dahl, R. A. *Modern political analysis*. Prentice-Hall, Englewood Cliffs, N.J, 1963.

Dencik, L. '*Peace research: pacification or revolution. Notes on intra-peace-research conflict*', paper delivered at the Third General Conference of the International Peace Research Association, Karlovy Vary, September 1969.

Deutsch, K. W. *Arms control and the Atlantic Alliance*, Wiley, New York, 1967.

Deutsch, K. W. *The analysis of international relations*, Prentice-Hall, Englewood cliffs, N.J, 1968.

Dietrich, W. *The Palgrave international handbook of peace studies: a cultural perspective*, Palgrave Macmillan, London, 2014.

Etzioni, A. 'Sociological perspectives in strategy' in *Transactions of the sixth world congress of sociology*, Vol. 2, 1967.

Freud, S. *Psychopathology of everyday life*, standard edition, Vol 6. Hogarth, London, 1901.

Fromm, E. *The art of loving*. Harper and Row Publishers, New York, 1956.

Fulbright, W. J. *The arrogance of power*. Penguin, Harmondsworth, 1970.

Galtung, J. 'Feudalism, structural violence, and the structural theory of violence', paper prepared for the Third General Conference of the International Peace Research Association, Karlovy Vary (mimeo.), 1969

Galtung, Jo. *Peace, peace theory, and an international peace academy*, International Peace Research Institute Oslo, International Peace Research Association Groningen, Gandhian Institute of Studies, Varanasi. PRIO Publications No. 23-28, Varanasi, (mimeo). February. 1969a.

Grier, W. and Cobbs, P.M. *Black Rage*, Bantam Books, New York, 1968.

James, W. *Varieties of religious experience.* Modern Library, New York (many editions since first published in 1902), 1902.

Kelman, H. C. (ed.): *International behaviour: a social-psychological analysis.* Holt, Rinehart and Winston, New York,1965

Kohl, H. *The open classroom: a practical guide to a new type of teaching.* New York Review, New York, 1969.

Large, J. *The war next door: second track intervention during the war in ex-Yugoslavia,* Hawthorn Press, Stroud, 1997.

Lederach, J.P. *Building peace: sustainable reconciliation in divided societies.* United Nations University Press, Tokyo, 1994.

Lederach, J.P. *Preparing for peace; conflict transformation across cultures.* Syracuse University Press, Syracuse NY, 1995.

Lederach, J.P. *The year in haiku* at http://www.blurb.com/b/6751573-the-year-in-haiku, Accessed 2015.

Lederach, J.P. *Moral imagination: the art and soul of building peace.* Oxford University Press, New York, 2005.

Lederach, J.P. and Lederach, A.J. *When blood and bones cry out: journeys through the soundscape of healing and reconciliation,* Oxford University Press, New York, 2011.

Lyon, H. C., JR. *Learning to feel-feeling to learn.* Charles E Merrill Publishing Company, Columbus, Ohio, 1971.

MacDonald, J. and Bendahmane, D. eds. *Conflict Resolution: Two Track Diplomacy.* Washington DC: Centre for the Study of Foreign Affairs, 1987.

Maslow, A. H. *Religions, values and peak experiences.* Viking Press, New York, 1970.

Maslow, A. H. *Towards a psychology of being.* Van Nostrand, Princeton, N.J, 1968.

McConnell, J. *Mindful mediation: a handbook for Buddhist peacemakers,* Buddhist Research Institute, Bangkok, 1995.

Mitchels, B. *Love in danger – trauma therapy and conflict explored through the life and work of Adam Curle.* John Carpenter, Charlebury, Oxon, 2006.

Myrdal, G. *An American dilemma.* Harper, New York and London, 1944.

Nash, P. *The major purposes of humanistic and behavioral studies in teacher education,* prepared for the working conference of the National Standing Committee on Humanistic and Behavioural Studies in Education, A.A.C.T.E., Washington, D.C. 14-15 April 1971 (mimeo).

National Advisory Commission on Civil Disorders, *Report,* Bantam Books, New York, 1968.

Otto, R. *The idea of the Holy,* second edition, trans. by Harvey. Oxford University Press, London, 1950.

Ouspensky, P.D. *In search of the miraculous,* Harcourt Brace & World, Inc., New York, 1949.

Perls, F. S. et al *Gesalt therapy: excitement and growth in the human personality.* Dell, New York, 1951:

Ramsbotham, O., Woodhouse, T. and Miall. H. *Contemporary Conflict Resolution,* Polity, Cambridge, 2016:

Ramsey, D. *Affective education and schools,* Harvard Graduate School of Education, Cambridge, Mass, 1971 (mimeo).

Rapaport, A. 'Models of conflict: cataclysmic and strategic' in Reuck, de A (ed.), *Conflict in Society.* Little, Brown, Boston, Mass; Churchill, London, 1966:

Reich, C. *The greening of America,* Random House, New York; Allen Lane, London, 1970.

Rigby, A. *Dmitrije Mitrinovic A Biography,* William Sessions Press, York, 2006.

Rigby, A. 'Training for cosmopolitan citizenship in the 1930s: the project of Dmitrije Mitrinovic', *Peace and change,* Vol. 24, 3, 1999, 379-399, 1999.

Rigby, A. *Dmitrije Mitrinovic: a biography.* William Sessions Press, York, 2006.

Steele, T. *Alfred Orage and the Leeds Arts Club 1893-1923.* Orage Press, Mitcham, 2009.

Rogers, C. R. *On becoming a person.* Houghton Mifflin Company, Boston, 1961.

Rogers, C. R. *Freedom to learn.* Charles E Merrill Publishing Company, Columbus, Ohio, 1969.

Rothchild, D. 'Unofficial Mediation and the Nigeria-Biafra War', in *Nationalism & ethnic politics,* Vol.3, No.3, pp.37-65, Autumn 1997.

Schelling, T. C. *The strategy of conflict*. Harvard University Press, Cambridge Mass; Oxford University Press, London, 1960.

Schelling, T. C. *Arms and influence*. Yale University Press, New Haven, Conn, 1966.

Schmid, H. 'Politics and peace research', in *Journal of peace research*, No. 3. pp. 271-31, 1968.

Schmid, H.'Peace research as a tool for pacification', in *Proceedings of the International Peace Research Association, Third General Conference*, Assen., 1970.

Schutz, W. C. *Joy: expanding human awareness*. Grove Press, New York, 1967.

US Department of Health, Education and Welfare. *Towards a social report*. US Government Printing Office, Washington, 1969.

Wilson, A.T.M, Trist, E.L. and Curle, A. 1990, 'Transitional communities and social reconnection: the civil resettlement of British prisoners of war', in Trist and Murray, H. (eds), *The social engagement of social science, volume 1, the socio-psychological Perspective*, University of Pennsylvania Press, Philadelphia, pp.88-112

Wikipedia. I also need to acknowledge, perhaps unusually for an academic, Wikipedia, as a source for making the links between Mitrinovic, Orage, Gurdjieff and Ouspensky, and their biographies, manageable, informative and accessible. Also for revealing the similarity between Adam's Black Cloud and Fred Hoyle's novel of the same name.

Woodhouse, T. *Peacemaking in a troubled world*. Berg, Oxford, 1991.

Woodhouse, T. Miall, H. Ramsbotham, O. and Mitchell, C. *The contemporary conflict resolution reader*. Polity, Cambridge, 2016.

Yarrow, M. C. H. *Quaker experiences in international mediation*, Yale University Press, New Haven and London, 1978.

Young, O. R. *The intermediaries: third parties in international crises*. Princeton University Press, New York, 1967.

Young, O. R. 'Intermediaries: additional thoughts on third parties' in *Journal of conflict resolution*. Oran Young (1967,1972) vol. 16, 3, 1972.

End notes for chapters 1–14

1. *In the Middle: Non-official mediation in Violent Situations.* Bradford Peace Studies, New Series Papers No 1. Leamington Spa, Hamburg, New York: Berg. 1986.p. 17 andp. 24

2. *To Tame the Hydra*, 1999, v.

3. This account of Richard Curle is from 'Memoirs of the Author', written by Adam in the introduction to *The Last of Conrad,* written by his father who was present at the death of Joseph Conrad. We have also drawn on unpublished family papers, including 'One Branch of Your Roots: Adams's Story'; and Cordelia Curle (1879 – 1970), a memoir by a family friend, Hallam Tennyson.

4. From Adam's Memoir (unpublished).

5. Boulding, Elise (1978). The Child and Nonviolent Social Change. In: Israel Charny (ed.), *Strategies Against Violence: Design for Nonviolent Change* (Boulder, CO: Westview Press): 68-99. See also Elise Boulding, 1989. *One Small Plot of Heaven: Reflections on Family Life by a Quaker Sociologist.* Wallingford, PA: Pendle Hill Publications.

6. Adam Curle Memoir: One Branch of Your Roots: Adam's Story. Unpublished, no date. While not named in this quote it is clear that the remarkable man is George Gurdjieff

7. There are many cases where modernist thought and innovation were inspired by the same search for inner meaning and undiscovered sources of feeling cognition and consciousness. This is too big a field to explore here, but one fascinating example is worth noting. In the history of art, the development of abstract art is usually associated with men such as Kandinsky, Mondrian and others. Hettie Judah has written about a Swedish female artist, Hilma af Klint, whose abstract work preceded that of Kandinsky but is only now being recognised with a major exhibition of her work in April 2016 at the Serpentine Galley in London. Af Klint's work explored the 'unseen' world, influenced by the discovery in science of electromagnetic waves and x-rays. See The Independent 21 February 2016 at http://www.independent.co.uk/arts-entertainment/art/features/ rediscovering-hilma-af-klin-the-original-abstract-painter-a6885826.html

8. This is a necessarily short and basic account of modernism and mysticism and apologies are made for any over-simplification. I am indebted to

friends and colleagues who have worked on this peace-politics- esoteric-mystic link over many years and whose thinking I have greatly benefitted from: Andrew Rigby, 2006. *Dmitrije Mitrinovic a biography* York: William Sessions Press. Also his article on Mitrinovic as an early cosmopolitan: *Training for cosmopolitan citizenship in the 1930s: the project of Dmitrije Mitrinovic,* Peace and Change Vol. 24, 3, 1999, 379-399. Tom Steele, 2009. *Alfred Orage and the Leeds Arts Club* 1893-1923. Mitcham: Orage Press. On Gurdjieff and Ouspensky see Gerald de Symons Beckwith, 2015. *Ouspensky's fourth way: the story of the further development and completion of P.D. Ouspensky's work by Dr Francis Roles.* Starnine Media & Publishing Ltd. I also need to acknowledge Wikipedia (perhaps unusual for an academic), as a source for making the links between these people, and their biographies, manageable, informative and accessible.

9. This quote is from Adam Curle's memoir, *One Branch of Your Roots: Adam's Story.* Unpublished, no date.

10. Others included, in 1946, 'The teacher face to face with himself in relation to the community'; 'Some methods of facilitating the resettlement of returned prisoners of war'. In 1948, 'A theory of psycho-social interaction; 'Human satisfactions in rural life'. In 1949, 'A theoretical approach to action research'; 'Participant action research with special reference to Rural communities'. In 1952, 'War crisis seen in terms of human relationships'; 'Education for Freedom'; 'The function of educational psychology'. In 1953, 'Children and their social relationships (Inaugural Lecture at Exeter). In 1955, 'The psychological theory of groupwork'; 'The contribution of psycho-analysis to the understanding of human behaviour'. See bibliography in Part 4 for full references.

11. See True Justice (1981) for Adam's account of Quaker beliefs and principles.

12. The extracts in Part 1, Chapters 2-6, relate to this theme.

13. For an account of the history of the emergence and institutionalisation of peace studies at this time see Ramsbotham, Woodhouse and Miall 2016, chapter 2.

14. Curle 1971, p.15.

15. Curle 1971, p. 15.

16. The extracts in Part 2, Chapters 7-10, relate to Peace with Work to Do - 2 and 3.

17. For more on this see Berman, M. and Johnson, J. eds. 1977, *Unofficial Diplomats*. New York: Colombia University Press. Also MacDonald, J. and Bendahmane, D. eds. 1987, *Conflict Resolution: Two Track Diplomacy*. Washington DC: Centre for the Study of Foreign Affairs.

18. Curle family documents, unpublished, courtesy of Deborah Curle.

19. The extracts in Part 3, Chapters 11-14 relate to this theme.

20. Curle, 1995, *Another Way* p. 132.

21. Curle, 1994 p. 96.

22. Curle 1994, p. 104

23. For an excellent account of peacemaking thinking and practice in Buddhism, see John McConnell, *Mindful mediation: a handbook for Buddhist peacemakers,* Bangkok: Buddhist Research Institute, 1995.

24. See Elise Boulding, 1990, p. 4 and p. 140.

25. Boulding 1990, p. 95.

26. Woodhouse, 1991.

27. This chapter is from *Making Peace*. Introduction: Peaceful and Unpeaceful Relationships. pp. 1-28. London: Tavistock Publications. 1971.

28. Thus Johan Galtung (1969a), in speaking of peace and violence, says: 'Violence is present when human beings are being influenced so that their actual somatic and mental realizations are below their potential realizations', and violence is defined as 'the cause of the difference between the potential and the actual' (p. 3). Galtung divides violence into personal, physical and psychological violence; and structural violence, by which he means uneven distribution of resources and uneven distribution of power over resources (p. 11). The absence of the former he calls negative peace and of the latter he calls positive peace or social justice. The two together constitute peace in the full sense. Thus, although he employs different terms, his concept of violence is close to mine, of the unpeaceful relationship in which, while there may be no overt conflict behaviour, damage is done to human potential and the seeds of future open conflict or personal violence are sown.

29. In 1940 infant mortality among non-white Americans was 12-5 per cent higher than among white Americans. In 1965 it was 9.3 per cent higher, but the maternal mortality rate, four times as high for non-whites as for whites, was relatively higher than it was in 1940. In 1965 life-expectancy for whites was 6.9 years higher than for non-whites; and, at the

age of 25, life-expectancy for non-whites was 11 years shorter than that for whites (National Advisory Commission on Civil Disorders, 1968, pp. 270-2). There is no suggestion that the greater mortality is due to genetic weakness (this possibility is examined and dismissed by Myrdal, 1944, pp. 140-4). Myrdal records that in the late 1930s registered infant mortality for black people was 96 per cent higher than for whites, and that this was probably an underestimation. One way in which the socio-economic handicaps of black Americans are demonstrated is in evidence that, for blacks, a relatively high level of occupation attained by the father is not often reflected in the son's employment. A government document shows that whereas a majority of the sons of white white-collar workers are employed at the same level as their fathers, this applies to only 10 per cent of the sons of black white-collar workers (US Department of Health, Education and Welfare, 1969, p. 24).

30. It should be added that Boulding's versatile genius has played over most aspects of conflict and peace studies.

31. It might also be noted that in his publication of 1967 Deutsch deals with large-scale issues of strategy.

32. At least among those concerned with peace research. See, for example, Schmid (1968) and Galtung (1969). Schmid (1970) rejects the concept, however, as likely to lead to pacification.

33. There is also a valuable discussion of power in Dahl (1963).

34. Albert Camus in 'Create Dangerously' (December 1957); quoted by Fulbright (1970, p. 71).

35. Chapter 4 is not included in this extract.

36. The discussion of The Firm is not included in this extract.

37. Not included in this extract.

38. Not included in this extract.

39. These case studies form Part 1 of *Making Peace* and are not included here.

40. Not included in this extract.

41. The most systematic exponent of this approach in psychology is Maslow (1968); see also Chiang and Maslow (1969).

42. This chapter is from Part II of *Making Peace*, 'Introduction: The Practice of Peacemaking', pp. 173-189.

43. The Faqir Mishkin were an impoverished people in the Hindu Kush area of Pakistan. Adam travelled in this area and encountered these people during his period working for the government of Pakistan during 1958. The case study is the subject of Chapter 6 of *Making Peace*.

44. Chapter 15 of *Making Peace*.

45. This process is outlined schematically by Dencik (1969).

46. This process is outlined schematically by Dencik (1969).

47. Not included in this extract but the subject of Chapter 10 in *Making Peace*.

48. As I write there is a split in the ranks of peace researchers between those who follow the line that might rather unfairly be characterised as 'peace at any price' and those who are prepared to countenance disturbances, amounting if necessary to physical violence, to change what Galtung (1969a) calls structural violence. I prefer to think in terms of applying the right peacemaking technique at the appropriate stage of the conflict. The works of Schmid (1969 and especially 1970) and Dencik (1969) are particularly relevant.

49. This chapter is from *Mystics and militants: a study of awareness, identity and social action*. London: Tavistock 1972. Chapters 6 and 7 pp. 92-109.

50. Belonging identity is defined in Mystics and militants on pp. 27-31 and 41- 49, and especially and in essence means 'that one's identity is secured more in terms of what one belongs to than in terms of what one is ... (or) ... one becomes what one belongs to.

51. Described in Shutz (1967).

52. Since I first drafted this passage I have read the work of Reich (1970) which, I found to my gratification, came by a different route to approximately the same conclusion.

53. This is interestingly reported and discussed by Andy Logan in 'Around City Hall', *New Yorker*, 6 June 1970.

54. This chapter is from *Education for liberation*, chapter 5, pp. 53-62. London: Tavistock. 1973.

55. The most comprehensive description of this rather vague field that I know of is Lyon (1971). I am equally indebted to the shorter but more critical assessment by Deborah Ramsey (1971).

56. I take this term from Ouspensky (1949). Negative emotions are those

which, like jealousy, anxiety, self-pity or irritation, leave us feeling weakened. They drain away some form of psychic energy and leave us less capable of creativity, empathy or purposeful activity.

57. This great work is an indispensable source for all who are dissatisfied with conservative psychiatric interpretations of human nature.

58. This chapter is from Adam Curle's inaugural lecture published by the University of Bradford in 1974. It was later re-published as *Peace with work to do: the academic study of peace*, James O'Connell and Adam Curle, Leamington Spa: Berg. 1985. pp. 9-28. This contains the inaugural lectures of the first two Professors at Bradford, Adam Curle and James O'Connell.

59. For more on mediation see Ramsbotham, Woodhouse and Miall 2016, Chapter 7, 'Ending violent conflict; Peacemaking'.

60. See also Judith Large, The war next door: second track intervention during the war in ex-Yugoslavia. 1997. Stroud: Hawthorn Press; and Barbara Mitchels, Love in danger – trauma therapy and conflict explored through the life and work of Adam Curle. 2006.

61. Lederach, J.P. 'Conflict transformation in protracted internal conflicts: the case for a comprehensive framework', in Rupesinghe, K. 1995: *Conflict transformation*, pp. 201-222; quote at p. 212.

62. This chapter is from *In the middle: non-official mediation in violent situations*. Bradford Peace Studies, New Series Papers No 1. Leamington Spa, Hamburg, New York: Berg. 1986. pp. 9-29.

63. The case study and transcription which follows has been omitted from this chapter for reasons of space, but it is used by Adam Curle to show how mediators can change misperceptions and misunderstanding by leaders of conflict parties and encourage them to begin to think about dialogue and resolution.

64. Yarrow 1978, quotes at pp298 and 299.

65. See Yarrow 1978 266-267.

66. This chapter is an edited extract from Introduction to antidote to alienation, Part III of Another way: positive response to contemporary violence. Oxford: John Carpenter. pp. 110-130. (1995).

67. See 'New challenges for citizen peacemaking' *Medicine and war*, Vol. 10, 96-105 (1994).

68. This chapter is from the Committee for Conflict Transformation Support, Newsletter, 14, Autumn 2001 http://www.c-r.org/downloads/newsletter14.pdf. Here, Adam describes an experiment to 'resocialise' ex-prisoners of war at the end of World War II and considers its relevance for the 21st century.

69. The account of the principles and practice of the CRUs is an adaptation of a chapter by A.T.M. Wilson, E.L. Trist and Adam Curle, 'Transitional communities and social reconnection: the civil resettlement of British prisoners of war', in Eric Trist and Hugh Murray (eds.), *The social engagement of social science, Volume 1, The sociopsychological perspective.* University of Pennsylvania Press, Philadelphia 1990, pp.88-112.

70. This chapter is from Tom Woodhouse, (ed.), *Peacemaking in a troubled world.* New York, Oxford: Berg. pp. 17-29. The chapter was originally delivered as a lecture at Queen's University Ontario on 15th February 1978 and subsequently published as occasional paper no. 5, 1978.

71. See Mitchels, 2006, p. 246.

72. Curle, 1999, p. 5.

73. Curle, 1999, the *Hydra,* p. 54.

74. Curle, 1999, the *Hydra,* p. 52.

75. On cosmopolitanism, see Ramsbotham, Woodhouse and Miall (2016), chapter 11. On peace cultures, see Dietrich, Wolfgang (2014). *The Palgrave international handbook of peace studies: a cultural perspective.* London: Palgrave Macmillan.

76. It is interesting to note that the term 'black cloud' was the title of a science fiction novel by the British astronomer Fred Hoyle. Published in 1957, but set seven years into the future, in 1964, when astro-physicists in England detected a large gaseous cloud which approaches the Earth. It comes to rest around the sun, and causes disastrous climate change and widespread human suffering. The scientists in the novel conclude that the cloud may possess a form of intelligence and is a superorganism with which they can communicate.

77. *Recognition of reality* p. vii.

78. Curle 2006, p. 9.

79. Both of the editors of this book have written about the importance of art, culture and imagination in peacemaking and acknowledge Adam as

a source of inspiration in this. See Ramsbotham Woodhouse and Miall (2016), Chapter 16 (*Conflict resolution in art and popular culture.* See also John Paul's *The year in haiku* (2015) at http://www.blurb.com/b/6751573-the-year-in-haiku; his *Moral imagination: the art and soul of building peace* (2005); and *When blood and bones cry out: journeys through the soundscape of healing and reconciliation*, (2011), written with his daughter Angela.

80. This chapter is from to *To tame the Hydra: undermining the culture of violence* (1999). Charlbury, Oxfordshire: Jon Carpenter Publishing. Chapter 5, Happiness, pp 37-49.

81. This is a reference to the Chakma people of the Chittagong Hill Tracts 'a charming, cheerful and highly artistic Buddhist people whose society and culture was virtually erased by the greed and firepower of Bangladesh.'

82. This is the Essex Hall Lecture for 1977, and was delivered in London on 13th April, 1977. Essex Hall is the headquarters of the General Assembly of Unitarian and Free Christian Churches. The lecture was founded in 1892, and is one of the leading events during the annual meetings of the Assembly.

83. The material in this chapter is abridged from two publications, *The fragile voice of love*, Adam's last book, published in 2006, the year he died. The text selected is from pp. 18-23. The poems at the end of the chapter are from *Recognition of reality: reflections and prose poems*, published in 1987.

About the authors

Tom Woodhouse was appointed as research assistant to the founding Professor, Adam Curle in 1974 and held the Adam Curle Chair in Conflict Resolution at the University of Bradford from 1999-2012. He retired from his post in October 2012 and currently is Emeritus Professor at the University of Bradford. He is also a visiting professor at the University Ramon Llul, Barcelona, the Open University of Catalunya, Barcelona, and at Chulalongkorn University Bangkok. His book *Contemporary Conflict Resolution* (co-authored with Oliver Ramsbotham and Hugh Miall) was published as a fourth edition in 2016.

John Paul Lederach is Professor of International Peacebuilding at the University of Notre Dame and currently Senior Fellow at the Humanity United Foundation. John Paul works as a practitioner-scholar, providing education, facilitation and training. He set up the Eastern Mennonite University's Centre for Justice and Peacebuilding and has authored over 24 books.

Other Books from Hawthorn Press

Confronting Conflict
A first-aid kit for handling conflict
Friedrich Glasl

Conflict costs! When tensions and differences are ignored they grow into conflicts, injuring relationships and organisations. So, how can we confront conflict successfully?

Dr Friedrich Glasl has worked with conflict resolution in companies, schools and communities for over 30 years, earning him and his techniques enormous respect. Here are tools to:

- Analyse the conflict symptoms;
- Identify the types, causes of conflict, and if it is hot or cold;
- See how personal chemistry, structures or environment influence the conflict;
- Understand how temperaments affect conflicts and what you can do;
- Acknowledge when you have a conflict, understand conflict escalation, how to lessen conflict through changing behaviour, attitudes and perceptions;
- Practice developing considerate confrontation, seizing golden moments, strengthening empathy and much, much more.

Confronting Conflict will be useful for managers, facilitators, management lecturers and professionals such as teachers and community workers, mediators and workers in dispute resolution.

192pp; 216 x 138mm; 978-1-869890-71-1; paperback.

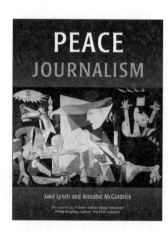

Peace Journalism
Jake Lynch, Annabel McGoldrick

Peace Journalism explains how most coverage of conflict unwittingly fuels further violence, and proposes workable options to give peace a chance. Here are:

- Topical case studies including Iraq and 'the war on terrorism' supported by theory, analysis, archive material and photographs;
- A comparison of War Journalism and Peace Journalism;
- How the reporting of war, violence and terror can be made more accurate and more useful;
- Practical tools and exercises for analysing and reporting the most important war stories of our time.

288pp; 246 x 189mm; 978-1-903458-50-1; paperback.

Common Wealth

For a free, equal, mutual and sustainable society
Martin Large
Foreword by Alastair Sawday

We know that we don't want a 'market state'. This turns our public services into businesses, uses relentless surveillance to secure compliance, destroys the planet for corporate growth and widens inequality. However, tripolar society is emerging as an alternative, where civil society, government and business push back the market, and work in partnership for the common good. *Common Wealth* tackles key challenges for remaking society by:

- building a sustainable local economy, vibrant culture and community;
- transforming capitalism for public good and for individual enterprise;
- securing permanently affordable homes for all through community land trusts;
- enabling social inclusion and individual initiative through the Citizen's Income;
- freeing education from bureaucracy and children from commercialism.

256pp; 234 × 156mm; 978-1-903458-98-3; hardback.

Organisations with Soul

A social path of schooling in the language of the human soul
Adriaan Bekman

Useful for advisors, managers, leaders and educators, this imaginative book reveals the timeless wisdom of the forgotten language of the human soul, and renews the wellsprings of inner life. Adriaan Bekman asks, 'How can we connect more deeply with others at work? And connect more wholeheartedly with our work tasks, so as to create mutual support, respect, meaning and growth?'

192pp; 234 x 156mm; 978-1-907359-30-9; paperback.

Hawthorn Press
www.hawthornpress.com

Ordering Books

If you have difficulties ordering Hawthorn Press books from a bookshop, you can order online at **www.hawthornpress.com** or you can order direct from:

United Kingdom
BookSource
50 Cambuslang Road, Glasgow
G32 8NB
Tel: (0845) 370 0063
E-mail: orders@booksource.net

USA/North America
Steiner Books
PO Box 960, Herndon
VA 20172-0960
Tel: (800) 856 8664
E-mail: service@steinerbooks.org
www.steinerbooks.org

Waldorf Books
Phil & Angela's Company, Inc.
1271 NE Hwy 99W #196
McMinnville, Oregon 97128
Tel: (503) 472-4610
E-mail: info@waldorfbooks.com
www.waldorfbooks.com

Australia & New Zealand
Footprint BookPty Ltd
4 /8 Jubilee Avenue
Warriewood
NSW 2102
Australia
Tel: (02) 9997 3973
Email: info@footprint.com.au
www.footprint.com.au

Hawthorn Press
www.hawthornpress.com